D1221759

UNTHINKING THE UNTHINKABLE

UNTHINKING

Nuclear Weapons

THE UNTHINKABLE

and Western Culture

JEFF SMITH

INDIANA
UNIVERSITY   *Bloomington & Indianapolis*
PRESS

Manufactured in the United States of America

Library of Congress Cataloging-in-Publication Data

Smith, Jeff
    Unthinking the unthinkable.

  1. Nuclear weapons—Social aspects—United States.
2. Nuclear warfare—Social aspects—United States.
3. Antinuclear movement—United States.   4. United
States—Civilization.   5. Criticism.   I. Title.
U264.S585   1989   355'.0217   88-45458
ISBN 0-253-35353-X

1 2 3 4 5   93 92 91 90 89

In memory of Henry W. Haas and George E. Smith
  and
To Mrs. Gladys Leonard Haas and Mrs. Emma Ostendorf Smith
  —with love and respect

CONTENTS

Acknowledgments

Early work leading to this book was helped along by a Fulbright Graduate Fellowship to Great Britain that I held in 1984–85. That what began as research collateral to my Fulbright project has, consequently, become a book in itself is perhaps an ironically literal realization of the Fulbright vision, which, according to J. William Fulbright, is to enhance international understanding with the aim of reducing the risk of nuclear war. In a recent article* Senator Fulbright said, "The personal benefits to the individual participants in the Fulbright program are readily recognized, but the effects of the scholarships on the political relations and the security interests of the nations involved are less obvious." I hope this book helps make them more obvious.

For help in connection with the Fulbright I am specifically grateful to Mary Martin of the University of Chicago, and Mr. J. A. O. Herrington, Capt. John Franklin (ret.), Mr. Stephen Selway, the staff of the U.K. Fulbright Commission, and Professor James Leahy, London. Also important at an earlier stage of my studies were Dr. and Mrs. Bela Erdoss, who kindly endowed the fellowship I held at the University of Chicago in honor of their daughter, Patricia Erdoss Maxwell.

I am also indebted to many friends and colleagues, some of whom read and helpfully commented on parts of the manuscript. Linda Blum, Paul Boyer, Debbie Brown, Dan Friedrich, Donna Gregory, Susanna Hawkins, Marcia Klatt, Miriam Luebke, David Morris, Susi Mowson, Leslie Ross, Betsy Rubin, Jon Siess, Doug Sugano, Keith Tuma, and Shari Zimmerman were all generous with their time and attention. So was Ann Dawson, who also helped me obtain public documents through the U.S. Embassy in London. Roberta Bell helped a great deal with data entry.

Some ideas in the book were tried out originally in articles, and for that I am grateful to several editors: Len Ackland, *Bulletin of the Atomic Scientists*; Richard Liefer, *Chicago Tribune*; James Wall and Linda-Marie Delloff, *Christian Century*; and James Nuechterlein, *The Cresset*, as well as the Fulbright Speakers' Bureau. For answering my unsolicited correspondence I am grateful to Dr. Martin E. Marty, Thomas Powers, and Jonathan Schell. Also to E. P. Thompson, who incorporated some ideas from what is here Chapter 5 in his book *Star Wars*.

For housing, employment, and forebearance while the book was in progress I am indebted to Mr. and Mrs. Edvin Eding and the Revs. Tom Bruch and Antti Heinola, International Lutheran Student Centre, London; Professors Charles Lynn Batten, Ray B. Browne, Chris Geist, George Gadda, Michael Hodd, and Ellen Strenski; and the Canal Cafe Theatre, London.

Finally, I have been the beneficiary of an unusually coherent education by a long line of socially conscious teachers, including (chronologically) Marylin Chapin, Ann Dennis, Richard McNally, Richard Foss, Mel Piehl, Marc Riedel, Warren Rubel, Carl Galow, Van C. Kussrow, Jr., James Combs, Theodore Ludwig, Kathleen Mullen, R. Keith Schoppa, Richard Maxwell, Gerald Mast, Robert Ferguson, and Wayne C. Booth. These teachers and others, along with Christ College at Valparaiso University and its deans, Richard Baepler and Arlin G. Meyer, encouraged me to believe

*"Fulbright Exchanges Enhance Our National Security," *Chronicle of Higher Education*, 10 Dec. 1986, p. 104.

that education should be both rigorous and concerned with the world. They helped me recognize that my main intellectual interest was my own culture and taught me ways of studying it. Another teacher, Mark R. Schwehn, specifically inspired my turning attention to the nuclear problem. And of course, I was able to benefit from these teachings by virtue of a home environment that was supportive in countless ways and that has been my first and ongoing forum for critical discussion. All the important values I hold were learned there, and this book owes most of all to the love and encouragement of my parents, Robert and Margye, and my sister, Ellen.

Introduction

This book looks at the problem of nuclear weapons from the neglected perspective of cultural history. Through analyses of literary and other texts, it tries to give a new kind of account both of the existence of the weapons and of certain features of the public debates over them. One of my interests is the irony that *anxieties* about the problems of war, weapons, and technology can help in certain ways to support the kinds of thinking that gave rise to those problems in the first place. I believe this irony can be seen in recent antinuclear thinking and also in historical developments of much earlier eras, when basic conditions for our present situation were being laid down. In fact, contemporary polemics on the nuclear question undercut themselves partly because they do not pay enough attention to those basic conditions and those earlier eras.

This was a feeling I had while following the last major round of public nuclear debates, in 1982–84 (the period of the nuclear freeze movement). As a student of humanities and cultural studies, I had learned to assume that texts and events of earlier epochs can speak to problems of today. I had also learned that any cultural situation has historical bases and antecedents. Most discussion of the problem (by those who assumed, as I did, that the existence of massive numbers of nuclear weapons *is* a problem) seemed to me to overlook this. Antinuclearists tended to move too quickly to the mode of exhortation, saving the analytic mode for inquiries into how the nuclear problem *affects* society, not how it was caused. In search of causes, I was able to find works that went halfway, but they always seemed to stop short of the really interesting questions.

For instance, there are historians who trace the origins of the present situation—but never, it seems, far enough back into the past. Histories that deal explicitly with nuclear weapons usually deal with the last fifty or so years, the period since atomic bombs actually showed up on the drawing board. But historians who limit themselves to that period are able to adduce only what I would call proximate causes of the nuclear problem, not remote or underlying causes. The more remote the cause, the further back in history its onset is going to lie. Feeling that the depth, even seeming intractability, of this problem suggested that the remote causes of it were important, I felt a need for historical analyses to be pushed further back.

I was also dissatisfied with most economic and psychological analyses. Though these sometimes get at underlying causes, they seem to suffer from numerous difficulties, which this book tries to detail. Many of them assign nuclear weapons to universal psychological tendencies: tendencies among human beings toward aggression, toward the creating of enemies, and so forth. Some, reflecting what are basically sociobiological ideas, suggest that these tendencies are genetic, but even studies that steer clear of that rather discredited premise sometimes end up with essentially the same universalistic conclusion. It seemed ever clearer to me as I read this sort of literature that the answer was somewhere in culture, not in genes (or their functional equivalents). For even if people are universally aggressive, they are not *only* aggressive, so one still must explain why aggression shows up where and when it does.

Moreover, I found myself frustrated by the uses made of clinical and therapeutic perspectives, and by the effect on psychological analyses generally of attempts to be therapeutic. That people at least tacitly support the existence of nuclear weapons is indeed a problematic psychological fact, and psychological problems do demand therapy. But again, it came to seem increasingly clear to me that you can't perform therapy on whole cultures without knowing something about culture. Too many therapeutic approaches lacked this dimension; they seemed to imply that the therapy of a culture is just individual therapy multiplied by the X million people who make up that culture. (These approaches also, in consequence, fell heavily into what I call the We problem—an issue discussed in chapters 2 and 4.)

Shortly before I finished this book I had a conversation with a psychotherapist that seemed to sum up these frustrations. The psychotherapist was explaining that there are certain "cognitive formations" and so forth that bring about the nuclear problem. People tend to project onto an "enemy" the qualities they fear in themselves, she said, stating a familiar psychological postulate. She also spoke to how this projection process might be curtailed. But when I pressed her to explain how millions of people might be persuaded to do that curtailing, she literally didn't understand the question. She assumed I meant to ask how the *Russian* people could be brought into the process, not how our fellow Americans could be. Therapists expect individual clients to come into the clinic for treatment, and the problem (essentially a political one) of getting the public at large into the clinic is beyond anything in the clinicians' training or orientation. Faced with this larger question, they quite logically speak as if taking up the therapeutic challenge is the job of each of us individually. That's true, and those (like this psychotherapist) who don't really need to change their ways will be happy to do so. But part of the public pathology, if we may call it that, is the failure of most people to see that they need this therapy.

At another theoretical extreme, there were (and still are) nominally psychological analyses underlying official policy itself. Deterrence theory, for instance, is based on a psychological theory about what sorts of fears and inducements people—in this case, Russians—are most likely to react to. There have been very elaborate versions of such explanations, some of them influential with policymakers. But such elaborations—for instance, Thomas Schelling's game theories—also beg the questions I assume to be most interesting. Though they deal with the causes of particular events or crises, they are not interested in the basic causes of the present situation.

Rational calculation or game theory might explain something of how people react within a game, but not why they play the game in the first place, not why they seek its particular prize.

Now, the nuclear field does have some so-called cultural analyses. These analyses are promising in that they at least begin with the term *culture*. But typically they mean by this term something much narrower than I am speaking of. When I tell colleagues interested in the nuclear problem that my work deals with cultural aspects, they initially think I mean the study of people who work at the Rand Corporation or Los Alamos National Laboratory (the people who do those rational calculations and theories in support of policy). The idea has been widely popularized that there is a "nuclear culture" that includes scientists, strategic planners, military officials, and even assembly-line workers at weapons plants. But of course, culture in that sense is really sub-culture, and I am sorry that *culture* has been taken over to refer to it. For this leaves us without a term in common usage to refer to the cultures that have ultimately authorized that subculture's work—Western (including, of course, Russian) culture and, in certain special ways, American culture.

So that is the culture to which I have turned attention. I have been somewhat anticipated in this. David G. Mandelbaum's call for an anthropology of the nuclear problem, Spencer R. Weart's examination of nuclear imagery, and certain works from the field of language and discourse analysis are recent examples of efforts that begin to define the field to which this book belongs. What is different here, broadly speaking, is the historical depth to which I try to penetrate (some four hundred years). In *By the Bomb's Early Light*, his book on American culture of the early nuclear era, Paul Boyer called for "ventures into even more tantalizingly speculative realms," and I see the present book as that kind of venture. Specifically, it tries to do three things. First it critiques various positions within the nuclear debate (chapters 1 and 2) and, by looking at underlying themes (chapter 3), tries to establish a new framework for the issues in that debate. Then it offers some ideas about remote causes of the current situation. These causes are located, first, in the period at the end of the Middle Ages when modern war and statecraft arose (chapter 4), and, second, in the nineteenth-century period of American industrialization (chapter 5). The latter chapter is also concerned with how cultural attitudes become public policy, and therefore it deals with how the older views showed up and were applied in a particular contemporary case—President Reagan's promotion of the Strategic Defense Initiative.

Finally, the book concludes (chapter 6) with further reflections on the current situation itself and with some suggestions for political (or metapolitical) orientations that might prove most useful for intervening in these dangerous cultural dynamics. I do not see this latter project as separate from the book's main concern of explaining culture and texts. Not only is scholarship pointless if it isn't at least indirectly addressed to issues in the world; but also, to look at our particular culture's history is to see attitudes that can only seem—especially against the backdrop of what preceded them—problematic. And it is also to see that history is alterable, that those problems need not be paralyzing.

Though concerned with history, the book relies most heavily on literary and textual analyses. Partly that is because I am more competent at such analyses than at any other. But there is also a more serious justification: the complexity of the interplay among cultural attitudes and anxieties can be more easily observed, I think, within the confines of a single text or group of texts. In a text the attitudes clash and combine (or both at once) in more decisive ways than they do anywhere else, except in the inner recesses of individual human minds. (In fact, chapter 5's SDI analysis assumes that the texts show us the interplay of attitudes actually present in a certain mind—Ronald Reagan's.) This approach makes the book historically selective and suggestive rather than comprehensive. My point is to identify some of the broad intellectual themes that underlie present circumstances, and to trace their complex interactions within popular thinking. I do not account for every cross-period or cross-cultural variation, as a single connected narrative might try harder to do. Nor do I deal at great length with how or why the themes arose, even though they too have causes.

In fact, here is where economic and other so-called materialist analyses would come back into play. I do not deny that cultural ideas do arise from material forces, but I do find it unhelpful to try to explain every particular policy, including today's nuclear policies, by pointing to such forces directly. Instead, I suggest that particular policies result directly from ideas, and thus only indirectly from material forces. Material forces produce particular policies only by taking certain cultural and intellectual forms rather than others, and it is these forms that must be looked at more closely. Choosing this approach necessarily means not dealing with every possible cause; a given policy or event might *also* have direct economic and other determinants. But no analysis deals with every possible cause, and it is necessary to focus on those that have so far been most neglected. On the nuclear issue the neglected area is culture. Believing this was my motivation for writing the book in the first place.

Through demonstration the book also aims to establish two truths. The first is that literary and film analysis, the disciplines in which I was trained, are highly relevant to the understanding of this particular real-world problem. That they have not been drawn on much by those writing on the problem is not entirely the fault of those writers, for unfortunately the disciplines do little to advertise the potential public relevance of their work. The sophisticated methods of cultural analysis they make available rarely trickle down into public discussion. But it is time to make sure they do, for otherwise nuclear writers and journalists will continue to base their work on commonsense premises that disciplinary inquiry has more or less shown to be untrue (for example, the premise discussed and criticized in chapter 4: that nation-states have existed for all time). This can lead to mistakes that neutralize the efforts of those writers, rendering them as irrelevant to the problem as are the ivory-tower academics who know the terrain better but refuse to let anyone else see their map.

It follows from the point just made that my claims, though based on the perspectives of academically specialized fields, nonetheless aim to speak to the nuclear problem publicly and not esoterically. Russell Jacoby, in his recent book *The Last Intellectuals*, has made the case very well that contributing to public discourse is what scholars ought to do. Frustration at the failure of so many, at least in my fields, to do so is a feeling I share with Jacoby and another motive underlying this book. Indeed, I would imagine that respecting the broader public enough to try to speak to it is inseparable, for me, from caring to understand, analyze, and criticize public attitudes in the first place (a large part of what this book is doing, concerned as it is with explaining how bad weapons policies have been produced by good people—our own friends, relatives, neighbors, and national leaders).

The second truth I want to establish is that engaging public problems is vital to those academic disciplines themselves, purely in view of their own disciplinary ends. In the field of English, the end in question is the better understanding of works of literature (and film). I want to show that engagement with the world is indispensible, not as some sort of gratuitous, civic-minded overlay—the English professor's equivalent of pro bono work—but as a central feature of literary analysis as such. Something like this idea is heard ever more frequently these days, but it never lacks for opponents, and acting on it is still very much discouraged by entrenched curricular and institutional boundaries.

The notion of discourse, of which I make extensive use, seems a natural bridge from the esoteric confines of English to the public dialogues of (and about) our culture. Discourse concepts have already begun to be applied to nuclear questions (though again, not in the particular ways I try to do). Discourse is not the whole of history, as I might sometimes seem to be implying. Many things exert pressure on the way we speak and act — economic dislocations, natural disasters, even the existence of nuclear weapons themselves (once certain discourses have taken the particular form that produces them). Again, it is a question of emphasizing that which hasn't yet been dealt with enough. Moreover, the discourse idea points the way toward close readings of the texts under consideration, something not yet done even in other works of cultural study on the nuclear problem. And it allows us to be (in fact, requires us to be) inclusive and eclectic in ways consistent with that breakdown of traditional boundaries. In this book, statements by President Reagan are treated as equally revealing a text as works by Shakespeare and Orwell, while Shakespeare's and other texts of earlier times are treated as equally relevant to the nuclear question as a Reagan speech or *Dr. Strangelove*. This variety of texts is used to constitute a new discourse, the one that makes up this book—a discourse of reflection and analysis on the nuclear issue.

We will deal further with issues of method, but first let us look at one of the key questions that has motivated the discourse and that helps us to define what exactly it is. We are interested in learning what developments in culture made nuclear weapons thinkable, with the hope of assessing whether and how we might, finally, unthink them. This issue is central, for nuclear weapons are machines, and machines, it has been said, are finally ideas—or, as I will put it, precipitates of discourse, physical embodiments of a culture's attempts to deal with certain questions. And one of those is a question that flashed into view in the bright light of the first atomic explosion.

UNTHINKING THE UNTHINKABLE

ONE

Ancient of Days:
The Question after Trinity

Let thine almighty aid
Our sure defense be made . . .
Come and reign over us,
Ancient of Days.
      —Eighteenth-century hymn

I.

The first atomic test was code-named Trinity and was thought of by its participants in religious terms. Its director, J. Robert Oppenheimer, equated the blast with images from Hindu and Christian poetry. An official report to President Truman said the detonation had released "forces heretofore reserved to the Almighty." For Winston Churchill it was a kind of Second Coming.[1] And some nuclear weapons since then have been given names like Atlas and Poseidon, names reminiscent of the ancient gods.

Such language expresses the feeling that atomic weapons are a radically new thing, so different from all other weapons and devices in the magnitude of their power as to be indescribable in everyday terms. To speak of something, even metaphorically, as somehow divine is to suggest that it stands outside normal categories of experience, that it exists on a different plane altogether. It implies that the thing, even if superficially invented by scientists, isn't really a human creation at all. In fact, by assigning it to the highest plane of being—a plane that exists in some form even in modern, secular thought—such language begins to imply that the thing actually partakes in the cosmos's forces of creation, that it somehow helps establish the world's conditions of existence.[2]

That is the obvious level of meaning. At another, less obvious, unconscious level, the scientists' and politicians' religious language suggests something quite different—almost the opposite, in fact. For religion has been around a very long time, and ideas about the divine go back much further than any of our modern scientific knowledge. They are among our oldest cultural artifacts, and objects describable in quasi-divine terms are therefore reflections or products of a long history of culture. Far from standing outside of or creating human experience, such objects, it might be said, partake in all the experience that has gone before.

So while in one sense religious language *obscures* the continuities between atomic weapons and scientific knowledge, making the bomb seem extraworldly, in another sense it calls attention to far deeper and more profound continuities. The language of the scientists at Los Alamos unwittingly established a relationship between the atomic bomb and one of the oldest of human ideas, that of God. It aligned nuclear weapons with our most fundamental systems of shared belief, systems that in any culture will feature some force or center like the one that we historically "cried unto" by that name. And thus the basic question that arose at the start and that has been with us since what Oppenheimer called the day after Trinity. The question is: Is the bomb basically a very new thing, or a very old thing?[3] Is it *prior to* (and perhaps the main cause of) the condition of our lives today, or is it the logical *effect* (not cause) of a history which is prior to it? Should it be thought of as the beginning of the modern age—or should it be thought of as the outcome of ages past?

The dominant view among professional U.S. nuclear strategists today is that it is neither. This leading think-tank view holds, first, that nuclear weapons are neither divine nor even very special, but simply instruments of policy and, potentially, of warfare; and therefore that their usefulness, and even morality, under foreseeable political and military scenarios can be rationally assessed, and their place in the nation's arsenal correspondingly fixed.[4] But the general public has endorsed this view only in the broadest and vaguest way, not in specifics. The majority allows that nuclear weapons may be—must be—an aspect of policy, but also misconceives the policy actually in force to be fairly simple: keep enough of the things around to be sure of not getting attacked. (Given this assumption, it puzzles people that the actual numbers have been so large—enough to kill everyone on both sides thirteen times over, and so forth.) The "hard-headed" calculations of strategists have never had much impact, not even with people who broadly support the nation's nuclear posture.

Instead, most people assume in some fashion that the bomb has an overwhelming, even transcendent significance. Politicians reflect this public view by always giving at least lip service to the idea that "a nuclear war cannot be won and must never be fought," as President Reagan put it (once he discovered that certain of the strategists' words and styles were off-limits to the president in public). And most members of the public repay that lip service by confining their enthusiasm for ideas like a nuclear freeze— anathema to the hard-headed planners—to occasional answers to questions in a Gallup poll. Yet the existence of even pro forma support of this kind confirms that majorities of people imagine the bomb to be in some fundamental sense different, a special threat. Most would agree that Oppenheimer's mystical murmur made some sense, even if by action (or inaction) they unwittingly allow the technical and policy communities to work from a notably different set of assumptions.

Thus we come back to the question—is the specialness of the bomb its transcendent newness, or its profound cultural rootedness, its ancientness of days? What most people think on this should be obvious. The more familiar assumption is that the bomb is new. Like those who first used the term, most people who imagine the bomb to be almighty would mean by this that it was a cause instead of an effect, a partaker of the cosmic rather than a product of culture. Hence, they would assume, we live in a new age. This is the view even of many who condemn nuclear weapons and the public's failure to oppose them more vigorously. (In fact, as I later argue, the assumption of newness is what leads them to condemn instead of trying to *explain*.) It has been a tendency of politicians, journalists and disarmament activists alike to look on August 1945 as a watershed in human history, since which things have never been the same. The dominant view has been that nuclear weapons are, in Jonathan Schell's words, "a basic change in the circumstances" of life.[5]

II.

So nuclear discourse thus far has consisted of certain views and combinations of views: that the bomb is a new thing that has worsened the human condition, or a new thing that has usefully transformed assumptions about war, or one that has dangerously *not* transformed such assumptions. On the other hand: that it is nothing particularly new, but just another device to be assimilated into the nation's arsenal. Or something more than a mere device, but also something our age was destined to have—hence not a thing to imagine being rid of. To each of these views there is a corresponding reading of history, ranging from (for example) Einstein's famous "Everything has changed save our modes of thinking" to strategist Herman Kahn's "war can still be fought, terminated and thought of as an experience to be survived" to the conclusion put forward by the Harvard Nuclear Study Group: "Like Adam and Eve, we have eaten of the tree of knowledge and have been cast into a world" from which nuclear weapons will never go away.[6]

But another view has been neglected in this debate. That is the view that the nuclear problem is culturally rooted. This view also involves a reading of history—argues, indeed, that history is at the heart of the matter—but a kind of history that has likewise been largely neglected. We have often been given nuclear histories in the narrow sense of dates, names, meetings, and memos. Usually such histories either begin or center around Alamagordo and Hiroshima, meaning that in effect they reinforce the notion that the bomb is new. On the other hand, we have seen a kind of history that ascribes the bomb to time immemorial—either by tracing it to the "elemental" violence in "human nature," or by writing it into stories of weapons development that go back perhaps to the stone age.[7] This kind of allegedly historical analysis has two effects. It either leads us to that complacent "professional" view that the bomb is just another, even potentially useful, device.[8] Or, it reintroduces the newness notion under another guise: somehow that unbroken line of weapons development suddenly got broken; we reached (for some reason) critical mass or took a quantum leap in destructive potential. Hence, the world did change in 1945 after all.

But none of these kinds of history explains cultural rootedness. To do that, we need another kind of history—a cultural history that analyzes (instead of fearfully dismissing) the unconscious, nonrational and self-contradictory springs of a society's behavior, the "region of culture where literature, general ideas, and certain products of the collective imagination—we may call them 'cultural symbols'—meet."[9] Cultural history is what is needed to meet the objection Bernard Brodie raises against most traditional histories in this field:

> Though we depend critically on the work of historians, we cannot regularly accept their judgments on motivation. This is especially true with respect to the making of wars, where we see so much behavior that does not appear to be rational.[10]

The same goes for the making of weapons. Standard histories of the kind mentioned above have trouble not seeing the bomb as new because they underrate the depth of the motives that produced it. As Brodie suggests, their theory of motives is too limited. They see motives as arising from the individual's life history or institutional position or from interrelationships among institutions. But they usually pass over that amazing interplay of underlying beliefs and commitments that provide the materials out of which motives are constructed in the first place.

For instance, here is a randomly selected paragraph from a standard history of the Manhattan Project and Hiroshima. The author is describing the early resistance of two top U.S. science officials, Vannevar Bush and James B. Conant, to the idea of pressing ahead with a nuclear project:

> Not until July 10, 1941, did an American physicist, returning from an unrelated mission to Britain, report to Bush in his office at Sixteenth and P Streets in Washington with a sketchy preview of the British findings. A formal report arrived a few days later. Bush and Conant set about studying it, but the scientists in London, reeling from the aerial Battle of Britain and still pounded by Nazi fire raids, had grown impatient. They wanted action.[11]

Part of why this seems so straightforward is that we share the "commonsense" theories of people and events that this passage encodes. We, too, assume that it makes sense for people in a region in which bombs are dropping to perceive their situation in certain ways ("they" are attacking "us"; our two peoples are "at war"; all normal comity is suspended, with no exceptions made in respect of ties of blood or culture "we" might have to "them," etc.). We grant that people would be "reeled" by such attacks, whether they or their kinsmen directly experienced the violence or not. And we see it as just sensible that they look to their state, and that the action they want would be comparably violent, if not more so. At the same time, we do not question that their counterparts in another, allied state might put other needs ahead of solidarity with these seeming victims.

But why is all this so? What more fundamental worldviews make these reactions seem natural, and where did those worldviews come from? How did they replace other reactions, like praying for deliverance or sending forth a lone champion—equally natural things to do in other times and places? What happened to those elaborate (and to us, quite odd-looking) courtesies that used to mark even some very bitter wars? It might be claimed that technological changes made all these older ways obsolete. But that just restates the question. Why was technology perceived as taking a form that *supplanted* rather than enhanced the old customs? (We certainly could imagine, say, a duel of lone champions in high-tech armored tanks. It still happens in the movies.) And why did people accept the new methods nonetheless? What cultural values was new technology *protecting* that offset its destruction of old, familiar ways of life (and death)?

There is no need for a cultural explanation if everything that strikes us as common sense is really common, cutting across cultures like the feeling that food satisfies hunger or that the ground is beneath one's feet. But if it is instead the shared outlook of our own culture and century, contingent on our own history, then there is every need for such an explanation—since "common sense" is such a large part of what apparently convinces people that nuclear weapons are sadly unavoidable today.

III.

Nuclear arsenals seem especially unhistorically contingent. They have sometimes seemed possessed of an almost mystical tendency toward "strange, apparently self-perpetuating increase."[12] One might note, for example, the phenomenon some have called retirement wisdom. Oppenheimer himself was a spectacular example, but to varying degrees retirement wisdom also seems to have beset associates of his like Leo Szilard and George Kistiakowsky, military officials like Admirals Hyman Rickover and Gene LaRocque, cabinet members Henry Stimson and Robert McNamara and colleagues of theirs like George Kennan, and many others. "Sometimes, after these people have returned to private life, they begin to sound worried themselves, and issue the very sort of troubled warnings that they ignored or explained away when they were still in office and might have done something," says Thomas Powers.[13] It is as if, says John E. Mack, there is a "group context of fear, [a] paralysis of initiative" that overtakes people while they are in the councils of power.[14]

Perhaps the seeming self-perpetuation of nuclear weapons is not an individual but an institutional matter. Certainly there are any number of nuclear instances of best-laid plans. President Eisenhower's squeamishness about targeting Soviet cities fails to change U.S. war plans in the short term yet, in the long term, provides the "'rationale' for each new and improved nuclear weapon" for decades thereafter. Secretary McNamara's attempts to bring civilian control to the nuclear growth industry wind up providing the Pentagon with rationales for further procurements. Attempts to scare the Russians out of MIRVing their missiles (installing multiple warheads) instead drive them to do just that. And President Carter's moves to drastically cut the nuclear stockpile instead turn out to have "left Ronald Reagan with all the defense plans and Presidential orders in place to carry out his harder line"; Carter's well-intentioned efforts prove to have "brought the two superpowers closer to being able to wage a nuclear war than they had ever been in the nuclear age."[15]

Today medium-range nuclear missiles (INFs) are dismantled under a historic treaty. But then it is reported that "the INF deal just happens to leave in place the precise Soviet conventional and tactical nuclear forces needed to justify a whole range of Pentagon procurement programs." Antitactical ballistic missiles, under development to shoot down INFs and, therefore, left briefly "in search of a threat to counter," are actually built *up* in the wake of the INF deal. Some other Soviet system is simply redesignated as the threat. "Thank God," says a Pentagon official, "we've still got a threat to justify the antitactical missile program!"[16] It almost seems as if, like always, "weapons came first and rationalizations and policies followed." Officials go on making military decisions for frankly nonmilitary reasons. They express powerlessness to do other than as they do. They seem concerned to discover "How much is enough?" yet "in language that defies clear comprehension . . . would have us believe that nothing is ever enough."[17]

These and many other ironies raise the possibility that something besides rationality supports the bomb, some "underlying malignancy that deforms human enterprise and aspiration," as Christopher Lasch has said (though we don't need to put it that strongly to be curious about it).[18] The ironies also suggest looking beyond the *conscious* intentions of the people involved—beyond, that is, the traditional concern of explanations that focus on the politics of the issue.[19] The malignancy (or whatever it is) is a *thwarting* of conscious intentions. Maybe it is also just the way of the world. Yet as long as rationality does prevail on other issues in our common life, we need to explain its seemingly frequent ineffectiveness where the issue happens to be nuclear weapons.

Actually there have been attempts at explanation, and two in particular have become common—the "interest" (or greed) theory, and the "blunder"

(or stupidity) theory. Both theories acknowledge the nonrational component in the kind of behavior I'm describing. Under the first theory, this
component is thought to be self-interest. The official who thanks God for a
threat to justify his program speaks volumes, it is argued, about the real
causes of nuclear stockpiling. His career is advanced by weapons procurement, and his friends in the military-industrial complex are directly profit-
ing from it. He himself might have hopes of profit too. Maybe he is even
plotting an actual U.S. nuclear strike, as antinuclearists like David Dellinger
have sometimes suggested.[20] Interest theories, analogizing from behavior
like this official's, give us a seemingly simple explanation for the actions of
large sectors of at least the leadership elites most directly involved in the
nuclear problem.

Really, though, such theories risk begging the crucial questions. Though
some are relatively more subtle and sophisticated, interest theories on the
whole presume a questionable psychology based largely on greed, and they
take it to be obvious that official greed naturally would translate into
support for nuclear weapons in particular, in spite of the many problems
these weapons also pose. Interest theories also don't explain indirect support for arms races, the kind of tacit public endorsement I mentioned
above—support which, even if vague, nonetheless is very widespread,
touching people well outside the circles of those who could hope to con-
cretely benefit from the weapons. Why do those whose interests aren't
served let those whose are get away with what they're doing? Our society
long ago cut off support to an unproductive aristocracy—why not to a
military-industrial elite which, in the interest theorists' own view, behaves in
ways that are even worse than useless?

It might be answered that there are aspects of "elite" policy that people
in general don't know about, and that this helps account for the policies'
public support. But, first of all, people do know quite a bit; if anything, the
public has an impression of nuclear weapons as infinitely destructive, an
impression even more potentially damning of their existence than would be
likely to emerge from most internal government debates. Certain officials,
like Ronald Reagan, have even gone out of their way to emphasize this
point for the public's benefit.[21]

Second, much of what people don't "know" is itself a problem for
analysis. If jurors in a civil-disobedience case don't "know" (after months of
intensive news coverage) that the U.S. was involved in mining Nicaraguan
harbors; if most citizens (as Robert McNamara points out) "would be
shocked to learn" that the U.S. has not foreclosed the possibility of being
first to use nuclear weapons; if a coworker of mine doesn't know that the
U.S. conducts underground nuclear tests—then the question arises, why?[22]
What does this not knowing consist of? Have people just coincidentally not
heard the facts, or have they for some reason managed not to retain or
attend to them? And if people *haven't* heard the facts—to which they have
remarkable access—why not? Because they don't bother to read news-

papers? All right, but why is *that*? Why wouldn't people want to investigate an issue which they do know involves the future of their lives and country—especially when they insist on being well informed on far lesser matters? Like relentless psychoanalysts we must probe each of these "failures," since each one is also a phenomenon in its own right. Hence each asks to be explained, beyond dismissive slogans like "people are manipulated" or "they concede these issues to experts" or "public opinion is dictated by the media."

Third, it is true that where large numbers of people *have* expressed desires for a change in policy, often nothing has happened as a result. But this, too, is a far from self-explaining fact. It is said that the public over-whelmingly supports a nuclear freeze, as shown by numerous resolutions and public-opinion polls. Yes? Then why didn't one occur? There have been several elections since those polls appeared; who besides the poll respondents have been voting for the anti-freeze officials? Clearly "support" can mean different things. There is an obvious gap between what the people feel (or tell pollsters they feel) and what officials do. But pointing to the gap is not explaining anything. It is indicating part of what needs to be explained.

Bernard Brodie has demolished the interest theory more systematically, pointing out its vulgar Marxist roots—even among some exponents, like President Eisenhower, whom few would consider Marxists.[23] I won't repeat his whole argument here (though chapter 2 will continue the demolition a bit further in its discussion of functionalist and leaders-versus-people ideas). Actually *interest* might still be a useful term if we expand the definition of it quite a bit. But Brodie rightly suggests that we not become so wedded to interest theory as to overlook the other hypothesis—that policy is sometimes just a product of stupidity.

Others, too, have pointed us in this direction, including the author of that history of Hiroshima from which I took that paragraph for analysis above. Unfortunately the blunder theory also risks begging the interesting questions. To say something is stupidity or a mistake is to say fairly little about it. It is a purely negative designation; it suggests that the act in question consists of failure or lack, that it has no *positive content*. But much of what look like mistakes in history in fact make sense at another level of analysis (as chapter 5 in particular will try to show). And even "pure" mistakes—"I thought doing X would accomplish Y but instead it gave us Q"—often have, nonetheless, some willed aspect ("I wanted Y"), some cognitive basis ("I imagined Y was a function of X"), and some tempera-mental or emotional component ("When it came down to it, I was willing to risk Q"). Plus, the emergence of Qs where Ys were intended is often not the accident or coincidence it seems; often it points to some hidden but impor-tant relationship between the intended and the actual results. In all these ways mistakes often have positive content. They are not just the lack of something but also the presence of something else.

The same holds true when there seems to be a gap between public support for something and actual policies, or (as is more common) when people in general appear to be expressing no position at all. This latter situation is often remarked on by antinuclearists, who work up ingenious theories to explain people's "failure" to act on a problem that endangers their world. One major such theory, "psychic numbing," familiar from the work of Robert Jay Lifton, Jonathan Schell, and others, holds that nuclear weapons are themselves the cause of this failure.[24] The threat these weapons pose paralyzes people in exactly those ways that keep them from opposing the threat. Psychic numbing theory is ingenious in that it joins the idea of the bomb as a new thing and a cause of our situation with the assumption that people currently *aren't* acting, that their behavior lacks positive content. The two ideas are used to explain each other: people aren't acting, and the bomb is why.

Psychic numbing theory has so taken hold that antinuclear writers these days frequently just assume that some such mechanism must be at work. What they apparently see as the alternative, that millions of ordinary people might simply be in the wrong, is evidently too troubling a prospect. But the theory has several problems. Like most bomb-as-new theories, it tends to isolate the nuclear issue from other areas of experience, since feelings about the bomb are thought primarily to *create*, not result from, other feelings. The theory's extreme forms claim that feelings in all areas of life are affected; much is read into contemporary children's mushroom-clouded nightmares and so forth, evidently in the belief that children of the past lacked dreadful and scary things to dream about. How one could prove, though, that since 1945 net levels of fear in the world have risen, or that esprit has declined, I cannot guess. Jonathan Schell, for his part, doesn't prove this; he simply infers it from the dreadfulness of the threat. Psychic numbing theory does have the virtue of trying to *name* the phenomenon, a first step toward assigning it content instead of writing it off as failure or lack.[25] But just barely, for *numbness* is really a nonname, a name for absence (the absence of feeling). So the theory's main problem remains its dubious central assumption that people's behavior today lacks positive content. Yet we all know that not to decide is to decide, or, as Robert Paul Wolff has put it:

> One of the first truths enunciated in introductory ethics courses is that the failure to do something is as much an act as the doing of it. . . . when a man who has power refrains from using it, we all agree that he has *acted politically*. Omissions are frequently even more significant than commissions in American politics, for those in positions of decision usually rule by default rather than by consent.[26]

There might be an argument over whether the citizens of Western nations do have power in Wolff's sense. But surely they do have it in some respect, for massive noncooperation or active resistance on their part (and maybe actions far short of these) would certainly make a given policy untenable. So if we are not seeing noncooperation and resistance, then again, that is a fact that needs to be explained. Wolff is right that omissions are significant, but that term and *default* are too simple. What people display is not a lack but a certain *form* of consent.

As loath as antinuclearists are to face it, there is more than numbness in remarks like that of the cabbie who kibitzed the 1987 British elections with this comment on the opposition leader: "Talks very well, he makes me sick. Ban the bomb and all."[27] Perhaps such remarks don't prove that ordinary people actively want nuclear weapons. But generally it seems that people want not to appear to *not* want them in some unseemly or culturally inappropriate way. There is an interest in being normal, an interest easily overlooked because (as the clumsiness of my last sentence makes clear) it is hard to put into language. Language names the nonnormal, that which sticks out, more easily than the normal; it is the record of things perceived to "be there" rather than to be lacking. Language therefore makes it hard to give positive content to a lack. Language is the naming of things but also the *refusal* to name some others, and the many ways it structures analysis are difficult to overcome.

Nonetheless, mistakes, failures, and seeming absences are as surely phenomena in their own right as are interests. All, therefore, are open to analysis. And the specific kind of analysis needed, the one that avoids the problems of the interest and blunder theories, is what I have called cultural history—the attempt to understand *why* interests exist in the form they do and why blunders happen in the way they do. Cultural history is an attempt to grapple with complex, even seemingly occult factors in human affairs. Since it involves probing behind interests and ascribing content to seeming mistakes, it has certain relations to psychoanalysis. I will argue, though, for suspending the familiar metaphor whereby whole cultures are assumed to have psyches. There is no one thing that any society "thinks" or "feels" at any given time, partly because people are divided within themselves and partly because they contend against each other. These facts both reflect the nature of culture and complicate it. People are divided within themselves precisely insofar as their thinking is the product of complex histories, each larger than the individual's. A given self is an heir to various of these histories at once—a nexus somewhere in that interplay of thoughts, commitments, and anxieties, often mutually contradictory ones, that are what we refer to when we say culture. And since, within that interplay, different individuals are located and constituted differently, they also contend against each other. As we will see, this is a complicated story, the sharpest contentions often involving just slight shifts in one's place within the network of intersecting cultural beliefs: this fundamental view of things crossed with *that* particular assumption, instead of the other one it was crossed with for one's predecessor or neighbor.

IV.

A brief illustration of this kind of complexity comes from the writings of Herman Kahn, an influential U.S. strategist who was closely associated with that hard-headed view that is now the main line of U.S. policy. Kahn worked on nuclear scenarios: If the Russians were to bomb New York City as a show of force, but did no other damage besides, what would be the "rational" American response? Kahn wanted the lecture audiences to whom he presented this case—he called it a thought experiment—to see the absurdity of massive retaliation and the relative costs of bombing Moscow (two of the options they were most likely to favor). Instead, he would suggest that the more thoughtful course was to bomb Leningrad; in fact this is what the Soviets would be expecting—they, after all, have their Herman Kahns too. Actually Kahn's overall point was that the U.S. might avert this scenario altogether (though, disturbingly, by developing a first-strike capability). Regardless, having posited the destruction of Leningrad, he is now confronted with the question of that city's people and their fate:

> The U.S. government might conceivably feel that the people of Leningrad were not implicated in the decision by their government to destroy New York City. Therefore, American leaders might want to punish the Soviet regime by destroying an important national treasure, while doing as little damage as possible to more or less innocent bystanders.
>
> Most people would argue, however, that citizens must suffer the consequences of acts taken by their government, whether they were explicitly consulted or not. One almost has to adopt such an attitude, even if it is close to the edge of immorality. There is almost no other rule that would work—at least in most such circumstances.[28]

I will have more to say later about the attitude expressed here; cultural history, I believe, can explain *why* most people would argue in the way Kahn correctly predicted. It can also interrogate that little word *work*, which carries a truckload of assumptions about what one's purposes might or ought to be. Clearly Kahn saw things as "working" to the extent they contributed to the paramount goal of meeting so-called national interests. He presumably thought this goal merely obvious. And in that sense, the ability of his argument to persuade the reader depends on a kind of common sense not unlike that on which the writer of a standard history must rely if his description of "reeling" British scientists is even to strike the reader as coherent.

But from a cultural-history perspective it is equally revealing that Kahn pauses over these moral caveats at all. By doing so he registers an anxiety about them that in its own way affirms how compelling they are. As I will later show, something similar happens to many of Kahn's opponents, but in reverse: while foregrounding the moral concerns, they unwittingly affirm versions of the entrenched, Kahnian view of national interest. They, too, have a common sense ensnared along with Kahn's in the complex, dialectical, and ironic interplay of cultural attitudes. It is much more than a simple matter of this view versus that.

Complexities of this sort multiply when we turn to more intricate texts, like the works of literature and film this book will examine. For a cultural historian, literature and film are major avenues into that interplay of cultural beliefs. A given text in these media, if it is coherent—and even more, if it is valued—is a nexus of beliefs in much the same way as is an individual "human subject" (the term preferred over *person* by theorists who want to draw attention to the self's having been produced by culture, just as are texts). Individual and text are both "cultural categories," as Robert Wuthnow puts it.[29] Reading one gives us insight into the other.

This is a subtler project, though, than traditional readings of literature designed to reveal how people think (or thought). The "beliefs" that figure importantly in culture are less unitary and closely bounded than that word has generally been used to mean. As Freud taught (and as Herman Kahn exemplifies), beliefs acknowledge their opposites, and disavowals are also affirmations. Stated views have a way of revealing the power of what they're excluding.[30] So what we are really after are beliefs coupled with refusals and driven by anxieties, all of which bring the beliefs into peculiar and unexpected partnerships, and occasionally rise up from underneath to transform a given belief into its opposite.

A better set of concepts for what I'm describing comes from the work of theorists like Michel Foucault, Richard Rorty, and others, who speak of "discourse" and "discursive practices," and of texts as "discursive events."[31] The interplay I spoke of (a Foucaultian word) is the crossing, recrossing, doubling-back, and occasional undoing of discourses. We look at a text in hopes of seeing the traces of processes like these. This procedure is a variant of the familiar notion that ideas move history, but based on more complex definitions of both ideas and history, which are seen as difficult to separate. Beliefs and ideas are acknowledged not to exist on their own, but always to be encoded in language. Cultural symbols (or rather signs) are recognized as not having any single, unitary meanings, but rather as shifting their "significations" depending on context, just as words do in a complex discussion. And history is looked upon as a flux of contending and self-canceling ideologies: shifting matrices of belief that do not just "reflect" concrete conditions or interests but also have their own (discursive) internal logic.

By this discursive view, human beings themselves are "networks of beliefs and desires" who make history by talking to each other, as Rorty puts it. The state of things at any moment is an arbitrary "contingency," the result of "a thousand small mutations" that work evolutionary changes in the culture by changing its discourses:

> The mind of Europe did not *decide* to accept the idiom of Romantic poetry, or of socialist politics, or of Galilean mechanics. That sort of shift was no more an act

of will than a result of argument. Rather, Europe gradually lost the habit of using certain words and gradually acquired the habit of using others.

The basic principles of, say, today's scientific outlook took hold when, "after a hundred years of inconclusive muddle, the Europeans found themselves speaking in a way which took these interlocked theses for granted."[32]

Rorty understates, I think, the extent to which views at least of the physical world are objectively provable, not just matters of semantics. Nonetheless, he makes two valuable points: that no collective mind decides what will happen in history, and that what does happen is in large part a function of what is taken for granted. As we will see, the habit of assigning a single mind to a whole people is a common source of trouble in nuclear discourse. In a way, it is the fundamental source of the whole problem of nuclear weapons. And against this idea of a single will, what in fact turns out be involved in deeply entrenched popular beliefs is a tacit agreement among people who on the surface seem to disagree with each other. In examining the roots of the nuclear problem, we shall see many examples of underlying agreement that makes the discourse possible, but that also then rises up in the form of concrete institutions and products of culture—which, in turn, people come to take for granted and assume they can't change.

In a discursive theory of history, history is looked at as in a way textual. As against the Marxist assumption that "a ruling class generates an ideology that suits its own interests" (the interest theory), the discursive view of history recognizes the involvement of everyone: "those ruling classes don't know how they do it, nor could they do it without the other terms in the power relation—the functionaries, the governed, the repressed, the exiled—each willingly or unwillingly doing their bit."[33] The discursive view sees structures of power in history as working the way the structures of ideas or symbols do in a text, affirming some things and anxiously negating others. In this way, the theory avoids the simplistic assumptions about history which, as we have seen, simply fail when applied to the issue of nuclear weapons.

In this view, nuclear weapons would be precipitates of the discourses of our culture. If machines are really ideas, then they are events in that flux of discourse. It is the discourses and their interplay that are happening in history; the weapons are physical residues of this process. "The way people talk," says Richard Rorty, "can 'create objects,' in the sense that there are a lot of things which wouldn't exist unless people had come to talk in certain ways."[34]

This is hardly to deny the weapons' physical reality, or their danger. No text is going to turn cities into firestorms or bring on nuclear winter. But if those things happen, they will be results of discourses and ideologies, and of the beliefs these generate at a given moment. They will be events within cultural history, as was the building of the weapons in the first place. So it only makes sense to study those other, more benign discursive events, the written texts of literature and of policy, while we still have a chance of seeing and perhaps reconstituting the discourses by way of them.

V.

This section will be of less interest to some readers, but it behooves me to respond briefly to academics in the disciplines I draw on who would deny that an inquiry into the nuclear problem also stands to advance the work of those disciplines. For, however acceptable they might find it as political analysis, there are specialists who would still see this book's project as having no relevance to a purely "literary" appreciation of the texts in question. Some of the texts to be analyzed here are almost never subjected to literary readings, nor are the literary works that are so subjected usually placed in their company. Traditionalists would hold there to be a fundamental difference between "great" imaginative works, serious polemical prose, popular or mass-media products, and press-conference remarks by President Reagan. (I list these in their traditional descending order of literary value—from the canonical to the near-canonical to the at-best-in-a-different-canon to the you-can't-be-serious.)

Yet as discursive events, written (or filmed) texts easily lend themselves to analysis side-by-side with political decisions and policies, which are even more obviously discursive events. So the discourse view of history and culture demolishes these traditional and canonical distinctions—even if in practice English professors who have taken up Foucault and related theories still pay more attention to Shakespeare than to Schell or *Strangelove* (let alone Reagan).

Likewise, the view demolishes the even more entrenched assumption that works are to be studied and grouped according to intrinsic qualities. *Intrinsic* is the classic professorial code word for "the safe literary categories of formal analysis—internal structure, consistency, thematics, tone and symbolism—that still constitute the overwhelming majority of all academic studies," as Dana Gioia has put it.[35] Relevance to an issue like nuclear weapons has not been among these familiar warrants for analysis. Guardians of tradition would say my textual readings here are "about" a political problem, and that this is importantly different from being "about" literature. For purely literary purposes, one might be allowed to study Shakespeare in relation, say, to Spenser or Ben Johnson; Shakespeare himself would recognize that link. Orwell might come into play since he also wrote fictions, and maybe St. Augustine, for "background" in dealing with theological "motifs." But to link Shakespeare to Schell—particularly if the point is a topic raised *by* Schell (unraisable, in fact, by Shakespeare, who never dreamed of nuclear weapons)—this, in literary terms, is beyond eclectic, it is arbitrary. It is supposedly to exit literary analysis in the direction of social science.

It should be obvious that we cannot seriously listen to works like *Dr. Strangelove* or *The Fate of the Earth* outside the context of our political concerns. To read these works outside history would be to not read them at all. But my point here is that the same is true of Shakespeare. A Shakespeare text is a discursive event, but there is no one discourse amid that intricate flux that it obviously belongs to; the one within which we read it depends on our purpose in reading it, and that purpose exists not in the text but in the world. Foucault-influenced critics like Terry Eagleton recognize that "perhaps some of the most interesting statements which could be made about Shakespearian drama would also not count as belonging to literary criticism,"[36] and that this is a limitation not in those statements but in traditional criticism: its denial that its "purely" literary readings have any particular worldly motive.

So admittedly when various texts are analyzed (as they are here) as events in a play of discourses whose concerns are power, virtue, the ends of society, and the nature of reality, it is true those texts "will be inevitably 'rewritten,' recycled, put to different uses, inserted into different relations and practices," as Eagleton says. But literary works "always have been, of course; [even if] one effect of the word 'literature' has been to prevent us from recognizing this fact."[37] What is arbitrary is not this way of organizing the texts but the belief that some *other* construction is obviously more true to them.

As I said, this view is increasingly taking hold. Even if Eagleton were dismissed as a politically interested Marxist, and his call for integrating literature with social life as a political ploy in some disreputable sense, we would still have to deal with the similar calls that have come from others, including non- and anti-Foucaultians.[38] Wayne C. Booth, a pillar of the academic English "establishment," has argued that training in English fails to connect with ethics, politics, and history, and that its graduates "have not learned how to tackle a serious historical or philosophical *problem*."[39] And in the same establishment forum as Booth, Robert Scholes said:

> We need to come out of our belletristic closet. . . . We need to aim at a broader grasp of our textual culture as a whole—all kinds of texts in all kinds of discourses and media—supported by a firmer grasp of the central tradition of Western thought.[40]

Some of the specific proposals that have been offered for doing this make use of terms much like those I have been using. There are calls for a "civilizational approach," for study of "currents of thought," and for English to broaden into "culture studies," "discourse theory," or "rhetoric" devoted to the whole "cultural conversation" and all its diverse "symbolic processes."[41] Some such assumption underlies recent efforts like New Historicism, as well as more established subdisciplines like popular culture and feminist criticism. In short, there is "considerable agreement" today

that in reading texts, historical circumstances are necessary even for "intrinsic" understanding.[42] We can only see what a novel like *1984* is saying about
modern politics by virtue of having reflected on real-world politics and,
therefore, on specific political issues. And some literary critics who know
this have already suggested that nuclear weapons should be such an issue.[43]

The disciplinary walls are also being chipped at from the other side.
Hayden White applies literary concepts like "trope" to historical analysis,
and Dominick LaCapra calls for historians to cultivate greater sophistication with texts, since texts are as vital to the historian as to the literary
critic.[44] There are also arguments in the field of history corresponding to
the arguments in literary studies over what the field is for in the first place;
some historians (like their counterparts in English) hold that there is no
such thing as studying the past for its own sake without some reference to
the issues of our lives in the present.[45]

In short, texts, history, and present-day problems are simply inextricable. Our interest in a text presumes an interest in history, and our interest
in history, in turn, flows from our concerns in the present. Conversely, a
discursive view of history requires that any engagement with history become an engagement with discourse. And since discourses necessarily
happen in time, any discursive reading of texts must be historical.[46] One is
seriously limited if one tries to work only within one's discipline, whatever
that means. It used to be thought that tending one's own little garden inside
academe was a way of beautifying the whole world, but today we at least
need to complicate that view. Not only does the world outside distractingly
clamor for attention (as always), but the garden itself is only what it is
because of hidden relationships to that world. One tends a garden because
of its beauty, but one only recognizes the beauty in the first place because of
a larger world in which the garden exists and which taught one what beauty
is. Cultural history presumes that no body of thinking can be kept from
direct involvement in historical problems by virtue of inhabiting some
institution; but that in fact, the institutional forms to which discourses give
rise *are* history and *are* problems.

VI.

When we take the cultural-historical view of texts, or the textual view of
history, we are apt to discover certain things in particular. One is the
remarkable complexity already discussed. Cultural texts do not reveal simply the views of our era or some other, but the debates and dialectical
tensions that structure the whole historical process that produces views. We
ought to be as interested in what a text denies (hence also affirms) as in what
it purports to say. This is why I spoke earlier of "rhetorical" analysis. By
pursuing the anxieties and exclusions in a text, we get, among other
insights, some answers to the question of why certain views either fail to
translate into action or ironically produce their opposites, while others—

and the policies associated with them—become dominant beyond all reason, seemingly intractable in their era of history. One of the answers is that *certain views are powerful because they synthesize the erstwhile* opposed *views of a given discourse.* They manage to incorporate within themselves both one position from a given cultural debate or epoch *and* the supposedly opposite view—thus, in a sense, temporarily settling the conflict.

This principle applies to some of the cultural attitudes that support the existence of nuclear weapons. It is as if the history of culture is a drive toward such syntheses, which, once achieved, establish certain assumptions for a period of time as all but unassailable, as "common sense." The cultural production of common sense is a key problem to be studied. It is the essence of any *dominant* ideology, which always involves the attempt to establish certain facts or conditions as *metaphysically* grounded—as mere reflections of the nature of things—instead of as products of (discursive) history, objects created by the simple fact that people had come to talk in certain ways.

But recognizing these consensus assumptions of a culture for what they are, we can also trace (or in looking to the future, envision) the *un*doing of them, as happens when a once unshakeable synthesis comes apart. This applies very directly to the nuclear situation, where we must wonder whether, even if machines *are* ideas, we are perhaps destined to be stuck forever with those ideas now that they're here. The notion of ideas as precipitating from discourse, and of dominant ideas as synthetic combinations of different precipitates, clearly argues that we aren't. Instead it argues that even seemingly unassailable problems are historically contingent—that is, dependent on certain historical conditions holding true, which they can't do forever. It is true that the knowledge of how to build nuclear weapons can never be taken away, but that's not what's important. That knowledge can do nothing on its own, and the contexts in which it becomes dangerous are vulnerable to changes in discourse. In an important sense, therefore, present policies can be unthought.

In fact, we can even guess as to the time frame in question (all such guesses assuming, of course, that no one actually *uses* the nuclear arsenals first). The rule of thumb for cultural history is that the facts about a culture are relatively *stable at the level of decades or generations, unstable at the level of centuries.* Of course these are analytical distinctions. History is changing constantly. But if periodized by decade or generation, the cultural attitudes we are concerned with appear more continuous than not; if periodized by centuries, more discontinuous. The formula answers the prevailing "time immemorial" and everything-is-new theories of history. It more faithfully captures the rhythm of that discursive flux, which, like a system of geological fault lines, takes a certain amount of time to shift, re-form, and build up pressure toward new shifts.

It is easy to forget how similar our world is to our parents' or even our grandparents' (though the similarity is recalled in folk wisdom: "the more things change. . . ." and "there's nothing new under the sun"). But the point is that *qualitatively* greater differences appear if we compare our world with that of two, five, or seven centuries ago. Viewed on time lines of that length, things are subject to definite ideological dislocation; there are even wholesale changes in what is taken to be common sense. Today it is "obvious" that the earth is round and the moon its satellite. Was that obvious ten years ago? Of course. Fifty years ago? Yes. Five hundred years ago? Far less clear: at that historical depth we have to take a whole new look at how various kinds of discourses were constituted (for instance, what status was given to concepts like science and fact) to get a sense of the prevailing answer to that question, or of whether the question would even have been understood.

If the perspective of centuries seems too long to be politically useful, recall the alternatives: nuclear weapons are a whole new phenomenon, changing the world utterly since 1945; or, nuclear weapons reflect conditions that have "always" existed. Conventional thinking has a tendency to jump from the frying pan of the former notion into the fire of the latter. A prominent antinuclearist once told me that we *have* to assume the bomb is something radically new, and not just "an enlargement or worsening" of evils that have been with us for all time, for that view would be too discouraging. This antinuclearist was replying to other writers (including some of the professional strategists) who have argued, to the contrary, that there is more hope to be found in learning to live with that which we can't get rid of. But aside from the fact that hope and discouragement are hardly grounds for deciding which *analysis* is right, both these views rest on absolutes that have no basis in any sophisticated reading of history. And in the end they reduce to the same basic claim: culture, human beings, have not really built and are not really responsible for nuclear weapons. Either the weapons themselves are the cause of things (having, through ineluctable "science," virtually built themselves), or the weapons are so deeply rooted in that ahistorical, time-immemorial kind of history that in effect they are part of nature, not culture. In either case, they are simply there, cast down on our unlucky world from somewhere beyond it.

Cultural history depends on rejecting both these mystifying, metaphysical views, and hence rejecting both implications contained in the question after Trinity (the bomb as source of essential reality in the contemporary world, and the bomb as rooted in an essential reality as timeless and omnipotent as God). It argues that nuclear weapons could not represent a fundamental change from past generations, for those generations laid down the cultural conditions for them. But those cultural conditions, in turn, *were* a change from the conditions of earlier eras, not permanent features of human existence. Nuclear weapons are neither wholly new nor timelessly old, but *historically* old.

But they are also not just logical outcomes of commonsense national planning, as the professional strategists would rationalize them and as most people vaguely accept them to be. (Nor, of course, are they simply a plot by a self-interested leadership cabal.) They are not ineluctable features of the world from now on. Nuclear weapons can be an old problem without at the same time being eternal. Other institutions, like slavery and duelling, also once seemed natural and also came at last to their crises. The crises didn't eliminate *knowledge* necessary to those practices, but they did eliminate other conditions, like the cultural desire to pursue them.

Looking beyond our usual, generational horizon of history, we can picture the existence of nuclear weapons as a crisis in just that sense. It is a fact of the present that poses a danger and so demands attention. But it is also one point on a longer time line of associated events—a point that might be a turning point (the original meaning of *crisis*), for there is a chance that the problem will diminish in importance as the time line is extended into the future. The "presentness" of nuclear weapons is no reason to see the world as basically changed, and their "pastness" is no reason to see it as never able to change.

VII.

Of course we can still believe that nuclear weapons have in certain ways changed the world. That idea can coexist with some sense of them as old and familiar, as the language of the Trinity scientists proved. The mistake is in seeing the change as total or qualitative. Since qualitative change, I am suggesting, does not typically happen at the level of the generation, it is fruitless to speak of pre-1945 and post-1945 as different worlds (the essence of bomb-as-new and extreme forms of psychic numbing theories). But it is also unnecessary. It takes nothing from the Wright brothers to recall the dreams of Daedalus or Leonardo da Vinci.

Perhaps no Leonardo ever sketched its plan (though Hieronymus Bosch came close), but global destruction, like flight, has its imaginative history: apocalypse is almost as old an idea as God. It has even, in limited ways, already been tried. Cities have been sacked and plowed under with salt. Peoples have been dispersed, sold to slavery, slaughtered. Whole national identities have been placed under bans. Machines are finally registers of human desire; and while nuclear weapons may be a technical jump upward in destructive potential, they are not necessarily a jump upward in desire.

On the other hand, those ancient (and, sadly, modern) genocidal acts are unique events in their own right, with particular cultural histories of their own. We need not obscure the differences between Carthage, Treblinka, and the potential global evil we face today. Cultural history is a record of differences and variations as well as continuities. We must especially avoid reintroducing the time-immemorial idea under another name—for instance by ascribing nuclear weapons to some timeless (that is, history-less) problem of war. War seems to have come down to us from the

Stone Age. Yet in important ways it hasn't. *Modern* war (which nuclear weapons, we will see, are characteristic of in other than just technical ways) certainly has not. War has "always" existed only if we adopt a flexible enough definition of the term *war* to make that true. The seeming intractability of something like war is partly a matter of semantics. It may be that we have too few words for war, as from the standpoint of Eskimos we are said to have too few words for snow.

To correct that limitation we must look at modern war in cultural-historical terms, and behind it at modern ideas of the state and technology. The point of expanding our own discourse on war is that we come to better appreciate its nuances, as the Eskimo pursues a connoisseurship of snow—and thus no doubt comes at snow from some position of power: for just having words for something can give one power. The Eskimo (still assuming that bit of folklore is right) is discursively able to get a feel for snow as something other than that which just comes dumping down on the world. Similarly, war (let alone nuclear war) should not be thought something that would just come dumping down. "Many things are technologically feasible that we have quite good reason to believe will not happen," says Brodie, making a point that everyone knows already, but that few will grant applies to the bomb as well as to anything else.[47]

But granting that evil doesn't have to happen is different from grasping the conditions of the good. Here we will examine the modern popular majority's view of what is good, or in the classic term of ethical discourse, its view of virtue. The assumption is that ordinary people's views do count, but that saying that tells us little. We still want to know just *how* they count, by what dynamic they are related to collective policies.

Hence, we will also examine the particular crossings of discourse that have characterized recent American culture, and in the process we will look at what virtue stands against—at some of the evils it rhetorically depends on and defines. Overall we will be trying to discover, and finally critique, the modern metaphysics of virtue: the modern view of what constitutes the fundamental nature of things, and hence of which human actions concord with nature—that is, which are good. (I am inclined to the view that good can be defined by concordance with nature, though as I will eventually argue, modern ideas of virtue—and hence much of what goes into constructing our present situation—have been based on a faulty view of nature, a wrong metaphysics; they have taken the historically contingent and erroneously held it to be eternal.)

Before all this, though, we will look more closely at antinuclearist arguments, since these are self-conscious efforts to stretch cultural discourse—to create new words and ideas and uncreate old orthodoxies. Antinuclearist discourse naturally incorporates elements of psychology, the need for which, in the nuclear debate, we have already established. Psychology is needed for giving content to mistakes or lacks, for exposing the thinking of "average" people and for charting the ebbings and flowings of desire on which the flux of discourse depends. Similarly, it is evident that we should look at theology, our culture's prototypical discourse on questions of life, death, existence, virtue and evil. Official nuclear policy has often been called a kind of secular theology, and though this is usually meant as criticism, it also points the way (like the question after Trinity) to a discursive analysis that we might find useful. As we will see, though, both nuclear theology and nuclear psychology have encountered considerable problems—and understanding these is a key to understanding the grip the weapons themselves have seemed to have on our culture.

The direction to move in is toward a much-delayed recognition that nuclear weapons are *not* autonomous metaphysical ultimates, but historically contingent products of certain cultural (hence discursive) conditions. This is not only the truly hopeful direction but the one most consistent with fact. For the fact is that at certain moments in history, people stop acting by inaction and start *really* acting. These then go down as history's revolutionary moments. Our own times are as specific and constructed, as historic, as any other. They are perceived by most people as normal, not revolutionary. But that is a description of this moment. It is not a statement of what truly *is* normal. It is not the essence of history itself.

TWO

Antinuclear Psychology and Antinuclear Theology

We must be prepared to analyze
clinically as a neurosis not only the
foreign culture we dislike, but also our
own.
　　　　　　—Norman O. Brown

I.

Suppose an unhappy patient were to visit a psychologist, and the conversation went something like this:

> PATIENT: Doctor, I'm convinced my neighbors are conspiring to kill me. This makes me extremely anxious. Moreover, I have wired my house with explosives and will blow it up if they try to get near me.
>
> DOCTOR: You are suffering from a syndrome called paranoia. You exaggerate the intentions of others and will only hurt them, and yourself, if you continue on this course. That will be fifty dollars, please.

Suppose the same person then sought advice from her parish pastor or priest, and the conversation went like *this*:

> PARISHIONER: Help me, Father. I live a life of strife and discord with those around me. The only way any of us has yet found comfort is by threatening each other's lives.
>
> PRIEST: Oh my, what you describe is terrible in God's eyes. Scripture clearly teaches that we are to love our neighbors as ourselves. Those who live by the sword shall die by the sword. Now, please go and sin no more.

We would not think much of that psychologist as a therapist, nor of the priest as a minister. When we think of individuals' problems, we have no trouble seeing that solutions require more than refutation or warning—more than the merely negative. The problems must be seen as having actual, positive content if the person is to be helped to live differently. Mere exhortation solves nothing.

Yet where the problem is a collective one, like nuclear weapons, this point is easily forgotten. Much antinuclear discourse, especially from psychological and theological perspectives, differs very little from the kind of "advice" imagined above.

We are isolating psychological and theological discourses here because of the obvious application they have to the nuclear problem. If the existence of nuclear weapons is rooted in culture, then it lies somewhere close to the "soul." Theology and psychology are historically allied methods for diagnosing the ills of the soul. Modern depth psychology, in particular, is in large part an attempt to give positive content to what was previously thought the merely irrational. So to the extent that nuclear weapons inspire collective soul-searching, they involve us in the terms and assumptions of psychology and theology. Any attempt to account for their deep-rootedness will necessarily borrow from one or the other discipline.

The pioneers of nuclear soul-searching have already recognized this. If they have not themselves been psychologists or theologians (and often they have been), then they have certainly availed themselves of the idioms of those disciplines. Thus, we find much prodisarmament writing that speaks of the "nuclear madness" or "fixation," of "deliriums" and "death wishes"; or, in the other vein, of "revelations," "idolatry," and "warnings" of "the wrath of God." It has even been suggested that the two approaches be combined into a single method of "psycho-theology" especially designed for the nuclear problem.[1]

Moreover, the use of such methods and language has led these writers to speak, quite logically, of either "repentance" or "therapy" as possible courses of action. But in practice, something tends to go wrong with efforts to lay out such solutions. Here is a typical passage from an essay on "The Social-Psychological Dimension of the Arms Race" by Morris Schwartz:

> I believe that the persons generating these [official] delusions and deceptions acutely feel the loss of security and stability [brought about by nuclear weapons], and that they feel afraid and powerless. They try to overcome and defend themselves against this feeling of powerlessness through a massive increase in nuclear arms, and they try to conquer their fear and reassure themselves by asserting that we can prevail if we do indeed multiply our nuclear arsenal.

This states a problem and begins to analyze it psychologically. But look at the paragraph's conclusion:

> Thus as we escalate the arms race we increase the very devices that are responsible in the first place for our loss of security, and are left with a greater sense of vulnerability and insecurity.[2]

Instead of following the analysis through, this last sentence just re-emphasizes the problem. In similar fashion, a great many disarmament polemics begin with the weapons, analyze the problem partway, and then end with, "And so we must get rid of the weapons": the advice of my imaginary doctor and priest. The obvious question is, How will people suffering from the ills described possibly be able to do that?

A more scholarly example of the same confusion can be seen in this passage from an article by psychiatrist John E. Mack: "We need to develop means of penetrating and exposing the make-believe [on the part of officials]. . . . Through accurate presentation of the facts, illusions are shattered and make-believe is undermined."[3] Here, paralleling the belief that the bomb is an autonomous problem, is the suggestion that people's feelings about nuclear weapons can be got at directly, that they exist in isolation from other feelings. And Mack's impulse to "penetrate" a troubling psychological mechanism is undercut by his assumption that facts will do the job— that you can argue people out of something they haven't been argued into. If this were so, we wouldn't need psychological analyses at all. Rationality is fine when the problem is in the mind—but not, unfortunately, when it is in the soul.

II.

I picked the foregoing examples not because they are especially mistaken but, to the contrary, because they are altogether typical. Antinuclear discourse involves a lot of preaching to the converted, apparently in the belief either that the discourse reaches more widely than it does (i.e., to the *un*converted) or that addressing an elite antinuclear audience is the same as addressing the whole body politic, the "we" which "must" change its ways. Or, the discourse assumes that taking issue with the other side *can* usefully be done in the same rational, straightforward terms with which one speaks to one's comrades—as if one could have a useful argument with people with whom one does not share basic premises.

I will call the outcome of these faulty assumptions the We problem. The We problem is the confusion that seems to exist about whom one is addressing, and what one can assume or hope to accomplish, when writing on the nuclear question. It is what turns Morris Schwartz's social-psychological analysis (and many others) back upon itself. Let us look again at Schwartz's paragraph to see just how this happens. Initially, Schwartz is criticizing not a "we," but a "they"—specifically, national leaders and their various apologists, who, he says, are responsible for such mistaken views as "We can recover from a nuclear attack." He clearly says that this *they* are trying to reassure *them*selves by thinking such thoughts.

But naturally when this "they" speaks to itself, it thinks of itself as "we"; hence Schwartz is entirely right to characterize that thinking as he does: "They try to . . . reassure themselves by asserting that we can prevail." Yet thereupon enters the We problem, for in the third and last sentence, this "we" in the heads of a detached and mistaken national leadership becomes a "we" which the writer applies to all of us—himself and his readers. This crucially shifts not only the blame for what's gone wrong but also, implicitly, the whole direction of the analysis. Yet Schwartz apparently doesn't realize he has made any transition at all.

It is not surprising that he wouldn't. The "we" of his third sentence is a characteristic pose that writers and speakers often assume for rhetorical purposes. It is consistent with the old debate-team wisdom that one should try to win the assent of one's audience by speaking as if on their behalf. (I use it selectively myself in this book.) The "we" pose is an especially comfortable one for political analysts to adopt when they wish to characterize the large-scale actions and beliefs of the public as a whole. Thus (again to take a typical instance) Garry Wills, in his excellent *Reagan's America: Innocents at Home*, speaks of the myths that "we" find appealing in the image presented by Ronald Reagan.[4] It is again a case of an easy transition being made between characterizing what Reagan, perhaps, *wants* us to believe—that, for example, "We have it in our power to begin the world over again"—and what "we," the real "we" actually out here, do believe. Perhaps too easy a transition, since Wills has been criticized for it by reviewer Jack Beatty:

> [I] squirm over Wills's use of those implicating words *us* and *we*. Who are the members of this "we" who fall for Reagan's flatulent promises ("begin the world over again," and so forth)? Clearly, Garry Wills is not among them. *He* is on to Reagan. "We," evidently, is the electorate. . . . Wills's "we" is only a literary device, but it is an inauthentic one. A writer should always test his "we"s against himself. Am I in there? he should ask. And if he isn't . . . then he should scrap his "we."[5]

Beatty might further have questioned whether labeling even the electorate a "we" makes sense. More than 37,000,000 Americans voted against Reagan in his 1984 "landslide," and many millions more didn't vote at all.

But then, Wills's use of the device is comparatively unobtrusive. Mainstream journalists carry it further, speaking of "our" not just having supported but having been "mesmerized" by Reagan.[6] (*Mesmerized* is a term commonly used to evade psychological analysis.) And the all-embracing "we" appears even in discussions that can *only* be meant for readers it can't possibly include. William Greider, for instance, analyzes the Iran-contra scandal in terms of how "we" have responded to Reagan's cold-war rhetoric and "allowed our innocence to become a form of self-deception. Our natural idealism is twisted into a simple-minded world view that is not only stupid but dangerous." This analysis is then published for readers of *Rolling Stone* magazine—probably not, by and large, members of this particular "we."[7]

In some uses the device becomes completely absurd. Chellis Glendinning turns *we* into *you* in announcing his program for "nuclear therapy": "My job is to ask you to explore your attitudes toward this global precipice we share."[8] (As if those needing therapy would be likely to seek out his book.) And Gail Sheehy in *The New Republic* implicates not just us, but *all* of us, in the Reagan achievement: "If Ronald Reagan came to assume that he was above reality, it was in large measure because we the electorate coddled him into believing it. . . . Under Reagan *we all* developed the habit of denial."9 This kind of language, reminiscent of the headline style made famous by *USA Today* ("We're dining out more often this year"), doesn't just mislead, it unconsciously plays into the hands of people like Reagan himself, by granting the kind of unanimity that Reagan's 1984 "America is Back" campaign was designed to convince "us" we had achieved. At its worst, the device reflects the kind of "history has ended" thinking that I will discuss further in chapter 6.10 (Of course it is not just Americans who turn up as "we"s. A 1987 British Conservative Party political broadcast argued that foreign ideas like socialism had been allowed to "creep into our thinking.")

In nuclear discourse the shadow of "we" often reaches absurd lengths. It involves not just subtle shifts from "them" to "us," but from the conditional to the (supposedly) actual:

> We can . . . respect the [reality] constructions of other people, and then try to create some shared constructions. But this means changing our own constructions, and if we refuse . . . then we have to resort to force, to some form of cruelty, to get other people to accept our constructions. So we beat our children, give greater powers to the police, send in the army to destroy those who oppose us, collect and use guns, bombs and the instruments of torture.11

It is not that this description of a psychological dynamic is wrong, but it certainly errs in its application in the last sentence. This is an error with many consequences, among them that it depersonalizes and dehistoricizes the dynamic: if we accept it we stop asking why *particular* "we"s at particular times and places beat their children or rely on bombs.

I said the We problem was a confusion about to whom one speaks and what one can assume about that audience. This view is based on my observations as a teacher of writing, where I have often observed what I think are these same underlying confusions among students struggling to write argumentative prose. Again and again, the specific failings of student essays—problems of organization, of relevance, of coherence, even of grammar—turn out at bottom to be problems in forming a clear mental picture of an audience. Perhaps the single most crucial thing students of writing must learn (particularly in academic settings, where there is no genuine audience) is how to answer the questions, *To whom am I speaking? Why? What am I trying to accomplish? What must this essay include, and in what tone and order, to accomplish that, to bring the audience along with me?* Students often find themselves at a complete loss because they don't know what kinds of ideas are possible, and what kinds of things it might be interesting to say. And this, in turn, is because they haven't clearly seen the shape of the discourse community they are struggling to join. They haven't known audiences in real life who are in need of knowing what they have to say.

In this condition, students sometimes appear as if they not only have no ideas, but don't know *how* to have them, and don't know an idea when they see one. I think this fact is closely connected to the supposed decline in student literacy and, more importantly, to the widely acknowledged political apathy and impotence of young people, to the almost militant insistence of many of them on not acting politically (which, of course, also *is* acting politically). What is important for us is to ask whether there are similar sources for the "apathy" of the wider public, and whether writers on the disarmament question are unconsciously participating in those patterns, perhaps for reasons like the students'.

III.

In *After Virtue*, moral philosopher Alasdair MacIntyre has argued that the ability to reason about moral issues has been lost from our culture during the past two hundred years. MacIntyre's analysis of the reasons for this is erudite and complex. But he mentions one consequence of this loss that should be of enormous interest to readers of disarmament literature. *Protest*, MacIntyre points out, used to have positive as well as negative meanings—as it still might if we speak, old-fashionedly, of "protesting our love" for something. But, as the premises of modern moral debate have become what MacIntyre calls incommensurable, the term has largely lost its positive meanings. Thus:

> The self-assertive shrillness of protest arises because the facts of incommensurability ensure that protestors can never win an *argument*; the indignant self-righteousness of protest arises because the facts of incommensurability ensure equally that the protestors can never lose an argument either. Hence the *utterance* of protest is characteristically addressed to those who already *share* the protestors' premises. The effects of incommensurability ensure that protestors rarely have anyone else to talk to but themselves. This is not to say that protest cannot be effective; it is to say that it cannot be *rationally* effective and that its dominant modes of expression give evidence of a certain perhaps unconscious awareness of this.[12]

If this is right, then the We problem in disarmament polemics—the problem, in effect, of antinuclear protestors talking to themselves—may be embedded in a deeper cultural problem (which, for that matter, might also account for much of the difficulty students have in learning to write). But it seems to me that where the nuclear debate is concerned, there are specific forms this problem takes, and therefore more specific reasons which we can assess for the We problem's appearance at awkward moments.

In the case of psychological antinuclear discourse, there seem to be three related problems. We might call them three roadblocks, since they tend to impose themselves one after the other: A writer who clears one will tend to get stopped by the next, or the next after that. First, a psychological analyst might have no *name* for the soul's sickness and, thus, no "handle" on it. Second, the analyst might have a name for it, but be unwilling to ascribe it to people in general. And third, he or she might admit that the sickness belongs to people in general, but feel forced to regard it, therefore, as an unchangeable "fact" of "human nature."

Notice how problem one creeps into this analysis by Edward Thompson, in his essay "Notes on Exterminism":

> There remains something, in the inertial thrust and reciprocal logic of the opposed weapons systems—and the configuration of material, political, ideological and security interests attendant upon them—which cannot be explained within [our usual political] categories.[13]

What is the "something"? Thompson tries calling it exterminism, which he defines as a certain "inertial thrust" within the "deep structure" of the Cold War. But to make up new names is really to *deny* that older terms make sense, or that the nuclear peril is part of some preexisting pattern after all. It is another way to abstract the nuclear issue out of the complexity of life and history, and to look upon the bomb as that "basic change," a cause of things rather than an effect. This is not really to explain the phenomenon, for explaining something ultimately requires linking it to known categories of experience. (Robert Jay Lifton's and Richard Falk's "nuclearism" concept reflects essentially the same problem.)[14]

Problem two is very common in discussions that speak of the "madness" or "paranoia" of the arms race. As often as terms like these get thrown around, almost equally often are excuses made for ordinary people.

This is where the We problem becomes most fully apparent. Notice, for instance, the confusion George Kennan gets into when he speaks in psychological language. "Can we not at long last cast off our preoccupation with sheer destruction?" Kennan asks. "For this entire preoccupation with nuclear war is a form of illness. It is morbid in the extreme." After a bit more such psychological-sounding analysis, Kennan concludes, "I decline to believe that this is the condition of the majority of our people."[15]

That's a relief—but then, who was the "we" Kennan was speaking to one paragraph earlier? Kennan clearly has not settled that point for himself. People in general seem implicated, yet they must not be. To our democratic way of thinking, holding the majority responsible for our predicament is even more unthinkable than nuclear war itself.

This is the point on which confusion about who the audience is joins with confusion about how it should be spoken to. Chapter 1 spoke of the arms race as the result of people's positive, though unconscious, decision to act (or not) in ways that would stop it. It is a tough thing to face, the idea that millions of people—one's own friends, neighbors, relatives and co-workers—might be participating in some gargantuan mistake. But even tougher is to stand back from these others and say, "*They* are making the mistake," while exempting oneself. At least in our culture, all one's training in etiquette argues against saying such things. The We problem arises in part, I think, from an effort among writers on the nuclear question to be polite and fair—as well as (they may think) less confrontational toward "the people," and hence more effective in persuading them.

But again, the problem is that politeness gets in the way of analysis. Only by standing back from a phenomenon (in this case, ordinary people's at least tacit support for nuclear arms) can you really study it. As I've said, what disarmament writing tends to do is to veer away from study toward exhortation—which is to say, to veer toward the natural position which a polite speaker will tend to take: Come on, folks, I'm one of you, and *I* can see this is wrong. So surely *we* can see it too, right?

In effect, when a speaker uses the "we" form of address in this way, he is saying, "You people have *got* to be more like me. I can't *believe* you're not all just like *me!*" It is like trying to get a foreigner to understand English by shouting it at him. In short, it is not really polite at all; it is a failure, rather, to acknowledge other people for what they are, warts and all, unwillingness to act and all, unconscious, acculturated desires and all.

A special form of this failure, and a special way of excusing the people, is to write off the nuclear "madness" as a characteristic of political and military leaders only. Under this strategy, the fact that the public condones what those leaders do is rationalized (recall the terms of chapter 1) as an *effect* of the arms race, a logical, defensive response to it, rather than as one of its chief causes. It is assumed that nuclear issues would be decided differently if submitted to "the conscience and the common sense of ordinary people," as William Stringfellow puts it.[16]

A good example of this attitude comes from Dr. Helen Caldicott. Caldicott sees "pathology" and "paranoia" at work in the arms race, but nonetheless prefers to ascribe these conditions to "strategists and leaders."[17] That congressmen elected by the American people regularly vote for more weapons is explained, she speculates, by their having "given up their souls and intellects" for "dinner at the White House and Gold Medal Presidential Commissions." Politicians, Caldicott adds, will have to be "trained" like children, by a public which allegedly takes a more mature view of the problem than they do. Again, it is assumed to be impossible that those politicians may be *representing* their constituents when they cast those pro-weapons votes.

And there is one other, related strategy for excusing the people: admitting that they might be wrong, but attributing this to ignorance on their part deliberately cultivated by elites—in simplest terms, manipulation by the media. Or more subtly, one can speak of the mass pathology as something passive, so that ordinary people become (in Jim Garrison's words) "victims of a compelling nightmare, hypnotized and magnetized" in a "dreamlike" state that resembles that of children following the Pied Piper. Superficially, this reverses Caldicott's formulation, in which people were seen as adults and the *leaders* were the children. But at bottom it is based on the same stern separation between the two.

Problem three begins when we attempt to close that gap between people and leaders. If we can finally acknowledge "human nature" as the problem, then ordinary people are at least as culpable as politicians. Psychologists David P. Barash and Judith Eve Lipton, in *The Caveman and the Bomb: Human Nature, Evolution, and Nuclear War*, express this view with their useful observation that "the nuclear arms race goes on because *people* allow it," and this is true in turn because of the residual "Neanderthal mentality" of our race.[18] Such a view, imputing responsibility to people in general, at least makes it less mysterious that the arms race has been led from the start by a great democratic society. It also holds hope, finally, for a solution. For by this formulation, the weapons stop appearing as an autonomous problem. They stop being causes and instead become effects, which means they in turn have causes which we can hope to act upon.

So here is where we began, with the need to fit nuclear weapons into older, preexisting patterns of behavior. That pattern, or, one might say, the prior phenomenon, is people's attitudes. If we can understand and change the attitudes, we can eliminate nuclear weapons.

Yet, somehow we end up further from the answer than ever. How on earth can you change human nature? Indeed, at this point the whole psychological approach seems to break down. That approach is based on an analogy between individual psychology, which one encounters in clinics and can hope to treat, and the collective psychology behind the arms race. And collective psychology cannot be brought into the clinic.

Perhaps this is why so few analysts even hazard stage three to begin with. Intuitively, they agree with Marcus Raskin, who says that to see the weapons as "not causes but effects," to ascribe them to human nature, gives us "a prognosis without hope."[19]

But such pessimism rests on a major unexamined assumption: the commonsense view that human nature is fixed and changeless. Barash's and Lipton's "Neanderthal mentality" is another nonname, like "exterminism," since it circularly avoids explaining anything. Literally, it just means "the kind of thinking people have had since Neanderthal times." But worse, a prehistorical mentality is also *ahistorical*, which means all but permanent. To say we've had something since Neanderthal times is to say we've had it forever.

Barash and Lipton are essentially biological determinists—theorists who explain social phenomena in terms of fairly simple models of the action of biological drives or states.[20] While they might argue for saying no to our inborn tendencies by use of our superior faculty of reason, they have no suggestion for how we might do this. They can only remind us of the urgency of doing so and note that "maybe" humanity will reach "the point at which, while unable to be saints but refusing to bow down to universal murder, we resolve to overcome the Neanderthal mentality and thereby transcend, if not overcome, our biology itself."[21]

This, again, is preaching to the converted. The reader has no doubt already said no, and might readily agree that "we" should resolve to do all this—but *he* or *she* is then left to wonder how to get *them*, those who aren't reading *The Cavemen and the Bomb* and who aren't aware of the problem, to join in such resolutions. The book offers no answer; the words just quoted are from its final sentence.

IV.

Two other possible ways out of nuclear psychology's conundrums are also worth noting, partly because they offer insight into another general problem of this whole discourse. First is the argument of Brian Easlea, whose book *Fathering the Unthinkable* specifically names, and hence explains and isolates, the problematic facts about "human nature." Easlea argues that it is not human nature as such but *male* nature and *masculine* psychology that give rise to the arms race, by foregrounding such traits as insecurity, aggressiveness, competitiveness, and men's allegedly intertwined desires to control women, property, and the natural world. He presents this argument specifically as a rejoinder to the Barash and Lipton type of argument:

> Since the extent and brutality of [men's] problematic behaviour have varied greatly both geographically and over time it is impossible to be satisfied with the pessimistic "explanation" that men are "by nature" part beast. We must therefore, and gladly, look elsewhere for explanations.[22]

That "elsewhere" is the realm of feminist theory, one of whose projects has been to reanalyze dominant institutions and activities of Western society (in this case, science and technology) in terms of how they rest upon, and perpetuate, the values of our historically patriarchal culture.

Feminism is a natural resource for depth analyses of the arms race. It is one of the few increasingly mainstream bodies of thinking which are willing to entertain seriously the possibility of widespread error: the daunting prospect—on which, as described above, so much antinuclear thinking has foundered—that hundreds of millions of people support policies which are dangerous and wrong. It might be said that *Fathering the Unthinkable* gets us halfway from leaders-versus-people to people-in-general: It assigns the blame for today's predicament to a much wider circle than the national leadership, but still to a *circle* or limited group which in some way resembles most of that leadership—namely, by being male.

The problem with this is, first, that by identifying the problem with the characteristics of that group, it tends toward reductionism: the sticking of too simple a label on too complex a range of phenomena. At bottom, masculinity is as imprecise a concept as Neanderthal mentality, and hence as difficult to make good use of. Easlea elaborates the concept somewhat by arguing that there are particularly masculine myths and desires, such as that of the "pregnant phallus," which constitute an identifiable male/patriarchal outlook on things; but it is difficult to know how to define these myths and desires except, circularly, by their specific manifestations. For instance, Easlea quotes Edward Teller, widely acknowledged father of the H-bomb, on the difference between "conception" and "execution" in the H-bomb's development, and then remarks that

> the belief that "the idea" is paramount, the execution secondary . . . is yet again an example of the supremacy of the belief in the supposedly "masculine" over the supposedly "feminine" in the process of conception and giving birth.[23]

This notion that conception is masculine and execution feminine derives from a feminist hypothesis that people in general analogize large areas of life to sex and gender-role phenomena. Thus, it is thought that people value conception because it is like insemination, a male function, and disvalue execution because it is like a woman's bearing a child. (The pregnant phallus would be men's subconscious wish that they could make children—or anything else—entirely on their own.) In the passage quoted above, Easlea is imputing these subconscious analogies to Teller, and thus "explaining" Teller's preference for conception: he values it, ultimately, because it is like insemination.

But it is also possible to argue that Teller values conception because it is like conception, and disvalues execution because it is like execution. It is possible that those values preexist, or are grounded in some other psychology altogether—and then, perhaps, that insemination is valued over childbearing by analogy to *them*. (In the same way, it is difficult to prove that people's attitudes toward nature follow from, rather than *give rise to*, men's views of women and sex.) Easlea's theory usefully tries to name and to isolate the problematic in human experience, and it introduces a vocabulary and an outlook from depth psychology to the otherwise rigid notions of human nature that leave us, seemingly, with no action to take. But it also tends toward the reductionism that even Freud himself recognized depth psychology could fall into. Even Freud knew that sometimes a cigar in a patient's dream really is just a cigar.

A lesser but related problem with Easlea's argument is that it tends toward the simplistic idea that the world we live in is constructed out of self-interest. By claiming that the model for scientific and political thinking is men's *oppression* of women, it implies that men act in ways intended to aggrandize themselves and that, at least until now, they have largely succeeded at this. This is the intellectual postulate known as *functionalism*: the assumption that given behavior or beliefs are what they are because they accomplish something, "function" in some way, for the people who hold them.

Superficially, functionalism is the *opposite* of simple human nature theories of behavior, those of the "Neanderthal mentality" type. Functionalism sees human personality as responding to circumstances at least as much as to genes. Yet finally it, too, tends to overlook the complexity of real behavior. I said that functionalism was a "lesser" problem in Easlea's book, but it is hardly so in antinuclear thinking or oppositional politics in general. To some degree functionalism could be held to be *the* intellectual problem of the whole political Left. Viewing people primarily in their *material* rather than their cultural relationships, left-political discourse ends up relying on commonsense psychological theories, like the interest theory discussed in the last chapter. People's behavior is seen as the logical response to definable external stimuli. Thus, the simplest answer to the question of people's ideological commitment to "the system" is that the system makes it worth their while; it offers benefits that favor conformity. People, in other words, find it *rational* to go along.

But as we have seen, nuclear weapons especially call this rationalistic psychology into question. And once it is discredited we are back to where we started: needing a psychology that will give some sophisticated account of people's complex and contradictory behavior.

To some extent, materalistic thinkers (including Marxists) understand this. But seeing the inadequacy of their own psychological categories, and insensible to the untapped resources of *depth* psychology, they argue for giving up altogether on looking into people's minds. This is the road temporarily taken in Joel Kovel's *Against the State of Nuclear Terror*. Kovel begins by noting the obviousness of the need for psychological analyses:

> We are fatally silent, yet have the voice to cry out. Therefore the silence is a thing of the mind, and we have the right, indeed the obligation, to think psychologically if we are to find a way out of the nuclear trap. In no other political situation has there been more need for psychological understanding.[24]

Kovel then discusses several psychological phenomena which he sees at work, including "the radical mystery of the state." The modern state forces our submission, partly on the basis of the several benefits it provides—"a carrot as well as a stick," as Kovel explicitly puts it. But, he recognizes, there is more to a radical mystery than mere bribery:

> In face of this mystery, our inertia becomes less baffling. The penalties for not believing in the state's beneficence are simply too high. One does not want a nice, kindly protector to turn into an ogre when that ogre has the power to end life on earth. But to question the state's version of things is to risk just this. . . . It would be deadly to underestimate the extent of our inner bondage to the established order, to the image locked inside us of a state that is our benevolent protector. It is scarcely an exaggeration to assert that we owe our sanity itself to

our acquiescence. For how could we . . . continue to function unless we believed in the virtue of our society?[25]

People (or "we") are "infantilized" by the state, forced to depend upon it as children depend upon their parents—and not just out of carrot-and-stick economic motives but, as this passage makes clear, out of deeply held psychological needs as well.

This explanation, while not so simply rationalistic as the crude "psychologism" Kovel rightly critiques, is nonetheless functionalist: it presumes that certain kinds of overtly irrational behavior serve, in the broader view, the rational purpose of holding society together and defining people's places within it. Thus, in looking at the ideology of sovereignty, it sees a real *need* on people's part for the false consciousness that props up the state. It sees such consciousness as serving, down deep, some real *function*. There is still a carrot, only one that lies buried in the earth rather than dangling before people's eyes.

Now, depth psychology also looks for sense in people's wrong-headedness, but sense of a far more complex and less easily rationalized kind. It asks why people behave in certain ways even when the only possible carrots and sticks driving them to it are pure fantasies. It looks for whole underlying worldviews (or, in my terms, metaphysics) which people adhere to quite apart from whether such views "function" in the narrow sense. Kovel eventually takes up depth psychology himself and says some useful things about the role of culture, the locus of "an entire attitude toward the world."[26] But this happens in the context of his appeal to "us" to learn to see politically instead of psychologically:

This means letting go of the categories of psychology [and] shifting our focus to society. . . . As a first step, it means seeing [our] experience as a form of *oppression*. There may be a psychology of oppression, but oppression itself is nonpsychological. It breaks the bounds of the self and makes us look at the other who is doing the oppressing.[27]

In other words, we need to return to more recognizably Marxist turf, to step *out* of the mind and into the structures of society, rather than *beneath* it, into the structures of the soul. Many other antinuclearists never think beyond society in the first place—hence the multitude of calls for "us" to throw off "our" reliance on nuclear arms. However true it is that structures of society are "nonpsychological," people's behavior with respect to them is a psychological problem of the first order.

This means, again, that we must put Marx aside at some point and turn to Freud. We must recognize the limits, not of psychology per se, but of rationalistic and functionalist psychologies that assume people respond to needs and stimuli in something like a one-to-one fashion, each stimulus X generating response Y. Moreover, we must open up for discussion the large historical questions that functionalist thinking of this sort fails to raise. Is it really true that "we," in all times and places, equally need to believe in the virtue of our own society, as Kovel seems commonsensically to point out? Looking more closely at the symbolic and unconscious transactions between people, in all their complexity, and at people's complex images of the state, we might find that the answer is no. It might turn out, rather, that to attribute special virtue to one's own society is a particular and explicable phenomenon, fed by currents of history that swell forward under some cultural conditions and recede under others—not just something "we" all crave (by nature) all of the time. What would be needed, then, would be an addendum to Kovel's "*general* psychology of technocracy," detailing *specifically* how certain tendencies identified by depth psychology have managed to get the upper hand in certain cultural situations. This detailing would be a true psychoanalyzing of our culture, and it would not even be so inconsistent with the socioeconomic kind of analysis inspired by Marx. For it was Marx who, by linking political history to economics, suggested that there are origins to be found in historical time for the political forces which today are the leading actors in the nuclear drama—forces (like the nation-state, to be analyzed in chapter 4) whose presence on the screen of history had once been assumed to be as magical, even divine, as those bright, giant images of early film actors must have seemed on the first movie screens.

V.

These are some of the problems of psychological antinuclear discourse. What about theological? If psychologists trapped by functionalism and the We problem are at a loss in the face of "human nature," we might hope that a better grasp of it would be shown by theologians. After all, the idea that humanity is collectively in a bad way is surely no news to theology, which knows full well that sinfulness appeared on Earth well before 1945. Surely theologians know better than to agree with Jonathan Schell, who calls the nuclear age "the second fall of man." The first fall, they would say, was plenty, and explains all subsequent problems—explains them, we would hope, in terms which theology has had more time than psychology to elaborate for us.

But what we actually find, when we turn to theological writings on the subject, are variations of the same problems we have just been discussing. First, the We problem. Paul Rogat Loeb has quoted Bishop Leroy Mathiessen, the antinuclear prelate of Amarillo, Texas, as saying that "whatever God *we* formally profess, we bow before, we tithe to, we place our trust in quite different gods—gods of metal" (emphasis added). In fact, Loeb's discussions with antinuclear activists suggest reasons for believing that theology might be *especially* prone to the We problem, precisely insofar as it holds *everyone* to have "sinned and fallen short of the glory of God," as St. Paul said. One activist, Marv Davidov, is quoted by Loeb as saying,

When we first got together [the church-based people said] "We are all just as guilty as Honeywell management. We are all guilty." And I said, "Wait a minute. Let me explain something that I've learned. The management at Honeywell profits from [building nuclear arms for the government]. They make millions out of murder. They're conscious of their choices. Therefore they're guilty in a different sense from the guilt that you're talking about. You may be guilty to the extent to which you pay your taxes or fail to act when you know. But you're not guilty the same way."[28]

The "church-based people" Davidov was arguing with were, of course, articulating the theological doctrine of sin and, in his view, confusing it with the more limited notion of *political* responsibility for existing nuclear policies. They were stuck in the We problem and also confused on the human-nature question—"sin" being, of course, one *theological* theory of human nature.

Classical theology has looked at sin as something that entered the world long ago, something that has *always* been part of the human condition. Logically, applying the concept to nuclear weapons should, therefore, tend to reduce the apparent specialness, or what I have called the autonomy, of nuclear weapons. Indeed, the sin concept as classically understood supplies us with a cause, of which nuclear weapons then become the effect. This should help us avoid the easier but less useful belief that nuclear weapons are themselves a new thing and a cause. From the theological perspective, all human self-destructiveness ought to be seen as an effect of the eating of the forbidden fruit of the Garden.

Yet this is frequently not how the concept is applied. Dale Aukerman, in *Darkening Valley: A Biblical Perspective on Nuclear War*, sees the splitting of the atom as "a postponed swallowing of the tough core of that original fruit." Although Aukerman allows for the fact that humanity already had fallen, he insists on treating nuclear weapons as something cosmic—as far-reaching as the fall of man. The bomb is not just one more earthly contrivance, but, finally, a *metaphysical* event. Like many theologians who take up the issue, Aukerman is less concerned with the cultural question of how *people* could permit the existence of nuclear weapons than he is with the spiritual question of how God could. True, he links the bomb with humanity's fall, but the whole distance from that event to the specific historical fact of nuclear weapons is traversed in a single metaphor, the swallowing of a core of fruit.[29]

This is what I have called the time-immemorial view of the bomb, and as I have noted, it comes to the same thing as saying that nuclear weapons are altogether new, a cause rather than a consequence of culture. Either human history has always been a history of self-destructiveness, ever since the beginning of human time, or it has not, and something new has come to pass since 1945. The usefulness of linking nuclear weapons to sin ought to be that it opens, rather than closes, investigation into the former idea.

I am aware of a potential confusion here. On the one hand, I have been criticizing those writers who assign responsibility for the nuclear threat to some "we" which includes even those who vocally oppose the weapons' existence. On the other hand, I am endorsing a recognition of nuclear weapons as sin. But isn't sin a condition in which (according to theology) we are all equally entrapped? So do these views contradict each other—doesn't the linking of nuclear weapons and sin logically lead to the view that we *are* all responsible for them? Indeed, since sin is a term for human nature, doesn't this linkage amount to the same thing as assigning the nuclear threat to human nature, a strategy I have criticized?

By one use of the term *sin*, yes, it does. But we have also certainly heard *sin* used to describe particular acts of particular people (not "we"s) who are asked and expected to turn away from them—even if (again according to theologians) they can only finally do this with some sort of divine help. The nuclear threat could be seen as such a particular act. I have tried to show that it *was* an action in the first place, even if often in the form of nonaction. Here, I am trying to suggest ways of further characterizing it as an act. Nuclear weapons are a consequence of a basic human nature (whether we call it sinful or not); *but* it is a mistake to view this basic nature as always predicting any particular action in a given case, just as it is a mistake to assume that a given person's sinful nature requires that that person will be, say, a child molester. There are different ways of sinning, and threatening to destroy the world need not be humanity's way.

Put more generally, where we run into trouble with our concepts is where we fail to use them as *explanatory* hypotheses. Psychological and theological ideas are powerful tools of analysis, but not if used in condemnation or preachment. Here I am stressing their use as tools. And the sin concept fails as such a tool if, like the We problem, it leads us away from making careful distinctions about the responsibility for and causes of the nuclear peril—if, indeed, it leads us to view the nuclear peril as itself a cause of how things are. To see nuclear weapons as a second fall, or as in some other way equal to the first fall into sin, is to place them outside history, and hence to encourage despair. Certainly, if nuclear weapons have cosmic meaning, they will literally be hell to get rid of. But the sin concept, used another way, reminds us that they do *not* have cosmic meaning—that they are simply the latest in a long series of preposterous human ideas, albeit a particularly dangerous one. We must look for the reasons why *certain* powerful factions among us have chosen this *particular* absurdity; in other words, search for *causes*. And we must remember that if something has reasons for existing, then it is not necessarily permanent.

Of course, it is unfair to accuse theologians of failing to analyze the problem, because metaphysical categories like sin *are* terms of analysis within their particular discourse (a discourse that assumes the reality of a higher realm). But there is another reason why, despite the potential power of the sin concept, theologians might have, if anything, a tougher time than psychologists in facing the nuclear threat analytically. Nuclear weapons, after all, sharply challenge the traditional Judeo-Christian belief in an omnipotent God. They seem to give humanity the power to short-circuit the Last Judgment, and, thus, they call that omnipotence into question.

There are several possible responses one might have to this problem. One is to hew to the traditional faith in a God who still holds the last trumpet, and who will ensure that humanity never does end the world on its own. Aukerman, for instance, has written of the "God who transforms attitudes" as the ultimate key to our deliverance from our peril.[29] Of course, if we can count on this God, it is hard to see what point there is in taking action ourselves. This is why politically aware theologians (and many ordinary believers) find themselves caught between trusting that God still holds the trumpet—and so doing nothing politically—or trying to do something, and thus in effect admitting to doubts about the power of God. If the theology of such people sounds peculiar, that just reflects the cruel force of this theological dilemma.

Another response is to argue that the trumpet really has been delivered into our hands. Some fundamentalist Christians apparently believe this, and quite happily look forward to the Bible's promises being fulfilled by a nuclear Armageddon. (For a while the last president of the United States gave disturbing evidence of being influenced by this notion.) But it is not just fundamentalists; there is also an antinuclear variant of this view, whereby writers like Jim Garrison have cast the nuclear peril as a "challenge" and "confrontation" of humanity by God, with God conceding to us His power to end the world. Again, the problem is that this view more readily leads to calls that "we" repent than to practical suggestions.

If we really took sin and the fall of man seriously, we would not be surprised that humankind has amassed the power to destroy itself. For we would see that it has been destroying itself little by little during its whole tenure on earth. What theologians call the sinful part of human nature has always sought more efficient methods for this, and now it has managed to find one. Let us not make Adam's mistake and imagine that this particular fruit of the Tree of Knowledge really does give us godlike power. Nuclear weapons are just one more tawdry, confused, frail human effort—maybe, like so many others, even a stupidly well-intentioned one.

Though this discussion deals with theology, I have tried to phrase the above in such a way as to show that the right view really is a *secular* one—a view, that is, which is equally available to nonbelievers, since it makes use of Christian beliefs not about the deity, but about humanity and culture. The right view (meaning the one most helpful in solving our problem) requires believing only, as C. H. Sisson has put it, that Christianity "has, even for those who are what is called sceptical, undeniable strengths in its far-reaching correspondence with the deeper reaches of human nature," and that our culture is heir to the worldview which Christianity gave to most of our ancestors. If we think of original sin as the archetype for our secular ideas about evil, including psychological ones, then theology provides the Western world with one of its most powerful frameworks for self-analysis. And it makes sense for anyone, Christian or otherwise, who is concerned about the nuclear peril to try to make use of that framework.

Evil was a point of contention in a seminal theological debate of some 1,600 years ago, between Pelagius and St. Augustine. Roughly speaking, Pelagianism rejected original sin in favor of a belief that evil arose from unenlightened error, which could be overcome by humankind's own, in-born spiritual potentialities, and not solely through divine intervention. Pelagianism pointed toward a possible utopia on earth, since it held that a properly enlightened (and fundamentally good) humanity would ultimately pursue worthy goals. Augustine led the way toward official ecclesiastical denunciation of the Pelagian view, which ever since has formally been regarded as a heresy.

But because heresies live on in cultural discourse, this foundational debate of Western culture has never really ended. "Even those who think of Genesis as literature, and those who are not Christian, live in a culture indelibly shaped" by interpretations of sin and the fall of man, says Elaine Pagels.[30] In our own secular era, the Pelagius-Augustine controversy continues in the arenas of literature and philosophy. Geoffrey Aggeler, a literary critic, has made this clear with reference to the novels of Anthony Burgess, novels which are self-consciously informed by the ongoing debate:

> If we are willing to share Burgess's vision and set aside, or at least look beyond, the narrowly theological aspects of it and view "Augustinianism" and "Pelagianism" in terms of their broad philosophical implications, we can see that the council of Carthage in A.D. 418, which condemned Pelagianism, was by no means the end of it. The debate has in fact continued in the West with periodically varying degrees of intensity down to our own time. Its more vigorous sessions include the fourteenth-century clash between Bradwardine and Ockham and the conflict three centuries later between the Jansenists and the Jesuits. Outstanding Augustinian spokesmen include Luther, Calvin, Jansen, Pascal, Racine, Hobbes, Swift, and Edmund Burke. Some of the more notable Pelagians are Shaftesbury, Corneille, Hume, Rousseau, Jefferson, Thomas Paine, Marx, Hegel, John Stuart Mill, Edward Bellamy, and most of the major English and German romantic poets. The validity of these classifications depends of course upon a willingness to view the debate in terms of its social and political as well as its religious implications.
>
> When the debate is viewed in broader terms, the nature of man emerges as the pivotal issue, and one can see that the diametrically opposed assumptions of Augustine and Pelagius could be taken as premises of diametrically opposed political philosophies as well as attitudes toward social progress as far removed as hope and despair.[31]

And if the disputes to which Aggeler alludes resonate with these ancient issues, it follows that American culture, a society of Puritans on the one hand and Jeffersonians on the other, of transcendentalists on the one hand

and business tycoons on the other, resonates with them to perhaps an unusual degree.

So it is easy to hypothesize that nuclear weapons do too. Here are devices which simultaneously reveal both the power and the weakness of human works, which argue for *both* the Pelagian and the Augustinian views. They are just machines, yet, at the same time, flaming swords held over our heads by angels. When that first atomic bomb was spoken of in reverential, religious terms, it was simultaneously an affirmation of both Augustinian humility toward God's power and extraordinary Pelagian pride in human-kind's. And if the bomb therefore stands at the shared apex of two central traditions of our culture, if it exists in the space of agreement above a dispute that constitutes one of our culture's most central discourses, then we have an explanation for the "tremendous internal momentum" which Jonathan Schell has noted in the arms race—and which drives so many writers on the subject into that despair I have already noted.

VI.

But at what level do these traditions actually work today, and where do we look to intervene in them? Again, the answer comes from leaving aside theology's exhortations, as we left aside psychology's, and looking instead at what religion teaches about cultural images and symbols. There are cultural "repertoires of values," says theologian Bernice Martin, and these values express themselves through a "hidden vocabulary" of symbols that "satu-rate" popular culture and structure its assumptions. Therefore, we need to look at

> the inchoate constellations of imagery, sentiment and identification which form archeological strata in our culture, sedimented deposits of unconsidered, im-plicit meanings lying beneath the surface of reasoned debate. . . . They stand unanalysed behind what counts as a good story, a proper response in a crisis, and so on.[32]

Notice that this also brings psychology back into the picture. Psychology is the basis for any science of cultural imagery. Sentiment and identification are psychological phenomena, and archeology a familiar metaphor for the probing of a troubled psyche.

It need only be added that we must intervene in the cultural sub-conscious not just to understand but to change it. Martin doesn't address this, but another writer, Ira Chernus, has suggested how we might. Cher-nus urges Christian churches, which are uniquely in touch with cultural symbols, to face up to the fact that the nuclear threat actually *attracts* people with its promise of a secular Armageddon.[33] With this argument he usefully recalls for us a basic truth about religious culture: that it has long looked with hope rather than fear on the prospect of the world ending.

Historian Perry Miller, in *Errand into the Wilderness*, argues that the belief in impending world destruction has been paramount in the Christian West, and that Newtonian physics provoked a serious crisis by suggesting there would be no such end. Newton himself studied the Book of Revelation in hopes of somehow restoring one.[34] So it makes eminent sense that Newton's heirs in this century, finally able to build an artificial doomsday system, have been granted society's full authority to go about just that task.

But sadly, Chernus's idea of a solution is unworkable if not dangerous. Disarmament activists, he suggests, should attempt to create in the popular mind an equation between nuclear war and hell, and between disarmament and heaven. Through such a change in the cultural imagery, we could "choose our own salvation as a political as well as spiritual act."

But what if a guilty, sinful people *likes* the idea of hell? And what kind of distortion of Christian theology would it be to tell them they can "choose salvation" by disarming? Even Pelagius didn't go that far. Besides, who would believe it? One year before the A-bomb, 1944, saw hundreds of thousands killed by war and genocide alone. Was that heaven? Were the trumps about to sound if the 1986 Iceland summit, where total abolition of nuclear weapons was discussed, had come out differently? If people carry the ancient debate in their bones, they're not likely to mistake a Pelagian dream, disarmament, for an Augustinian one, divine redemption.

But the basic point, that nuclear policies are not likely to seriously change until cultural imagery changes, is absolutely right. It is only necessary that this be done with full understanding of that imagery in all its historical complexity. Chernus may be right to say that churches should be about this task. Certainly, psychologists, anthropologists, and other social scientists ought to be about it too, and so should literary and film critics, the custodians of those works in which the cultural subconscious has been given expression over the years. The next chapter will look at specific cases of such expression, assessing them within the general framework established by these psychological and theological insights into culture. It will try to show what that framework can contribute, not only to our better understanding of films and books about nuclear weapons, but also to our better use of such cultural products in getting hold of the problem, to which they give us a unique kind of access.

THREE

![black bar]

Perpetrators and Prophets: Nuclear Weapons and the Discourse of Human Power

American films often tell more about
their times than their filmmakers
consciously intended.
                    —Peter C. Rollins

We need an ethic.
                    —Edward Leroy Long, Jr.

I.

Normally when we think of war movies (like normally when we think of war itself), we imagine men in uniform fighting battles, blasting enemies, sinking ships, and so forth. That the war has begun is a given; that it will end in victory for "our" side is usually in doubt—or at least is held to be for purposes of the narrative. The progress and outcome of the battle, therefore, are the progress and outcome of the story too.

Nuclear war movies are different, in the same way that nuclear war is imagined to be different from conventional war. The actual fighting is assumed to be distant, mechanized, and virtually instantaneous, hence of no storytelling interest. As against, say, a World War II movie, the battle in a nuclear war film is a kind of mathematical point with no dimensions, which the line of the narrative may approach or recede from, but not spend time passing through. The story ends up being about either the events leading up to that point, or the events following.

The actual movies (or novels, for that matter) that have been based on nuclear-war themes follow this principle exactly. Surveying the field, we find two fundamental categories, or (to use the formal term of analysis) two genres, corresponding to these two possibilities. On the one hand is a genre comprised of films like *On The Beach, Testament,* and *The Day After,*[1] which deal with the aftermath of a nuclear war. (*The Day After* gives equal time to the period before the war starts, but basically just to introduce the characters whose crisis arises afterwards.) In this postholocaust genre, the protagonists of the story tend to be ordinary people, and their problem,

42

naturally, is survival or, more generally, dealing with the war's physical and psychological consequences. We could call this genre the cinema of victims.

On the other hand are films like *Fail-Safe, Dr. Strangelove: Or, How I Learned to Stop Worrying and Love the Bomb, WarGames*, and *World War III*, which we might call the preholocaust genre. Here, the main characters tend to be officials—generals, diplomats, and presidents—whose problem is to avert a nuclear war that threatens imminently to begin, partly through their own actions or the actions of those they command. This, then, would be the cinema of perpetrators.

Postholocaust, cinema-of-victims movies tend to be meditations on the human spirit—on the enduring (or nonenduring) power of civilization and its values, of family loyalty, and so on. Preholocaust movies, as we will see, have at least as much to say about the human spirit, though less explicitly. The immediate issue for the cinema of perpetrators is the question of nuclear war's *causes*. It is the implied cause in each story that drives the plot and poses the problem for the characters who are trying to prevent the war.

We can further subdivide this genre, therefore, according to just what those implied causes are. Films like *Fail-Safe* and *World War III* might be called agonized-president stories. Implied by these films is the theory that nuclear war could happen by accident (*Fail-Safe*) or misunderstanding (*World War III*). Accident and misunderstanding are what ensue when the technical and diplomatic systems, respectively, fail. In each case, the cause of the war is clear; it is some kind of manifest error by the system, and the problem is to convince the Russians that this is the case before they retaliate. The plots of these films are about the trade-offs and quid pro quos—in *Fail-Safe*, for instance, the destruction of New York City—that are required to set things right when the system makes a mistake. But the system itself is not fundamentally called into question—except maybe in the sense that it is seen as too vulnerable to error.

Finally, two films—John Badham's *WarGames* and Stanley Kubrick's *Dr. Strangelove*—comprise another subgenre. As opposed to agonized-president, this subgenre is comprised of frantic-president or, maybe, system-out-of-control stories. In these, the focus is on efforts to rein in the nuclear war machine itself. That machine (in *WarGames* it is a literal machine, a computer) is seen in these films as taking on a mind and will of its own. Frantic-president stories imply that nuclear catastrophe would not occur out of "mere" misunderstanding or accident. Rather, the cause would be some problem inherent in the system itself.

By positing such a problem, these last two films in particular most explicitly present us with theories—theories of how the nuclear predicament arose, of exactly what kind of predicament it is, and of whether and how we might get out of it. It would pay, therefore, to look most carefully at these two films.

Surprisingly, what we find is that despite their superficial similarities, which place them within the same subgenre, *WarGames* and *Dr. Strangelove* are based on philosophical assumptions that are diametrically opposed. This philosophical gulf is only hinted at by the most obvious and striking difference between the films—the fact that *WarGames* is a "serious" adventure tale while *Dr. Strangelove* is a satirical comedy. For the real difference is one of underlying viewpoints, and if anything, the more sober outlook belongs to the black-comic *Strangelove*. To get at that view we must examine how each story unfolds.

Like all preholocaust stories, both films center on events at the high levels of command. In *WarGames*, the serious suspense tale, David Lightman, a teenage computer whiz, "hacks" into the North American Air Defense (NORAD) computer and starts a nuclear-war-game countdown that the computer mistakes for the real thing. While trying to avert the countdown (in company with a young love interest, Jennifer Mack), David is arrested by the FBI and confined at NORAD. Using his technical know-how, he escapes in time to track down Professor Falken, designer of the NORAD computer program and the only person who has a chance of persuading it to terminate its "game." Falken turns out to have faked his own death in order to live in disillusioned exile from the human race, which he had come to see as intent on nuclear extinction. Inspired, though, by David's and Jennifer's youthful idealism, he returns to NORAD and, at the last moment, helps David find a solution to the computer's murderous threat.

In the comic *Strangelove*, a deranged Air Force officer, Jack D. Ripper, launches a nuclear squadron—including a B-52 bomber piloted by Major "King" Kong—toward Russia in response to the fluoridation of water, which Ripper imagines is a Communist plot aimed at Americans' "precious bodily fluids." While Ripper's hapless aide, Captain Mandrake, fruitlessly argues for calling off the air strike, President Merkin Muffley and his staff chiefs (including General "Buck" Turgidson) hold a crisis meeting in the Pentagon War Room. There they discover that they don't know the planes' recall code, and that the bombers will trigger a Russian "doomsday machine" recently installed by Russia's Premier Kissov. Through a series of accidents, Major Kong's plane manages to elude a combined Soviet-American chase and to drop its bomb, thus indeed setting off the doomsday machine. Back in the War Room, meanwhile, American officials console themselves with the advice of their top civilian advisor, Dr. Strangelove, who suggests that the officials, at least, can wait out the next hundred years of radioactive devastation in relative comfort at the bottom of "some of our deeper mine shafts."

As these plot summaries suggest, *WarGames* frequently returns us to people and places in the real world—parents, suburbs, David's bedroom at home—as though underscoring that the problem is not in that world but in the high command. *Strangelove* never shows such an "everyday" world beyond the stifling interiors of War Rooms and B-52s. *Strangelove*'s world is all high command. The lack of a normal world free of the high command's hysteria forces our attention to what's wrong with people themselves. If *WarGames* embeds NORAD in the real world and keeps the two distinct, *Strangelove* embeds the whole world in the angular confines of the Strategic Air Command.

Strangelove similarly blurs *WarGames*'s sharp distinctions between reality and games, and between machines and people. Problems arise in *WarGames* only when games are confused with reality, as they are by the computer and its inhuman way of "thinking." In *Strangelove* the only reality we see revolves around the "game" of nuclear preparedness, and the machine that threatens humankind is this whole system, including bomber, crew, threat boards, posturing generals, and incompetent statesmen. Again we are forced inside the people to probe their symbiosis with their tools—a symbiosis epitomized by the crippled figure of Dr. Strangelove, who is more adept at managing his wheelchair than at using his own hands.

In short, *WarGames* externalizes the nuclear threat. It implies that something essential to humankind lies outside the ominous system. This human quality is represented by David Lightman and his technical competence, which is what saves mankind from its manufactured Goliaths. Since the competent are also the good (one becomes capable by being serious, humble, and chaste), technical skill will always serve, never oppose, other values. For all its late-model hardware, *WarGames* is really the old American outlaw myth. When I saw the film in a crowded theater, one of the biggest bursts of applause it got came during a scene in which David hot-wires a pay telephone—an act of both cleverness and illegality. David, it seems, wins the right to do this, to ignore the mundane rules, security systems, and politics of his machine-ridden world, because he knows that world so well: the way movie detectives know city streets and movie cowboys know shortcuts to the pass. People welcome his raids on that secure world because they trust that his purposes are theirs too.

In the end, David's mastery allows him to "reeducate" the NORAD computer, proving that machines can be humanized if they're turned over to adolescents, computer nerds, or other genuine human beings. David saves civilization from itself by staking out for human values the wild and woolly microchip frontier.

WarGames says, Machines can be like people: we're saved. *Strangelove* says, People are too much like machines: we're doomed. In *Strangelove*'s world, competence, as Thoreau put it, is as likely to serve the devil, without intending to, as God. Human competence built and serves the machines, which take on a life of their own. Bomber commander Kong shares with *WarGames*'s David a kind of good ol' Yankee know-how, which he demonstrates by getting the plane through and, at the last moment, hot-wiring its broken bomb-bay doors (as David hot-wired the phone). But in *Strangelove* such adroit achievements merely hasten disaster. Unlike David, Kong lacks—indeed, everyone in *Strangelove*'s world lacks—an overall grasp of things, such as would make their human actions an intervention against the machine, instead of a mere turning of its gears. And in any case, there is no more room in the world for outlaws: Major Kong's cowboys-and-Indians approach to "nuc'lar combat" just looks anachronistic and ridiculous. An open, frontierlike realm of human mastery and freedom is not to be found—neither on the ruddy horizon, as Kong imagines, nor, as in *Wargames*, on some blinking blue screen.

Moreover, where *WarGames* unself-consciously appropriates American myths, *Strangelove* very deliberately uses old movie conventions to attack such myths. The B-52's flight toward Russia builds suspense the same way old World War II movies used to, suggesting that what the nuclear army does is an extension of what armies have always done—and that's just the problem. Eventually these old-movie conventions are turned back against us, insofar as they get us to cheer on the plane (as we would cheer on the heroic air crew of a World War II movie). They make even our *real* real world complicit in the destruction of the world on screen.

II.

In the terms used in chapter 2, *WarGames*'s belief in a human spirit separate from the war machine is clearly Pelagian. By contrast, *Strangelove* takes the Augustinian position that there is no way to separate the human spirit from its works, and that humanity's predicament today is historically continuous with its predicament throughout history: The Pelagian belief in "progress" within this earthly life is an illusion. Of course, *Strangelove* could also be read as a critique of a kind of Augustinianism, a certain limited kind that could be said to have built the war machine in the first place. This limited or, as I will call it, naive Augustinianism would endorse our taking measures against each other here on this sinful earth—measures including, ultimately, the building of nuclear deterrents. When I argued that nuclear weapons stood at a shared apex of Augustinian and Pelagian cultural assumptions, the kind of Augustinianism I meant was naive: a kind whereby one gives up hope for rationality and virtue in human affairs and *therefore*, instead, embraces irrationalism or amoral pragmatism, the philosophies of, respectively, Strangelovians like Jack D. Ripper, Buck Turgidson, and (combining the two) Dr. Strangelove himself.

But the Augustinianism of *Dr. Strangelove* as a whole (as opposed to its individual characters') is not naive. It is, rather, a kind of Augustinianism that sees the human spirit as such—not just that of our enemies—as suspect. The human spirit negates and undercuts itself. Reflecting this, *Strangelove*'s ending is the inversion of *WarGames*'s: it shows a beautiful dance of mushroom clouds as humankind erases itself. And by making this beautiful, by inviting us to appreciate it, *Strangelove* further suggests that we, the viewers, are complicit in the world's destruction. What is unflinching about the film, finally, is not just that no "out" is provided and the war really does happen, but that responsibility for this is assigned to everyone involved; there are no heroes. *Strangelove* implies that all who support or have condoned the present political system are guilty when the world finally blows up—guilty, and perhaps even gleeful; and that includes those of us in the audience who root the plane along. At bottom, says *Strangelove*, the system's problem is no mere accident. It lies not in our stars, but in ourselves. We *built* the system and will finally use it for the purpose for which it was designed. The system embodies the positive desires of human-kind, the "strange love" that lies at the root of everything we do and that is both the best and the worst of us. The only difference between this kind of behavior now and similar human behavior in the past is that in previous eras, the strange love was not vested in machines of quite such ultimate power.

Actually, *WarGames* comes close to this notion of strange love at one point, in its depiction of Professor Falken. Falken has—in naive Augusti-nian fashion—given up on the nuclear-armed world and, like a medieval monk, taken to the hills, where he nurtures a peculiar obsession with dinosaurs (the prototypes, he believes, for the soon-to-be-extinct human race). Young David and Jennifer must rescue him from this incipient strange love. David and Jennifer are just on the brink of discovering nonstrange love, which, it seems, is permitted them by the same virtue which drives them to rescue the world. (They specifically resist the tempta-tion to give up on this demanding responsibility in favor of each other's embrace.) Their youthful joy in living is what touches Falken and restores his love for the world. Where the "heroes" of *Strangelove* are sexually twisted, the heroes of *Wargames* are pure of heart—full of love which is not strange, love which seeks the right objects and which guides the will into the right pathways. What sets this film apart from *Strangelove* is the belief that such love will finally prevail.

Schematizing the films as Augustinian and Pelagian is made possible by the fact that these ideas of love, strange and not strange, are in their origins religious concepts. They are, in effect, Augustinian original sin and Pel-agian grace. Augustine defined original sin in terms of the inability to desire good even when it can be seen, and the positive insistence, instead, on desiring evil—evil not just for others, but for ourselves. Where Pel-agianism holds that evil can be countered by enlightenment, or better knowledge of the good, Augustinianism argues that not just desire but even the ability to know and understand is corrupted by sin. In *Strangelove*, the most knowledgeable character on the scene, Dr. Strangelove, is also the most clearly evil. (That he is also a mad-doctor type familiar from fiction since at least *Frankenstein* suggests just where the Augustinian view has been kept in recent eras, and from where a filmmaker like Kubrick might be drawing it.)

Ultimately, Pelagian notions of humanly willed grace, like Augustinian notions of sin, can come in either naive or sophisticated versions. A naive Pelagianism would be one which linked grace, or human perfectibility, or utopia to some particular political philosophy or program, and so justified sacrificing everything to that program (as naive Augustinians are ultimately willing to sacrifice everything to hold off an evil adversary). *WarGames* is more naive in its Pelagianism than *Strangelove* is in its Augustinianism; it is more a product of common wisdom and less one of critical insight. But it is not Pelagianism in its grossest form, and, as I noted above, to some extent it is, therefore, cognizant of the same problems as *Strangelove*—particularly the possibility (in *Strangelove*, the inescapability) of loving strangely. Indeed, what these films finally teach is that the more Pelagian and Augustinian views tend one way or another, toward complete naiveté or complete sophistication, the more they tend to converge.[2]

III.

If we now turn to analyzing two of the most sophisticated and significant arguments thus far raised against the nuclear peril, Jonathan Schell's (*The Fate of the Earth* and *The Abolition*) and Freeman Dyson's (*Weapons and Hope*),[3] we again find the Pelagian and Augustinian archetypes useful up to a point. In many ways, the purpose of *The Fate of the Earth* is the same as that which Geoffrey Aggeler attributes to Pelagius: a desire to awaken mankind from a "sinful indolence" that is held to be the problem of the age.[4] In Schell's view this indolence results from the bomb, which thus is presented as a radically new thing in history, a "revolution" in human affairs comparable to man's fall from grace. By inventing the bomb, we have "eaten more deeply of the fruit of the tree of knowledge," changed the fundamental human condition, and enlarged our power to the point at which it now threatens "both history and biology." And this threat is permanent, since "a basic scientific finding," like nuclear chain reactions, "catch[es] the world by surprise and, once established, becomes universal and permanent" (101), thus taking on "the character of destiny for the world" (105). Science, in short, transcends culture and history—to a large extent, it *creates* the latter—and this is the key to understanding the nuclear threat, which, for Schell, originates in scientific knowledge, *not* in "social circumstances" (100).

Moreover, science is felt by Schell to be unidirectional. Hence, "it does not seem likely" that some new invention will appear and neutralize nuclear weapons, "for it is in the very nature of knowledge, apparently, to increase our might rather than to diminish it" (106). Science is "irreversible progress" (220). (As we shall see, Dyson and, in a different way, President Reagan both have disagreed with Schell on this particular point.) All in all, nuclear weapons present us with a great irony: humankind's advancing powers coming to threaten humanity itself (111). We have, just recently, proceeded "from tearing society apart to tearing the natural world apart" (123), and "the question *now* before the human species is whether life or death will prevail on the earth" (113, emphasis added).

There is no notion here that the world was fundamentally diabolical to begin with; Schell sees a stark change as having occurred, and his language even tends to make it sound like a freak accident:

> One might say that after billions of years nature, by creating a species equipped with reason and will, turned its fate, which had previously been decided by the slow, unconscious movements of natural evolution, over to the conscious decisions of just one of its species. When this occurred, human activity, which until then had been confined to the historical realm—which, in turn, had been supported by the broader biological current—spilled out of its old boundaries and came to menace both history and biology. Thought and will became mightier than the earth that had given birth to them. Now human beings became actors in the geological time span, and the laws that had governed the development and the survival of life began to be superseded by processes in the mind of man. Here, however, there were no laws; there was only choice, and the thinking and feeling that guide choice. The reassuring, stable, self-sustaining prehistoric world of nature dropped away, and in its place mankind's own judgments, moods, and decisions loomed up with an unlooked-for, terrifying importance. [113–14]

The fundamental change is that "death, having been augmented by human strength, has lost its appointed place in the natural order" (113). This, clearly, is as portentous an event as the entry of death into the world in the first place, and Schell chooses his words accordingly, describing the onset of the nuclear age as a second fall of man:

> According to the Bible, when Adam and Eve ate the fruit of the tree of knowledge God punished them by withdrawing from them the privilege of immortality and dooming them and their kind to die. Now our species has eaten more deeply of the fruit of the tree of knowledge, and has brought itself face to face with a second death—the death of mankind. In doing so, we have caused a basic change in the circumstances in which life was given to us, which is to say that we have altered the human condition.[115]

As the first fall made us mortal, the second has made us "sick" (8), a sickness Schell identifies with our pushing the nuclear threat out of mind; and as death has influenced the shape of life since the first fall, so the nuclear threat is "a backdrop of scarcely imaginable horror lying just behind the surface of our normal life, and capable of breaking into that normal life at any second" (46).

This "omnipresence" of the threat is especially important because normal life is not as "impressively extensive and solid" as it seems from day to day (65). Life is a "mystery" (73). It depends on the hope of continuity and is fundamentally altered in character when this hope is thrown into doubt; we "experience" extinction "in all the moments of our lives" as long as we permit it to be possible (147). Schell works from a psychological theory which holds that in the long run, if we are dull and cold toward life in its entirety we will become dull and cold toward life in its particulars—toward the events of our own daily lives—but if we are alert and passionate about life in its entirety we will also be alert and passionate about it in its dailiness. [148]

So, fundamentally, Schell worries not just that a sizable nuclear exchange could extinguish mankind, but also that by mortally threatening the human future we undercut the source of meaning and value for our lives in the present. That source, he says, is what Hannah Arendt called the common world, definable as the sum of everything human or (more simply, I think), as culture. The meaning of existence, for Schell, is to be found only in culture. By building the bomb and threatening the existence of our whole race, we have lost track of the source of values, which is ourselves. The nuclear threat represents mankind's new desire to elevate "some particular standard, goal, or ideology" over the source of all such values, mankind itself, and even over the natural order which produced mankind in the first place. It is a threat that we will enlarge some partial and limited cultural goal until it swallows the whole of culture and, with it, all goals, including itself. In Schell's view, we threaten now to foreclose the future because we fail to recognize that "mankind is to be thought of not as something that possesses a certain worth . . . but as the inexhaustible source of all the possible forms of worth, which has no existence or meaning without human life" (129).

IV.

The first thing to be said about Schell's analysis is that it rests, like so much other antinuclear thinking, on a dubious psychology. That the "spectre of extinction hovers over our world and shapes our lives" (169) is unproven, despite much writing in this same vein by such analysts as the psychologist R. J. Lifton. The idea is, in fact, unproven both in the linkage it postulates between future and present and in its assumptions about cause and effect, since it imagines, once again, that *nuclear weapons are themselves a cause.* To believe that "boundless relief and calm" will return once we begin to protect the unborn is to imply that such a calm existed before the nuclear age, a belief which no serious reading of history—certainly Western history— could possibly sustain.

Not surprisingly, given the thinness of its psychology, *The Fate of the Earth* is very poor at explaining where nuclear weapons came from in the first place. As noted, Schell generally ascribes the problem to "science" or "knowledge," as though science and knowledge simply "progressed" (in this case, with ironic results) apart from any particular human motives. Schell is quite explicit about this:

Political actors, who, of course, include ordinary citizens as well as government officials, act with definite social ends in view. . . . Scientists, on the other hand (and here I refer to the so-called pure scientists, who search for the laws of nature for the sake of knowledge itself, and not to the applied scientists, who make use of already discovered natural laws to solve practical problems), do not aim at social ends, and, in fact, usually do not know what the social results of their findings will be; for that matter, they cannot know what the findings themselves will be, because science is a process of discovery, and it is in the nature of discovery that one cannot know beforehand what one will find . . . while science is without doubt the most powerful revolutionary force in our world, no one directs that force. [104–5]

It is not clear that anything like the "pure" science Schell posits here actually exists, or if it does, it certainly is not in itself a problem. Schell seems to be aiming for the idea that there is a *discourse* of science, with an internal and inexorable logic of its own. But the nature of such a discourse is very much open to debate, as Thomas Kuhn and others have shown, and in any case it would be the actions of human agents of that discourse that posed whatever problem we would need to be concerned with. On this Schell is weakest, for whatever the status of pure science, there certainly do not seem to be pure scientists in his sense, and *certainly* not in the story of nuclear weapons, in which the world's leading physicists preoccupied themselves with social ends early and often:

> Gaseous diffusion was one of the ways of separating isotopes, which depended on membranes or "barriers" with very fine pores, yet strong enough to stand a pressure difference and inert enough to withstand the very corrosive uranium hexaflouride, the only known gaseous compound of uranium. . . . the electromagnetic method pioneered by Lawrence . . . needed for its magnet coils more copper than was available in wartime, so that the coils were instead made of silver borrowed from the U.S. Treasury. The third method of isotope separation, liquid thermal diffusion, was proved by Philip Abelson rather late. . . . 5

This is a summary of just one aspect of the Manhattan Project, which overall is the story of the *intertwinedness* of "pure" and "applied" breakthroughs. $E = mc^2$ is back of all this somewhere, but is hardly what is *causing* the bomb; equally important appears to have been the U.S. Treasury (in more ways than one). We might say that Schell is confusing different types of "cause" (formal, material, efficient, and final) or, in economic terms, that he is overlooking the role of *investment* in science—the fact that even "pure" scientists depend on "political actors" to pay for their labs and their research professorships.

If the problem isn't science but, rather, certain ways in which science is pushed for certain purposes, then drawing attention to science explains nothing. But there is an additional problem too: it leads Schell into many familiar analytical traps. For example, leaders-versus-people: "We are encouraged" by "the upholders of the status quo" to "inure ourselves" to our predicament (161–62). To account for the plain fact that "we" have readily taken to such advice, Schell oddly suggests that "we have so far had no better idea than to heap up more and more warheads, apparently in the hope of so thoroughly paralyzing ourselves with terror that we will hold back from taking the final, absurd step" (184). The phrase "no better idea" is a revealing one here, suggesting as it does the surrender of psychological analysis: what humankind is responding to, when it erects a system based on faith in deterrence, is not some belief or motive but the simple lack thereof.

At the outset I implied that Schell was superficially, but only superficially, Pelagian in his call for a reformation of earthly life. What keeps him from thoroughgoing Pelagianism is primarily his belief in, as his own title puts it, fate: a basically self-defeating quality overarching human experience. Schell's fate is more Augustinian- than Pelagian-sounding. Yet at bottom Schell is no Augustinian. Augustinianism, as outlined previously, is a philosophy of will, and Schell positively denies that people have willed themselves into their current dilemma. Augustinianism also holds contemporary problems to be reflections or manifestations of the ultimate Problem, the fall of man. To an Augustinian one bite of the apple was enough, and ever since then humanity has needed saving from its own desires.

Schell denies both these premises. For him it is not will that rules human destiny but, again, the products of mind, and these products—knowledge, science—are not intrinsically fallen. Science led *to* the fall rather than followed from it.[6] It is simply that certain particular products of mind happen to be evil, and one of these, the one which appeared in 1945, happens to be evil enough to have spoiled the "calm" of earlier eras. As to why scientific knowledge would suddenly come to endanger the knower, when it didn't fundamentally do so before, Schell has no explanation. Yet the true Augustinian would be concerned precisely with the question of *why* man's "judgments, moods, and decisions" loom up so "terrifying" before nature, as Schell puts it. Indeed, the Augustinian would argue that the terror infuses as well as threatens nature—the *world* is fallen too, not just human will.

But for Schell, it is possible for human beings to live in harmony with nature, and for most of history they did so until suddenly becoming "actors in the geological time span." Claims like this, so unarguable-sounding to Schell's lay readership, are in dramatic contrast with the conclusions of serious historians, especially those who have studied early Christian civilization. Lewis Mumford, for instance, argued in his classic *Technics and Civilization* that the key Western invention was not the atomic bomb nor anything like it, but the clock. With their roots in tenth-century monastic discipline, the clock and Western timekeeping, said Mumford, make possible the regimentation of human energies characteristic of the modern technological regime.[7]

And Lynn White, Jr. has pushed the technological horizon back still further, claiming that Western people became actors in the geological time span with the invention of a certain kind of plow. In "The Historical Roots of Our Ecologic Crisis," White points out that the tilling methods of the early Near East were inappropriate to the recalcitrant soils of northern Europe:

> By the latter part of the seventh century after Christ, however, following obscure beginnings, certain Northern peasants were using an entirely new kind of plow, equipped with a vertical knife to cut the line of the furrow, a horizontal share to slice under the sod, and a moldboard to turn it over. The friction of this plow with the soil was so great that it normally required not [like earlier plows] two but eight oxen. It attacked the land with such violence that cross-plowing was not needed, and fields tended to be shaped in long strips.
>
> In the days of the scratch plow, fields were distributed generally in units capable of supporting a single family. Subsistence farming was the presupposition. But no peasant owned eight oxen: to use the new and more efficient plow, peasants pooled their oxen to form large plow teams, originally receiving (it would appear) plowed strips in proportion to their contribution. Thus, distribution of land was based no longer on the needs of a family but, rather, on the capacity of a power machine to till the earth. *Man's relation to the soil was profoundly changed. Formerly man had been part of nature; now he was the exploiter of nature.* Nowhere else in the world did farmers develop any analogous agricultural implement. Is it coincidence that modern technology, with its ruthlessness toward nature, has so largely been produced by descendants of these peasants of Northern Europe?[8]

I am quoting at length here because I believe this is the kind of argument we too seldom see, and that its rarity is what makes the casual excesses of a Schell, his easy assumption that only *recently* have we "altered the relationship between man and the source of his life, the earth" (94), sound like mere common sense. Whatever the final truth of their claims, White and Mumford bring to the discussion a rather more subtle view of humanity's relationship to the earth and of how easily it might be altered. (Plowing the earth is as much a relationship to it as is unleashing on it "the basic power of the universe.") White and Mumford, and other careful historians, force us to consider the possibility that there is less that is new under the sun than Schell imagines, and that modern technology *as a system of attitudes* has a surprisingly long history. Schell is perhaps the most eloquent spokesman for a whole tradition of received wisdom that gets the matter back-to-front. This tradition assumes that the machines we have today are new phenomena, created not by social forces but by "knowledge" and put, as soon as they appear, to the service of social institutions that date back into some trackless and unscouted past. White and Mumford suggest that the machinery is the old phenomenon, and in the next chapter we will examine the counterpart argument: that it is the *institutions* those machines serve which have grown up far more recently than Schell imagines—and thus in a past which is open to study.

So we have, in Schell, a modified Pelagian denial of the Fall. It might sum up Schell's beliefs better to call them humanistic, with humanism understood as similar to the Pelagian affirmation of man but not necessarily rooted in any particular sense of hope. Humanism is the belief that, in Schell's words, "there is no principle, whether practical, ethical, or divine, that overarches mankind and would offer a justification for its self-destruction" (136). The second part of that formula—that nothing would justify self-destruction—sounds so commensensical that it obscures the radicalness of the first part: that nothing overarches humankind. Schell emphasizes at many points that he believes that values exist only within human life and that, absent some solution to the nuclear crisis, "nothing else that we undertake together can make any practical or moral sense" (172–73). Humanism rests on the disillusioned feeling that the universe offers no larger meanings: "The qualities of worth find in us their sole home in an otherwise neutral and inhospitable universe" (128). Human history is that "which alone offers the hope of saving anything from time's destruction," a goal Schell assumes to be the basis for our well-being in the here and now— for the "nonhuman universe" would simply "drag" all human achievements away (163). Indeed, Schell has a tendency throughout *The Fate of the Earth* to use words like *marvels* in reference to civilized activities (181), and *darkness* in reference to everything outside or beyond the human world in either space or time.

In sum: *The Fate of the Earth* presents biological existence, culture, and scientific mastery in the abstract (recall *WarGames*) as standing *apart* from the "judgments, moods, and decisions" that give us the bomb. Hence the book calls for conserving what is fundamentally human (the common world) over against any "particular standard, goal, or ideology" that we might be tempted to treat as the "sum" of all existence. But it could be argued that mankind has scarcely done anything *but* treat partial, temporal ideologies as cosmic sums of existence, and that biological life and culture have routinely gone by the boards in the process—and, moreover, that this has been going on since well before 1945. It could also be argued that culture, the common world, is nothing *but* the erecting of limited human goals and ideologies as sums of existence: the "reifying" of those goals, as some contemporary theorists would put it. For if it isn't, why would the growing power of the human mind necessarily bring about a problem like the nuclear threat? Why are there "no laws," as Schell puts it, in the human mind? This lack of an explanation seems the logical consequence of Schell's having no theory of the will. (In fact, there are "laws"—psychology is the science of discovering them—but they are laws of the fallen, sinful will, and hence are not *rational*.) What Schell fails to take seriously is the idea that human history is, as Norman O. Brown has put it, the history of a neurosis, or in James Joyce's colorful phrase, a nightmare from which one tries to awaken. Hence, Schell has trouble acknowledging that people themselves create the problem. (He thinks people "psychically numbed.") But even if Schell were right about the threat, he would be wrong about how anxious people are likely to feel about it. For how many times has civilization been thought to hang in the balance before? It is a common worry, arousing either an ordinary, unapocalyptic anxiety, or a desperate anxiety aimed at moving people to do what Schell would consider the wrong things.

In the end, Schell acutely judges that the specific bearer of most of the "standards, goals, and ideologies" for which nuclear weapons have been built is the sovereign state, and that the threat of world destruction owes to the state's insistence on a right to wage war in defense of its ideologies and its self-defined standards and goals. But from another view, in which all of history is seen as corrupted by willful error, national sovereignty would simply be the latest in a long line of such ideologies. In *The Fate of the Earth* Schell cannot engage the sovereignty problem because he believes that government arose in the first place for human betterment, rather than as an instrument of exploitation, class dominance, Oedipal trauma, or what have you. Hence it remains a puzzle that sovereign nations today threaten mutual annihilation to stay sovereign. The bomb itself Schell looks to as cause rather than consequence of the "ludicrous" failure of politics "even to aim at the basic goals that have traditionally justified its existence" (161)—as if politics traditionally had humanistic goals, and as if its self-defeating quality were anything new.

To save the common world (which, for Schell, is not the source of our problem to begin with), Schell calls for dropping our normal quotidian concerns and taking immediate action "to reinvent politics: to reinvent the world" (226). The world is organized at the moment around sovereign states that inevitably make war with the most extreme methods available. Hence we are in a bind:

> The fissure that nuclear weapons have created between our political selves and our moral selves is precisely delineated by the fact that as long as there are nuclear weapons in the world we are compelled to choose between a position that is politically sound but immoral and one that is morally sound but politically irrelevant. [*The Abolition*, p. 77]

As we will see in chapter 4, sacrifices of morality to "political soundness" are the essence of the modern system of state sovereignty, in which the state's claims have become morally limitless. On that, Schell is right. But this "fissure" has not been "created" by nuclear weapons. It long predates them and is part of what makes them possible. Put Schell's way, our bind is truly tragic: if the presence of nuclear weapons compels us to choose between morality and political relevance, then that is to say it compels us *not* to have both at once. And since not having both at once is precisely the problem,

Schell is really saying that nuclear weapons force us not to solve the problem of nuclear weapons. It is bomb-as-cause taken to its circular extreme: they cause even *themselves*. But this all follows from Schell's premise, that weapons created the fissure. Fortunately, the premise is wrong.[9] Cultural history teaches that the fissure creates the weapons, not the other way around.

Schell's work makes clear that positing a moral dilemma is not the same as providing an *ethic* that clarifies what one can morally do. Schell gives us things to do, but they are revolutionary things that really involve leaving the realm of normal behavior altogether, not managing it tolerably well. (This is somewhat less true in *The Abolition*, his sequel to *The Fate of the Earth*, but not entirely; the quotation just analyzed is from *The Abolition*.) To find an ethic we must look to an altogether different kind of argument.

V.

I have suggested that it may be possible to see the bomb not as a by-product of misplaced reliance on certain meanings, but as *central* to the whole, historic mission of mankind to mean. It is possible to see it not as representing the *failure* (as Schell puts it) of "consciousness and will," but as the positive, desired *achievement* of a consciousness and will that are radically flawed. Schell denies that we "love the bomb," à la *Dr. Strangelove*. He is aware of claims that innate human violence and a "territorial imperative" require for all time a system of nuclear-armed states. But he rejects such ideas of "some dark and ineluctable truth in the bottom of our souls," and instead calls on us to "delve to the bottom of the world" for a global political solution, like world government.

"Territorial imperative" is a reference to the best-selling pop anthropology of Robert Ardrey, another author much admired, not coincidentally, by Stanley Kubrick, maker of *Dr. Strangelove*. Among other things, Ardrey's books attacked the notion that the nuclear problem can be solved by world government. But Ardrey is not a worthy opponent for Schell. His naive Augustinianism is more level with that of the real-life Dr. Strangeloves, those professional strategist-advocates of deterrence and the nuclear stockpile. Kubrick's Augustinianism is more sophisticated, even if it, too, seems to offer little hope. But likewise more sophisticated is the theory offered by Freeman Dyson in *Weapons and Hope*, a book whose very title directly confronts the question of hope.

Dyson's analysis looks very unlike Schell's effort to "delve to the bottom" for ultimate truths about the world. Instead Dyson skims, horizontally, through history—which, he assumes, still "proceeds at its old slow pace"—in order to explore how "the cultural patterns of the past persist." "Central to my approach," says Dyson, "is a belief that human cultural patterns are more durable than either the technology of weapons or the political arrangements in which weapons have become embedded." Thus, "the main theme of the book will be the interconnectedness of past and future," and its purpose will be to foster the "hope that we can find practical solutions" to the nuclear problem (3).

Dyson claims to "look to history as a source of understanding." History, he explains, "never repeats itself, but it offers wisdom to those who are willing to learn. It teaches its lessons in the form of parables." Dyson then offers a number of these parables, principally drawn from the two world wars.[10] They involve looking at the different meanings attached to weapons by different interest groups—warriors and "victims"; diplomats, pacifists, "scholar-soldiers," scientists, poets, and the Russians; arms controllers, defense advocates, and proponents of "technical follies."

These groups are historically conceived, and the various opposing ideologies they represent long predate nuclear weapons. Dyson is more interested in how present policies grow out of long-standing ways of thinking than he is in how ways of thinking have been remade by those policies. Ideas, for Dyson, are prior to technology. Hence technology is always political. (Contrast this with the fact that *The Fate of the Earth* asked us to transcend politics, and that *WarGames*, in line with those old American myths, posited an apolitical technics that could be apolitically mastered.)

The theory that emerges from Dyson's analysis explains our peril in terms of converging dynamics. For Dyson, a physicist who has advised the British and American governments on weaponry, there is a dynamic to warfare, a dynamic to policymaking, and dynamics to technology, arms control, international relations, and even the human soul. So far these dynamics have militated in favor of nuclear weapons, but each could also militate against them. For instance, in technology there is a good dynamic whereby defensive weapons gradually replace weapons of mass destruction. In international relations there is a bad dynamic whereby the Russians, following their historical experience, unwittingly scare us with their strategic doctrines of "first strike," and we, following ours, scare them in turn with tactical doctrines of "first use." (In *Strangelove* the Russians build their doomsday machine out of fear of a "doomsday gap.") And nuclear weapons are themselves an equivocal dynamic in history, having inhibited world war at the cost of risking world destruction. Says Dyson,

> The arms race remains, as it has always been, a bundle of paradoxes, a Pandora's box with hope at the bottom. On the one hand, it is a monstrously wasteful and mindless outpouring of resources for destructive ends. On the other hand, it sets limits to destruction and opposes brute force with discrimination and intelligence. It made superbombs possible and it made them obsolete. It made nuclear weapons cheap and it made the means of their delivery expensive. It made big countries overwhelmingly strong and it made them powerless to fight one another. Many people believe that "stopping the arms race" would lead us to a more stable and peaceful world. Perhaps they are right, perhaps not. The arms race is a tool which can be used for either good or evil purposes. To stop it altogether may be a worthy long-range goal. But our more

urgent need is to guide the arms race intelligently, to use it, in conjunction with moral outrage and diplomatic negotiation, to hasten the obsolescence and retirement of weapons of mass destruction. [43–44]

Dyson, a weapons designer himself, here speaks in a way very reminiscent of the professional strategists, like Henry Kissinger and Herman Kahn, with their seeming willingness to suspend judgment over the weapons themselves and their insistence that the moral problem the weapons pose— if any—is centered elsewhere. Dyson agrees with the strategists that one goal is a "stable balance of power" (271). But there is an important difference in emphasis. When Dyson speaks of "use"—an ethical concept: how-can-we-make-something-of-what-we're-stuck-with—it is not the weapons he proposes to "use" properly, as the strategists might have it, but the arms race itself, "guiding it intelligently" to its own self-destruction.

Similarly, Dyson is concerned throughout his book with what I am calling ethical problems, for instance the question of building defenses (24– 27). Besides proffering "hope," a practical, stoical orientation of mind (hope is like wisdom, but "cheaper"), Dyson's book represents what he calls a quest for "concept." Concept is the "ruling principle" of policies (228). It might also be called policy's doctrine or premise, except that when Dyson makes his actual preference (Live and Let Live) known, it turns out to be not just an intellectual postulate, but a moral one too. It is Dyson's recommended way of "making the best of a bad job" and "finding the practical rather than the ideal solution to a problem" (310).

Concepts, and especially Dyson's Live and Let Live, are based on explicit recognition of the reality of original sin: we need concepts because we can't trust human will. Here, too, is a link to the professional strategists. The difference is, the human will they don't trust is purely Eastern European, whereas Dyson allows that we can't trust anyone's. This is reminiscent of Dr. Strangelove, which emphasized not just the venality of "our" side along with theirs, but, underlying this, the equivocal nature of even positive human urges. Believing ourselves to be the good guys, we nonetheless can't trust ourselves because even when someone tries to do good, things are as likely as not to come out for the worse.

Strangelove made this point not only about technical skill, but even more comically, about such noble traits as propriety—as in President Muffley's memorable outburst, "Gentlemen! You can't fight in here! This is the War Room!" As this irony suggests, in the real world bad tendencies get the better of good. However individual relations are governed, institutionally it's the savage or wrongheaded impulses that rule. This was the essence of Strangelove's satire, and it is also the point made by many of Dyson's parables. People can be well intentioned, well informed, or effectual, but never all three at once; they rely on machines that function well but only at the wrong times; they follow orders when the orders are mistaken, then take "initiative" when the right ones come through. Dyson's view isn't quite so bleak, but his tales told from experience do reinforce the sense that in humankind's collective life, at least, it tends to choose the worst of all worlds. Thus, J. Robert Oppenheimer advocates small tactical weapons in Europe in hopes of forestalling a crash "Superbomb" buildup; in the end we get the world-threatening Superbomb *and* unstable tactical deployments which make its use more likely. George Kennan, a hero of Dyson's, argues in 1944 for a stabilizing postwar balance of power; the U.S. pursues grander schemes of world order (including international control of atomic weapons), and when these fail we end up with both the balance of power and a destabilizing arms race—a situation Dyson likens to Europe's in 1914. And in the 1980s we get both the MX missile and a makeshift basing system that belies the missile's original purpose and invites a Soviet preemptive attack.

Similarly, we can look at that phenomenon of "retirement wisdom" and wonder why, in the case of Oppenheimer, Kennan, Einstein, Admiral Rickover, Robert McNamara, and others, lucidity about the nuclear peril has always seemed to correlate with a lack of influence on policy, and vice versa. It does seem that while individuals may be wise, institutions and nations, and individuals as members of same, have a gift for turning wisdom to folly.

With an eye to all this, Dyson explicitly invokes "original sin" as a historical explanation, and as a factor to be weighed in evaluating possible courses of action (260–71). His recognition of sin highlights his Augustinian inclinations, which bring this analysis closer than most to uncovering the problem's psychic roots. Next to the ignorance and paranoia most authors recognize as factors in the arms race, Dyson, perhaps surprisingly, sets fun, adventure, and beauty. Nuclear explosives, he has said elsewhere, "have a glitter more seductive than gold to those who play with them." We must realize that there are military men "happily looking forward to the days after the SIOP [nuclear-war plan] is executed," just as Major Kong was ecstatic as he war-whooped his way to Armageddon.[11] This, then, would be the really troubling "dark and ineluctable truth" (as Schell put it) in our souls: not the will to violence or some territorial imperative, but the fact that even our *better* instincts move us to "love the bomb."

Such an insight suggests a far different program than does naive Augustinianism. Naive Augustinianism requires that we surrender to the eternal need for a huge store of deterring armaments; it assumes that since dark truths created the status quo, they also dictate its perpetuation. One reply to this is Schell's effort, which is to shift the burden of proof away from those who favor sharp breaks with present policy and onto the naive Augustinians. Accomplishing the shift requires holding the peril before us and demanding that we face it until we have it thoroughly abolished. But another reply would be a more sophisticated Augustinianism, one in which no one is excused or held to be above the sinful tendencies of humankind. This is Dyson's reply, although, as with Schell's, we do violence to it if we settle for applying this simple label. Dyson's, after all, is the argument for hope—more a Pelagian than an Augustinian feeling or tone, as Schell's stress on fate was more Augustinian than Pelagian. A different schema altogether, really, is needed to account for what nonetheless remains the very striking opposition between these arguments.

VI.

What truly separates Schell and Dyson is that they write in distinctive literary modes, or genres—genres which, when fully understood, turn out to be even older than the Pelagius-Augustine debate, though equally of religious origin. They are, in fact, two of the modes of discourse that we find in Judeo-Christian Scripture. This should not be surprising if we understand, as Northrop Frye says, that "the Bible is the model for serious writing" in our culture and "clearly a major element in our own imaginative tradition, whatever we may think we believe about it."[12] Frye has described the Bible's influence on later literature in his critical study, *The Great Code*, a book premised on the belief that "there is no . . . excuse today for scholars who, in discussing cultural issues originally raised by the Bible and still largely informed by it, proceed as though the Bible did not exist" (xvii).

Proceeding as though it did, we discover that Schell and Dyson can best be explained in terms of what Frye calls types. In the Bible these types include seven "phases of revelation," appearing in this order: creation, revolution or exodus, law, wisdom, prophecy, gospel, apocalypse. By this typology, Dyson's call for hope is a species of *wisdom*—the term Dyson himself uses (along with its counterpart and opposite, *folly*). Wisdom, says Frye, is based on assumptions of persistence and tradition: "The sense of continuity, or persistence in the right ways, relates primarily to the past: wisdom facing the future is prudence (Proverbs 8:12), a pragmatic following of the courses that maintain one's stability and balance from one day to the next" (121). Wisdom argues that "only when we realize that nothing is new can we live with an intensity in which everything becomes new" (124). Eventually, wisdom grows into a playfulness and joyfulness (125), very much like the *comic* view of life that Dyson enjoins upon us. And wisdom uses the same literary approach for "instruction" that Dyson self-consciously borrows, the parable—or, in its predecessor forms, the proverb and fable (122).

Superficially, if Dyson's mode is wisdom, Schell's would seem to be apocalypse, but in fact it is more revealing to see it in terms of the forerunner to apocalypse in the Biblical revelation: the type which Frye calls prophecy. Prophecy is a counterpart to wisdom, "the individualizing of the revolutionary impulse, as wisdom is the individualizing of the law, and is geared to the future as wisdom is to the past" (125). Prophets tap the channels of communication between the conscious and the unconscious and provide a comprehensive view of the human situation, surveying it from creation to final deliverance. . . . It incorporates the perspective of wisdom but enlarges it. The wise man thinks of the human situation as a kind of horizontal line, formed by precedent and tradition and extended by prudence: the prophet sees man in a state of alienation caused by his own distractions, at the bottom of a U-shaped curve [which] postulates an original state of relative happiness. . . . The wise man's present moment is the moment in which past and future are balanced, the uncertainties of the future being minimized by the observance of the law that comes down from the past. The prophet's present moment is an alienated prodigal son, a moment that has broken away from its own identity in the past but may return to that identity in the future. [128–29]

Compare, here, Schell's characteristically Judeo-Christian idea that our lives in the present gain meaning from the whole span of history, especially from how it might end. Schell's belief about the consequences of modern science are a prophet's warnings of a rupture in history and of a break between humanity and its future, hence "its own identity."

At the same time, Schell himself uses scientific findings in his effort to outline the consequences of nuclear war. The first part of his book, in fact, accords with Frye's observation that in modern society, prophecy

may come through the printing press, more particularly from writers who arouse social resentment and resistance because they speak with an authority that society is reluctant to recognize. . . . In the modern world, therefore, what corresponds to prophetic authority is the growth of what we called earlier a cultural pluralism, where, for example, a scientist or historian or artist may find that his subject has its own inner authority, that he makes discoveries within it that may conflict with social concern, and that he owes a loyalty to that authority even in the face of social opposition. [128]

Frye would probably agree to adding journalists to his list of latter-day secular prophets—especially such journalists as Schell, who insist on the "inner authority" of scientific demonstrations that a nuclear war could destroy all human life. Indeed, in the modern world, prophecy in Frye's sense seems most aptly to lend itself to warnings of ecological catastrophe. The modern prophet is, as Ibsen made clear a hundred years ago, "an enemy of the people" who demands the public be told when there's poison in the city's water.

And finally, prophecy *is* linked to the last phase of revelation, apocalypse. Apocalypse, says Frye, makes use of the same materials as prophecy, namely portentous events (135), though it does not limit itself to describing things that are going to happen but, rather, describes events that are "the vision, the model, the blueprint that gives direction and purpose to man's energies" (139–40). "All these incredible wonders are the inner meaning or, more accurately, the inner form of everything that is happening now" (136). This, too, is reminiscent of Schell, who in essence argues that the threatened nuclear holocaust is the inner form or, revising the formula slightly, the inner *non*meaning of life in the present. "Man creates what he calls history as a screen to conceal the workings of the apocalypse from himself," says Frye (136). Schell might say that by concealing the workings of the apocalypse from himself, man sets up a screen between himself and history (everyday reality). In the end, what is apocalyptic about Schell — and that is perhaps the way *The Fate of the Earth* is most often described—is this assumption, beneath his prophetic warnings, that historical reality is defined by its future or outcome (whereas Dyson, like the wisdom writers, believes it is controlled by its past).

VII.

The difference or, more precisely, the antitypical character of prophecy in relation to wisdom very much accords with the gap between Schell and Dyson. Dyson is not concerned with inner forms and meanings but with a different concept altogether of what drives history, a concept that (iron-ically) is more like the "fate" in wisdom literature than is anything in *The Fate of the Earth*. It is a concept arrived at through a conscious refusal of the prophet's call to perfection, as Dyson suggests:

> Our task is not to choose the best possible path for the world to follow. The world will choose its own path, driven by forces which are largely beyond our control. Our task is to choose tools, people, and concepts which will enable us to give the world an effective push in the direction of survival, whenever it comes to a fork in the road. [286]

As an ethicist instead of a prophet, Dyson disagrees sharply with Schell on two particular points: everyday forgetfulness, and the assumption of sur-vivability. Unlike Schell, Dyson sees it as a *good* thing that we can forget about nuclear weapons and go on about our daily lives: this is what leaves us some space in which to find a solution. And unlike Schell, who thinks that since we can't be sure of a nuclear war's outcome we must simply assume it would destroy the whole race—and therefore must not in any way plan to fight one—Dyson sees the same uncertainty as dictating that we take ra-tional steps to limit a future war's damage. These ethical emphases are finally what constitute Dyson's idea of hope, a virtue "to be practiced whether or not we find it easy or even natural." Hope is the ethic Dyson urges upon a nuclear-armed world. Compared to prophecy, ethics takes a narrow view of the nuclear danger because it sees the world as fallen regardless of this threat. But conversely, it asserts that the world's having fallen into the "knowledge of good and evil" requires, and permits, rigorous efforts to limit evil and choose good.

In the end, as Frye suggests, ethical wisdom complements prophecy. By showing us the height to be scaled, prophecy inspires our own confession of guilt for our present circumstance. Thus, it reaffirms our ethical power to make new choices.

Given this complementarity, it is not surprising that Schell's later book, *The Abolition*, follows out his own prophetic logic to the point of also searching for an ethic ("a deliberate policy"), one whereby we still heed the prophet's call to perfection but also balance it within the total framework of daily life. In a sense, *The Abolition* reveals a crucial accretion of Augustinian insights in Schell's thinking. It is sympathetic to the dilemmas of "political realism" that undercut his earlier calls for a reinvented world. In essence, Schell independently discovers Dyson's Live and Let Live strategy, in which existing weapons are treated as bargaining chips in negotiations for a nuclear-free but defensively armed world, with cheating to be deterred by eventual, not instant, rearmament and retaliation. Besides promoting this approach, both Schell and Dyson also stress that a nuclear-free world might become an arena in which creative things could happen politically—perhaps movement in the direction of world government or toward some other final answer to the problem of war. This is the ultimate ethical wish: not just that human activity can be spared the pointlessness in which nuclear weapons drape it, but also that it can turn around and convert that pointlessness into some kind of lasting sense and value.

That is as far as nuclear-war movies take us toward insight, and as far, I believe, as antinuclear polemics take us toward "deliberate policy." My point here has been to suggest that we get the most out of what these sources have to teach us if we recognize them as a reemergence of ancient themes and styles of debate. But we are at our own fork in the road. All the material just analyzed still leaves us without a true historical account of how long-standing cultural assumptions arose and attached themselves to those particular objects that worry us today; and though light is thrown on these issues by the Augustinian-Pelagian and wisdom-prophecy schemas, the question is not answered by them because, finally, they are analogies, not causal accounts. We need to search for actual causes—lines of influence whereby these ancient beliefs and discursive modes became the pattern of our actual thinking today. And we need to search for "deliberate policy" in the context of the agencies that make policy in our real world today: in particular, the modern state. That search will be the work of my next two chapters.

FOUR

"A Largess Universal": War, Technology, and the State in *Henry V*

In dealing with the State, we ought to
remember that its institutions are not
aboriginal, though they existed before
we were born: that they are not
superior to the citizen . . . that they all
are imitable, all alterable; we may make
as good; we may make better.
—Ralph Waldo Emerson

Stranger engines for the brunt of
war. . .
I'll make my servile spirits to invent.
. . . I see there's virtue in my heavenly
words.
—*Doctor Faustus* (Christopher
Marlowe, 1594)

The State and War
I.

There is one institution in our world which, it is said, "monopolizes the means of violence," and it is this institution, and only this one, that has built and deployed nuclear weapons. This institution is the nation-state. True, other agencies—the National Guard, the local police, Brink's, the school principal —might have a certain authority to use force, even deadly force. But like James Bond, all these agencies are *licensed* to kill (or detain, or punish, or whatever). In other words, their authority is ultimately established by the state. And while there are countless cases of force being used by unauthorized agencies—indeed, it is feared that even nuclear weapons might one day turn up in private hands—such uses of force are considered criminal and terroristic, meaning that they, too, are defined and judged against the state's presumptively exclusive claim on the means of violence.

That the state enjoys such a status almost everywhere in today's world is thought to be a gain for "civilization" over the days of private warlords or of gunfights at the OK Corral. But nuclear weapons show us the dark side of this civilized principle. The state's right to use and to sanction violence is based on a kind of circular logic: what the state authorizes is legal because *legal* means "authorized by the state." And since for most people, most of the time, *legal* also means "acceptable" or even "justified," state authorization can be seen as establishing the justice of a thing as well. Hence the vague feeling most people have that even the use of nuclear weapons could, under certain circumstances, be just.

People have not always felt this way about the state and its authority, just as they do not feel this way today about other social institutions. If, say, a large corporation were suddenly to announce that it was building nuclear weapons, people would not only be aghast; more significantly, they would be puzzled. They would wonder why a private agency thought it needed or was justified in such a policy. Questions like this are sometimes raised about state policies too, but it is much harder to get people at large worried over them. A private agency that makes a certain decision is assumed to be acting for itself; the state, most of the time, is assumed to be acting for *us*. Its policies are not thought to reflect particular interests, but rather are seen as "our" policies, as expressions of our common "will."

Now, an agency that speaks for the people as a whole could well be thought to be authorized by them and, hence, under their control (as the Declaration of Independence says governments are). Yet, ironically, the notion that the state represents everybody has the effect of reinforcing the feeling that its actions are beyond ordinary criticism—that while other institutions must be authorized by higher authority, and must answer to standards higher than their own (usually, the state's), the state can authorize whatever it likes. The existence and needs of the people are natural facts, and therefore the institution that is thought to represent the people takes on an aura of naturalness too. Nature, which lays down the basic conditions of life, is—rightly, I think—taken by people to be the ultimate source of any rational system of values. So to be natural is to partake of the metaphysical source of values itself. It is to be unmeasurable against some higher system of values, since no such higher system exists. Something like this condition is at the heart of the modern state's so-called sovereignty—the power it has been conceded to be sole judge of its own actions.

Thus, as a matter of everyday practice, people accord the state almost unlimited moral authority—partly because they consider it to represent them and partly because they consider it *not* to represent them, but, rather, to issue directly from nature. More generally, people think of the state not as a particular institution, created in time and changing over time, but rather as a metaphysical given, a simple reflection of the way things are. (The word *state* itself suggests a kind of vacancy, since we also speak of the state of something as being just how the thing is.) All this makes a kind of sense, for if something is a given, there isn't much practical point in arguing against it, nor is it really rational to try. One prefers, rather, to simply presume that the thing is just, and that whatever it does or creates is also likely to be just.

Of course, historically what may have happened is the reverse of this. People may have decided that the state was a good thing, and *therefore* come to see it as natural. But at some point, the origin of this whole complex of ideas was forgotten; the state grew in power and pervasiveness until it became very difficult to think of as simply one more feature on the social landscape. Certainly when people today survey that landscape, they see all sorts of particular institutions and policies, but they tend to overlook the most fundamental fact of all: the existence of the state. This they take for granted, just as in surveying the physical landscape one might notice trees and houses, and maybe even streets, lawns, or meadows, but not the "ground" as such. The ground is simply that which grounds: that on which everything else happens to stand.

Similar kinds of blindness obscure people's views of war and technology. These, too, are human agencies—indeed, in the modern world, they are concomitants of the all-encompassing state—yet they are seldom thought of as such. Rather they are regarded as part of the natural way of things— givens of modern life which, therefore, it is generally not rational or worthwhile to criticize. When Jonathan Schell, for example, ascribes the existence of nuclear weapons to "science" and its inevitable progress, he in effect assigns them to the nature of things. But in fact, not only is science also a particular cultural institution, it is not even the true source of nuclear weapons. The development of such weapons required the concentrated efforts of states—indeed, of two emerging superstates. Neither is it a simple accident of how knowledge progresses that no political institutions of previous centuries ever developed nuclear weapons, nor any comparable single instrument of destruction. Schell's view (and that of everyday common sense) would have us believe that political elites of earlier eras would have built such weapons if they, too, had just had the requisite technical know-how. But people have never availed themselves of every technically feasible means of violence; they do not even do so today. When they make an exception of sorts by allowing states to stockpile nuclear weapons, this is a specific historical fact, and it demands to be specifically explained.

What we need to do is to problematize the state, war, and technology— that is, treat them not as unavoidable facts to be simply accepted, but as problems to be analyzed and solved. For each rests on the other and on a whole set of prior conditions. Nuclear weapons depend not just on the moral authority and resources of states, but on states' tendency to enter into a certain type of conflict (like the world war for which the bomb was developed). They also depend on the widespread belief that technology can and should serve the aims of such conflicts, that it should reflect the commitments of its sponsoring states. And even to the extent that nuclear weapons rest on "science," there is still the problem of explaining why scien*tists* cooperated in putting their discoveries to such a use. There is, in other words, the problematic ability of the state to command this kind of loyalty, even among professionals with their own disciplines and credos. All these conditions are historical inventions in their own right.

Currently people problematize *certain* wars, states, and technologies: the Vietnam War, Iran, nuclear missiles. But even antinuclearists, looking behind these particulars, are liable not to see any larger problematic of which each is a part. They are liable to *see* nothing at all, in exactly the same way that one doesn't see the ground in a landscape. Again, Schell's widely influential work provides a useful example. *The Fate of the Earth*'s ringing conclusion, "The task is nothing less than to reinvent politics," rests on the belief that

> [The] way of thinking [that makes nuclear extinction possible] is supplied to us, unfortunately, by our political and military traditions, which with the weight of almost all historical experience behind them, teach us that it is the way of the world for the earth to be divided up into independent, sovereign states, and for these states to employ war as the final arbiter for settling the disputes that arise among them. This arrangement of the political affairs of the world was not intentional. No one wrote a book proposing it; no parliament sat down to debate its merits and then voted it into existence. *It was simply there, at the beginning of recorded history*; and until the invention of nuclear weapons it remained there, with virtually no fundamental changes . . . I shall refer to it as a "system"—the system of sovereignty.[1]

This laudable attempt to explain war by linking it to the state undercuts itself by de-historicizing the state, and so de-historicizing war as well. (Schell says we are taught this kind of thinking, but he also seems to take it as true.) Hence nothing is really explained at all. War comes from states—but where do states come from? Like other antinuclearists who abhor the bomb—the ultimate creation of modern, state-sponsored warfare—Schell, ironically, manages to assume that war and the state are permanent. Hence the despair so often noted in *The Fate of the Earth*, its inability to suggest any nonutopian solutions. Once you grant the state as a given, you end up granting many other things too. Worse, you at least pave the way toward seeing those things as legitimate.

Of course every age has had a political authority higher than any other. But this authority was not always the state—certainly not a state possessing the peculiar characteristics of sovereignty. Schell's failure to see this is the key to the failure of his analysis. He can't suggest how to reinvent politics because he doesn't believe politics as we understand it was ever invented to begin with. But it was. The consensus it is built on is so firm as to seem timeless. Yet modern politics is simply discourse, and discourse can always be deciphered. States and their war policies are not mysterious, fixed edifices, thrusting up through the millennia like Stonehenge. They are products of cultural history, and once we see this, the problem of reinventing them appears in a whole new light.

II.

In one sense Western political theory has problematized the state for a long time, ever since it gave up the idea that the state was ordained by God. Perhaps since Machiavelli and certainly since Marx, it has been possible to view the state as one particular instrument of political power. For Marx it was an instrument characteristic of a particular historical phase. Its purpose was not to serve some general will, but to further certain limited economic interests, namely those of an exploitative capitalist class that was destined to be overthrown.

The value of this analysis, even for non-Marxists, is that it points toward a specific moment within history when the modern state arose: in the Western world of a few hundred ago, when the system now known as feudalism was giving way to new cultural forms in what chauvinistic moderns have labeled a Renaissance. The state as we know it has no continuous existence dating back further than that, despite what Schell, and common wisdom, would have us believe (though, arguably, the modern state was prefigured by the Roman empire and had counterparts in such non-Western cultures as China).

Familiar as this idea—of the state as a historical invention—is in some circles, it has yet to fully penetrate the nuclear debate, even among writers critical of prevailing attitudes (as Schell makes clear). And inquiry into it has yet to be fully informed by cultural history.[2] If the state as we know it dates to the early modern period, then exploring that period ought to give us insight into the collective urges which the state came to embody and from which it continues to draw its strength today. And one route to such insight would be the careful reading of cultural artifacts from that period, artifacts which, as always, were produced by the same discursive interplay that fosters the attitudes that give rise to policy, and with which we are therefore concerned.

Specifically, we will here examine modern attitudes toward states, war, and technology through an analysis of Shakespeare's *Henry V*, a play that appeared in 1599 and that has stood ever since as one of the great epics of state power in war.[3] *Henry V* is the story of a medieval war retold early in the era of modern war, by a mainstream but unusually sensitive observer of life in the latter era. And as a work in the first rank of our literary canon today, it apparently encodes beliefs, hopes, and anxieties still recognizable, even compelling, to many members of our own society.

Henry V dramatizes the exploits of a medieval king who ruled England in the early 1400s, some two centuries before Shakespeare. The central event in the play is Henry's successful invasion of France, which occurred during what we now call the Hundred Years' War and which temporarily won for England most of northern France (to whose dukedoms Henry claimed to be the rightful heir). The memory of Henry's surprising victory at Agincourt in 1415 serves Shakespeare as the basis for a heroic, patriotic, and popular tale about his own nation triumphant under one of its most revered kings—the rough equivalent, in today's terms, of an especially successful, stylized film depiction of D-Day.

It has been said that *Henry V* is more about war than any other Shakespeare play.[4] Henry's war is both the most heroic thing about him and the most troubling, waged as it is with the two terror weapons of the late middle ages, the cannon and the longbow. (The longbow was considered dreadful enough to have been banned by the medieval church for use against Christians.) Still more troubling for Shakespeare is that the war is waged on the basis of certain attitudes which, he accurately saw, must underlie and accompany the use of such weapons.

It seems that Shakespeare goes out of his way to draw attention to this problem. Needless to say, he makes no effort to be "historically accurate"; that notion didn't really exist yet. Shakespeare's Henry, therefore, is less a medieval than an early modern king, a bearer of the attitudes that Shakespeare (and others of the time) believed made for kingly success and national strength, ever and always. Shakespeare's high regard for those attitudes reflects what were thought to be, in his era, fundamental values crucial to both statecraft and war.

Those values closely match the actual conditions of emerging sovereign states. Sovereignty appears on the scene at a point in history at which communities are coming to be identified with fixed cultural and territorial boundaries and are seeking new principles of internal coherence.[5] *Henry V* depicts a society in just this condition—again, not Henry's society really, but Shakespeare's own—and a war with just such consequences. The turn of the seventeenth century was a period of economic transition in England, when new classes were acquiring power and social change was occurring quickly enough to throw old lines of power and privilege into doubt. English society was still comprised of the traditional classes—king, priests, nobility, minor gentry, servants—but "what is [newly] in question is the mode of their interrelation. The age is ripe for theories of authority," as Alasdair MacIntyre has put it.[6] The new notion of state sovereignty would be just such a theory, and *Henry V* gives us a foreshadowing of that theory's emergence, qualified by a deference to the old order that still claimed recognition and respect. Looking toward both the closing and the coming age, the play reflects the anxiety of the transition, as well as anxiety about the changing character of warfare. Ultimately, what makes it coherent is a brilliant synthesis in which Shakespeare tries to get these two anxieties to answer each other.[7]

III.

The play's anxiety about war can be glimpsed at once in the much-discussed scene at Harfleur. Henry and his army have landed in France and laid siege to this fortified coastal town. The length of the siege is taking a toll on his men, and Henry sees a need for a bold stroke to force Harfleur's surrender. So he takes an action that all by itself raises most of the key moral questions posed by warfare in our own time. Shouting across to the town's defenders, he issues this famous ultimatum:

> If I begin the battery once again
> I will not leave the half-achieved Harfleur
> Till in her ashes she lies buried.
> The gates of mercy shall be all shut up,
> And the fleshed soldier, rough and hard of heart,
> In liberty of bloody hand shall range
> With conscience wide as hell, mowing like grass
> Your fresh fair virgins, and your flowering infants.
> . . . Therefore, you men of Harfleur,
> Take pity of your town and of your people
> Whiles yet my soldiers are in my command. . . .
> If not, why, in a moment look to see
> The blind and bloody soldier with foul hand
> Defile the locks of your shrill-shrieking daughters;
> Your fathers taken by the silver beards,
> And their most reverend heads dashed to the walls;
> Your naked infants spitted upon pikes,
> Whiles the mad mothers with their howls confused
> Do break the clouds, as did the wives of Jewry
> At Herod's bloody-hunting slaughtermen.
> What say you? Will you yield, and this avoid?
> Or, guilty in defense, be thus destroyed?

[III.iii.7–14, 27–29, 33–44]

There is a certain familiarity about this threat for citizens of a nuclear-armed state. It is a threat of civilian destruction that stands in direct opposition to another medieval doctrine, that of the "just war," which specifically outlawed looting, wanton violence and the massacre of noncombatants. Yet it stands very much in line with the problem nuclear weapons pose today. This is no coincidence. Siege warfare has been called the closest analogue in Shakespeare's time to modern, total war involving the whole population; it would naturally tend to raise the same moral issues as strategic bombardment.[8] And it would tend to be rationalized in similar ways. Among the rationales that have been offered for Henry's speech is a kind of deterrence theory: Henry is just bluffing in hopes of avoiding the horrors described, which are in fact avoided.[9] By this rationale, Henry's thinking has the same moral coloration as the contemporary idea that nuclear weapons have kept the peace in Europe for forty years.

But by the same token, we can ask of Henry's claim (as some have asked of postwar Europe), exactly what kind of peace is being kept? And can it be acceptable to threaten actions which, on their face, would be immoral if carried out? Henry leads an invading army, and he himself compares the terror it poses to one of history's greatest crimes, Herod's genocidal attempt to kill Jesus Christ. Shakespeare's original audience would have recognized all this. It would have accepted Henry's description of war's terrors as true. And most remarkably of all, it would have known that Harfleur (like most of Henry's conquests) would by their own time have been ceded back to France anyway! Yet, that audience still accepted Henry as a hero. All in all, Henry's threats and his ability to get away with them are at least as morally perplexing as today's policies of nuclear threat, and perhaps even more so. As with the latter, one wonders what made them even conceivable in the first place.

The answer to that question lies in the positive vision of war that the play also strives to present. In fact, the play's overall pattern of justification for Henry's war takes us to the center of our own, modern struggle with the dilemmas of sovereignty and war. War is the occasion for Henry to take visible leadership of his whole people and, in the process, to accomplish two key purposes of the new, sovereign state. First is the unifying of disparate regions which, in the presovereign, "segmentary" state, remain separate principalities forever prone to disharmony. (One of the keystones of sovereignty is the idea of states as more or less unified cultures, each inhabiting a single territory.[10]) According to Shakespeare, Henry brings about this unification in two ways. His war is explicitly an effort to join historically linked dukedoms; and, the waging of it brings common cause to the different nations of the British Isles themselves. By Shakespeare's time, the first of these efforts had long since spent itself; conquering France had turned out to be an overextension of British power, and a violation of what would eventually come to be accepted as the logical modern boundaries of the two states. As Shakespeare well knew, the British were eventually to meet their match in France's own hero of nation building, Joan of Arc.

But the second effort was to prove central to Britain's emergence as a modern state. This was, specifically, the internal unification among ruling families (some of Henry's father's old adversaries sign on for Henry's war) and, most significantly, the precarious uniting of four distinct nations—English, Welsh, Scottish, and Irish—that Shakespeare dramatizes in *Henry V*'s meeting of the four captains (III.ii). Actually, the best that had been achieved among these four peoples by 1599 was the strained peace reflected in the captains' tense banter; Scotland had been recently at odds with England, and the Irish issue has yet to be fully resolved even today. But this fact further points up the urgency with which the call to union must have been felt. If Shakespeare extolled the less territorially logical annexation of France, it was partly by way of underscoring the need for greater unity within. (A few years after *Henry V*, Shakespeare was to write a great *tragedy* about another king, Lear, who divides rather than unites.)

Besides uniting regions, Shakespeare's Henry also attempts, and more definitively achieves, the forging of a new social order out of the "ranks" of traditional society. *Henry V* precisely reflects the situation described by MacIntyre: a world of traditional social landmarks whose proper relations to each other have been radically cast in doubt. In many ways these landmarks—people in their older social hierarchies, from the king on down—still exist and are respected in the play. Only members of the nobility hold higher ranks in Henry's army, and they are singled out by name when, for instance, the death toll is read. (Common soldiers, literally those not "of name," are merely counted.) The French nobility are similarly respected, if only in the sense that there is greater exultation when they are killed than when French commoners are (IV.viii.79–105). Thus, the play betrays a medieval outlook in which the high-born of different nations have more in common with each other, all other things being equal, than they have with the common folk of their own respective countries.

But all other things are not equal. The play, like the early modern state, puts a wholly new value on intra-national comradeship. Importantly, this new value is perceived to be humanly liberating, for along with it comes a leveling of the different ranks. Nationality is to replace rank as a social identifier. *Henry V's* most famous speeches extol this new vision of social equality. In one of them, Henry holds aloft the promise of the new order in order to convince his soldiers that their desperate plight (they were badly outnumbered at Agincourt) is really a valuable opportunity. War, says Henry, provides chances for social climbing:

> This story shall the good man teach his son;
> And Crispin Crispian shall ne'er go by,
> From this day to the ending of the world,
> But we in it shall be remembered—
> We few, we happy few, we band of brothers:
> For he today that sheds his blood with me
> Shall be my brother; be he ne'er so vile,
> This day shall gentle his condition;
> And gentlemen in England now abed
> Shall think themselves accursed they were not here,
> And hold their manhoods cheap, whiles any speaks
> That fought with us upon Saint Crispin's day.

> [IV.iii.56–67]

This speech radically declares that it is better to be a vile (socially low-ranking) war hero than a gentleman who stayed at home. War actually makes the vile gentle. The arbitrariness of honor and "ceremony" (social prestige) is a recurrent theme in Shakespeare, including elsewhere in this play;[11] but here, that arbitrariness is given a positive cast: honor and prestige are rewards to which anyone, not merely the highborn, can aspire. In the new social order, they are pragmatically based on accomplishment.[12]

In fact, what Henry really promises is heroism of a narrative kind—in the "story" that good men will tell. One becomes hero of a story through one's deeds, so here, too, is support for Henry's radical vision of social leveling. Shakespeare makes use of the fact that, however far short of realizing that vision the real world fell, the theatrical "world" confirmed it even as it was uttered. The vision could be seen in practice right up there on stage. Social leveling was not just a theme but a *style* of Elizabethan theater, where low comedy (associated with socially low characters) was interspersed with high epic, and commoners held forth alongside nobles. Henry *proved* that deeds were what counted by being the hero himself in a story called *Henry V*, a play in which ordinary soldiers are permitted to argue with the king (though not in blank verse, which was still reserved for the nobility). Such an equating of persons made Elizabethan theater a laboratory for the mixing of social classes, and for experimentation with new notions of individual human worth—notions we scarcely notice today for the simple reason that we share them.[13]

IV.

So *Henry V* outlines the coming new age and hints at what its audience should find compelling about it. And it paints its main character as heroic to the extent that he respects the old values but champions the new. Henry is depicted as making the social assumptions implicit in theatrical realism a kind of general social policy for Britain. Nor is this process undercut by the fact that the play, for all its mixing of classes, still depends on the mystique of its central character, a character who happens to be the king. For this, too, reflects a truth about the changing society. In the real history of Europe the elevation of the king was one device for dashing the older feudal hierarchies, and for clearing the way to a new concept of the state as a single "body politic." Just so, in this play Henry is the source and the guarantor of the new, pragmatic, egalitarian social order. In Shakespeare's view, the colors and contours of old social rankings are not washed over by economic change, as modern theory would have it; Shakespeare lived long before Marx. Instead, those colors are bleached to a uniform brightness in the glare of virtuous kingship. Henry shines with "a largess universal, like the sun" on everyone equally, "mean and gentle all" (IV.i.chorus). The body politic defines itself at first by projecting the king as an image of itself. Hence, we see here the onset of the now familiar, and very important, notion that a ruler embodies the whole state.

Early written formulations of the theory of sovereignty present similar ideas and even express them in similar language. For two key political philosophers, Shakespeare's older contemporary Jean Bodin (1530–1596) and his younger one, Thomas Hobbes (1588–1679), it was the essence of sovereignty to replace law understood as tradition, custom, or reflection of God's natural order with law as we understand it today: the will of some sovereign authority, enforceable regardless of whether it accords with nature or custom. And for both theorists, what characterized law in this new sense was its equal applicability to all, regardless of social status. A sovereign's legal power is "binding on all his subjects in general and on each in particular," said Bodin. And Hobbes even used the same metaphor of the sun that Shakespeare applies to Henry:

> For in the sovereignty is the fountain of honour. The dignities of lord, earl, duke, and prince are his creatures. As in the presence of the master, the servants are equal, and without any honour at all, so are the subjects, in the presence of the sovereign. And though they shine some more, some less, when they are out of his sight, yet in his presence, they shine no more than the stars in the presence of the sun.[14]

But this formulation immediately suggests one possible objection to the the new king-centered politics. Doesn't a sovereign so elevated become a remote, inhuman abstraction? And if so, how can he be able to embody anything, let alone to command the kind of loyalties that would emotionally compensate people for the loss of their familiar landmarks?

Shakespeare tries to answer this objection with his image of Henry as, in Henry's own words, a "plain fellow." Presented elsewhere by Shakespeare (notably in *Henry IV, Part I*) as human to the point of vulgarity, Henry is seen experiencing his kingly duties as a burden. The king, in short, comes down to earth by being the servant of his society. This is forcefully expressed in the remarkable first scene of act IV, in which Henry disguises himself as a soldier to impart to his troops "a little touch of Harry in the night." The scene is structured as a tour through the social hierarchy, dukes to captains to common soldiers and back to dukes. It contains numerous reflections on the arbitrariness of social ranks. When Henry, for instance, is challenged in the darkness by one of his sentries and claims to be "a gentleman of the company," the sentry retorts that he, too, is "as good a gentleman as the emperor"—to which Henry replies, "then you are better than the king" (lines 37–43). Here Shakespeare is punning with terms like *good* and *better*, which in his time could refer both to the "quality" of one's birth and (as we would use the terms today) to one's inner qualities of character. And in the soliloquy that closes the scene, Henry ruminates on the problems of being what Hobbes called a "mortal God," charged with the thankless task of guarding society's well-being. All that distinguishes the king from anyone else is an arbitrary ("idle") quality called "ceremony," Henry notes; and by burdening him with great tasks, this quality merely underscores his human limitations. The very thing that elevates the king also links him to common humanity.

This clever, if convoluted, argument might allay one fear about the brave new world of sovereignty. But there is also a deeper anxiety to be dealt with, and act IV, scene 1 takes on this anxiety too. In medieval thinking, kings could be held to account for violations of divine or natural law and of community tradition. If, under the new dispensation, monarchy becomes absolute—a quasi-divine power in its own right—this would seem to make the king all the more culpable for what happens in his realm; the more powerful he becomes, the easier it would seem to be to assign to him that troubling quality with which *Henry V* is everywhere preoccupied— "fault."

Codified in the Middle Ages by Thomas Aquinas, the view that the king could be faulted was well-established in the real Henry V's time, some two hundred years before Shakespeare. We find it expressed, for instance, in Philippe de Mézières's letter to King Richard II of 1395, written when the real Henry V was eight years old. Mézières, a French nobleman, appealed to Richard for peace between France and England in the real-life Hundred Years' War, arguing that "if your royal Majesty should triumph in person over your enemies, the greater the victory, the greater the number of slain, and, in the ordinary way, the souls of most of them will be borne to Hell, and all by your fault." Mézières also believed that the king must weigh a war's "countless ills and cruelties" in the scale alongside whatever political reasons he had for waging it. The king was answerable to God, "Who made you lord of peace and not of war," and would be better off giving up his war aims than taking a risk that all the "cruelties" they brought on might go for naught.[15]

These are serious issues. Mézières's view contradicts the whole political justification Shakespeare gives for Henry's war, and all his appeals to see it as some kind of socially upbuilding enterprise. It is therefore extremely interesting to find that Shakespeare himself has taken arguments very like Mézières's and put them into the mouth of one of the soldiers, Williams, who debates Henry in that key scene of act IV. If the war proves unjust, says Williams in the course of that debate, "the King himself hath a heavy reckoning to make" for all the ruin it brings and for all the souls it sends to hell (130–42). Moreover, Williams is troubled that mere subjects cannot judge the rightness of the war, nor do anything in reply were the king to somehow betray them:

> You pay him then! That's a perilous shot out of an elder-[pop]-gun, that a poor and a private displeasure can do against a monarch! You may as well go about to turn the sun to ice, with fanning in his face with a peacock's feather. You'll never trust his word after! Come, 'tis a foolish saying. [IV.i.192–197]

Through Williams, Shakespeare calls his own "sun" metaphor into question. Here the king/sun is not the source of life and warmth, but a distant celestial object whose actions it is useless for mere mortals to protest. Contrary to what one might think or hope, a society's willingness to view the king as the personification of itself actually cuts away the traditional ground for criticizing him.[16]

Clearly, these challenges cut to the core of Henry's whole enterprise. That Shakespeare presents them at all indicates how troubled it was possible to be over the political conditions that made possible such allegedly glorious wars. "Fault" becomes a pervasive source of tension in the play, and the more it is excused or apologized for, the more one senses serious doubts—as if the king, or the playwright, doth protest too much.[17]

To answer this particular problem, Henry presents a long speech of self-defense (IV.i.143–80), his "God's beadle" speech. Here he defends himself and his war on two grounds, both utterly contradicting the medieval, Williams/Mézières view. First, says Henry, the king is not responsible for the fate of individual souls caught up in his actions, and second, the war is actually a good thing to the extent that it does sort out good souls from evildoers. War is God's beadle (constable), his instrument of divine punishment.

Apart from its invocation of the deity, this speech makes it as clear as ever that Shakespeare's Henry is a figure of the 1590s rather than the 1390s, and that those two hundred years had seen major shifts in the Western world's views of state power. For here Henry begins to combine, in what would come to be a key modern assumption, a theory of sovereign unaccountability with a related theory that warfare is in and of itself a morally coherent enterprise. And the key modern element upholding both theories in Henry's mind is the idea that the struggle into which he has pressed his troops is really nothing special as human undertakings go, no more unusual a danger to their souls than if they were servants on a routine mission. "The King is not bound to answer the particular endings of his soldiers, the father of his son, nor the master of his servant; for they purpose not their death when they purpose their services," Henry says (151–54).

But it intuitively does seem that soldiering "purposes death." So either Henry is just being disingenuous, or there is some other theory of purposing at work here. One such theory would be: War follows naturally from statecraft (as errands follow from servanthood), and statecraft follows from state purposes, which are not just factors to be "weighed," as Mézières had said, but which rather are supreme over all other considerations—authorized, in effect, by nature (since the people consitute a natural reality and the sovereign's role is to safeguard the people). Caught up in such reasoning, Henry might well manage to overlook a central problem with his servant analogy: the fact that soldiers, unlike servants, are usually coerced, and in this sense don't really "purpose their services" to begin with.

Out of such logic seems to come the striking assumption whereby Henry's threat to Harfleur, perhaps his greatest transgression of traditional moral norms, is excused—and so also comes a key element in the way of thinking that makes nuclear deterrent postures thinkable today. Acting on behalf of the state, the sovereign does not really "act" at all. If anything, he oversees the natural consequences of his victims' actions. It is they who are "guilty in defense," guilty in the sense that they oppose the natural order of things—an order that has come to be embodied in him. In lines I omitted from the Harfleur ultimatum, Henry says,

> What is it then to me, if impious war,
> Arrayed in flames, like to the prince of fiends,
> Do, with his smirched complexion, all fell feats
> Enlinked to waste and desolation?
> What is't to me, when you yourselves are cause,
> If your pure maidens fall into the hands
> Of hot and forcing violation?
> What rein can hold licentious wickedness
> When down the hill he holds his fierce career?
> We may as bootless spend our vain command
> Upon th'enraged soldiers in their spoil
> As send precepts to the leviathan
> To come ashore.
>
> [III.iii.15–27][18]

The rhetoric of this is striking. Henry claims that it is war itself that does "all fell feats," and wickedness itself that careers toward its victims; and though he has led the invasion, he claims to be "bootless" in the face of both. As in the lines quoted earlier ("the gates of mercy shall be all shut up"—by whom?), he obscures his own role—indeed, claims to have no role. The active agents are, rather, "licentiousness," "impious" war, or, in the same nonspecific sense, "the fleshed soldier" (not *Henry's* soldiers particularly, but some soldier archetype). These agents must simply be expected to do what they by nature do.

The soaring rhetoric itself indicates the experimental quality that this line of argument apparently had even for Shakespeare. Henry's words, after all, contradict other claims made on his behalf—such as his orders to his troops *not* to mistreat townspeople (III.vi.104–10), and his view of war as anything but "impious" (IV.i.164ff.). And the very fact that they are presented is, again, a kind of backhanded apology, an acknowledgment-by-exclusion of traditional moral concerns.

Yet the arguments remain. Henry holds up war as simple reality, and thus he asks us to take the power he wields for granted, to stop thinking of it as power at all, to stop "seeing" it. "What is't to me?" This refrain both shrugs off Henry's power and universalizes it. If the king's ability to unite and inspire shines like the sun, his ability to destroy and punish simply rains (or reigns), indifferent as to the objects upon which it falls.

V.

What made such a view of war acceptable? Why, historically, did Henry win the argument and not Williams (or Mézières, or Thomas Aquinas)? We have already seen that the new view of war was embedded in a view of sovereign power that was considered socially upbuilding, even reformist. But likewise in the vanguard of enlightened thinking was the new, if somewhat diminished, concept of the individual subject. If ordinary soldiers couldn't question the king's actions (though of course Shakespeare ironically says they can by letting them speak with Henry unawares), they also couldn't vouch for those actions. Hence, they couldn't reasonably be responsible for them. "The subject," said Shakespeare's compatriot, Francis Bacon, "should not suffer for his obedience."[19] Instead, all was to be embraced and excused by the hand of the increasingly powerful monarch. As Shakespeare's soldier Bates puts it, "We know enough if we know we are the King's subjects. If his cause be wrong, our obedience to the King wipes the crime of it out of us" (126–29). (Of course, as Bacon saw, there was a practical benefit for the king in this law too. It tended to keep subjects in the attitude of Bates: not "busy[ing] themselves to pry" into whether the king was right, as they were likely to do if they were in danger of being punished.[20])

That attitude on the part of the king's subjects is disturbingly close to the modern excuse, "I was just following orders." With the subject's responsibility for his acts folded into the state's, it becomes easier for that responsibility to simply disappear. Political actors in an event like a war can shift responsibility around in a kind of shell game—the soldier shifts it to the king, and the king takes it on as part of the paternal burden he is so noble for bearing (in effect, shifting it back to the people). The king intends the act, but only on the people's behalf; and the people carry it out, but only because the king ordered it. "Fault" bleeds away from the people to the sovereign, and from the sovereign to nowhere—to nature itself.

The subject's diminished moral role has a still more disturbing outcome. This is implied in Henry's view of the French and their relation to *their* king. When the French Dauphin mocks Henry by offering to bribe him with tennis balls, Henry paints the consequences—the coming invasion—as follows:

And tell the pleasant Prince this mock of his
Hath turned his balls to gun-stones, and his soul
Shall stand sore charged for the wasteful vengeance
That shall fly with them: for many a thousand widows
Shall this his mock mock out of their dear husbands;
Mock fathers from their sons, mock castles down;
And some are yet ungotten and unborn
That shall have cause to curse the Dauphin's scorn.

[I.ii.282–89]

The Dauphin's guilt and responsibility are the paradoxical counterpart to Henry's own innocence. If the fact that sovereign and community have become inextricable—that the king is in a sense the country—can be used to excuse everyone on our side (the shell game), so too can it be turned around, as Henry here does, into a totalizing of guilt on the other side. Just as Henry embodies his people and so is freed of all fault, the Dauphin is held to embody *his* people, so that his actions call down punishment on them—even the most unarguably innocent of them, the unborn. Mézières's and Williams's essentially medieval view had been that the king could not escape responsibility for what he did to the people; Henry's essentially modern view is almost the reverse. It is now the people who cannot escape responsibility for what the king does.

Note that Shakespeare hits most squarely upon the new notion when confronting his Henry with a serious moral problem. It is as if the slaughter of innocents could be justified by nothing in existing tradition, nothing short of a whole new theory of authority. Shakespeare was unusually prescient about sovereignty to precisely the same extent that he was unusually sensitive to the moral dilemmas of war and willing to state these as starkly as possible.

Without the view, which begins to emerge in Shakespeare's time and comes full-blown down to us, that the people of a state are responsible and, hence, punishable for that state's policies, there may never have been any strategic bombing policies or nuclear weapons, at least not of the size and numbers that today threaten the existence of whole societies. There may never have been philosophers or strategists like Herman Kahn (at least none who were listened to) reassuring us that allowing for mass punishment is the only rule that "works." But as long as there have been—as long as, in fact, most people seem tacitly to accept such views without question— we may consider ourselves in the grip of a fairly radical (and historically quite peculiar) theory of sovereign moral unaccountability and of the enemy's collective guilt.

Yet this theory has become so accepted that one of its manifestations is now second nature for most of us: the anthropomorphizing of groups of people, especially national groups, which I earlier called the We problem (see chapter 2). Nations are treated as coherent entities, as though they were individual organisms, feeling and willing and behaving the way persons do. The We problem and the modern view of the state go hand in hand. Sovereignty involves, as F. H. Hinsley has put it, a "conception of the body politic as a single personality, in which both Ruler and People were absorbed."[21] As it has become our culture's preeminent theory of authority, anthropomorphic conceptions of the state have become ever more taken for granted in modern thinking.

Those World War II terror bombings, which caused civilians to suffer in ways that would have seemed diabolical even to Henry, prompted political writer Dwight Macdonald to explore this mode of thinking in a series of essays on what he called *animism*, after the ancient inclination to assign human qualities to the nonhuman world. For Macdonald, modern animism is "the theory of the 'organic state,'" and it is a view symptomatic of the increasing power of nation-states.[22] It especially serves the purposes of state leaders in wartime, who need to convince people that the state and its actions are merely extensions of people's own individual purposes—and, conversely, that enemy peoples are mere extensions of enemy states. Macdonald critiqued the use to which animism was being put during the war to justify the terror bombings (soon to culminate in Hiroshima and Nagasaki), as well as to undergird demands for the postwar punishment of whole peoples as if they were "the guilty accomplices of Hitler."[23] He ridiculed one American newsman who took this attitude toward the Germans:

> A German girl, member of the Hitler Maedchen, was taken on an enforced tour of Buchenwald [in 1945]. "She moaned, with tears running down her face: 'It is terrible what they have done to these people.'" The reporter comments, in evident disapproval: "The pronoun she used was 'they,' not 'we.'"[24]

But Macdonald was equally distressed by supposedly positive uses of the same attitude when it was applied to "our" side:

> The people of London are constantly being applauded for their "heroism" by war propagandists, and doubtless many individual Londoners did show heroic qualities during the bombing raids. But others doubtless also showed mean and cowardly traits. . . . When journalists salute the "heroism" of the Londoners or of the Russian people—they really mean a kind of collective heroism which can never exist actually, since as a collectivity the people of London had no alternative except to endure the bombings. As a Cockney retorted to a war correspondent: "Everyone's sticking to it? And just what the bloody hell do you think anyone can do? You'd think we had some bloody choice in the matter!"[25]

It is clear enough what is false about animism when one reflects on how the Russian people would be treated by U.S. war propagandists *today*. But false or not, the habit of imagining collectivities "which can never exist actually" is embedded in the very language with which most people routinely refer to states. As Brian Martin has pointed out, there is an "unstated identification of states or governments with the people in a country" in political discourse today, the identification I called the We problem and which Northrop Frye (whose Biblical criticism was discussed in chapter 4) calls, revealingly, the royal metaphor, since its prototype would be a statement like "Henry invaded France." People make such statements all the time. As Martin points out, they routinely say "China invaded Vietnam" when what really happened was: "Chinese military forces, mostly conscripts, were ordered by the rulers of the Chinese state to invade territory which was claimed by rulers of the Vietnamese state as exclusively theirs to control."[26]

And as this translation makes clear, the simpler, animistic version inscribes whole political theories. For that version rests on assumptions about how states are controlled, and what relations they have to "their" people.

Moreover, by failing to draw attention to, or problematize, these theories, the animistic version subtly endorses them—meaning modern political discourse, constructed as it is out of such animistic statements, also routinely endorses them.

At that, "China invaded Vietnam" is modern animism in its most obvious form, in which states are simply made singular subjects—metaphorically treated as if they "did" things, acted as wholes. Animism enters modern discourse in more recondite ways too. For instance, there is this remark by former Senator Barry Goldwater on the Gulf War: "If the Iraqis and Iranians want to fight it out, and it's going to go on forever, let 'em fight."[27] Here, Iraqis and Iranians are at least plural; the statement seems to imply that there are lots of each, as in fact there are. But it also still presumes that these individuals all share the same purposes. To hold that large groups of people "want" anything, the way that individuals want things, is as unconsciously metaphorical as to say they "do" things.

Still more advanced animism combines the singular conception of a people with the belief that whole peoples can have a single feeling. The *Los Angeles Times* reported recently that "Europe is not sure about the answers to such [defense] questions. It is not even sure which are the most relevant. But it is suddenly in the mood to ask all of them at once."[28] As the content of the article made clear, what was actually happening was that different questions were being asked all at once by different parties and officials in different nations of Europe. But instead of sticking to this fact, the report assigned all the views at once to "Europe," thus making Europe seem incoherent—and, thus, undercutting the reporters' own effort to characterize the thinking in Europe.

Animism of this sort ultimately becomes comical. Note this capsule item that appeared in *Newsweek* at the start of the last presidential race:

> Like Gov. Mario Cuomo himself, New Yorkers are ambivalent about his running for president. A new poll by the Marist Institute for Public Opinion will show 45.9 percent of state voters feeling Cuomo should run, 44.5 opposed.[29]

This statement was produced using all the principles just mentioned. First, New York State was construed as a single, animistic entity. Its "opinion" in a poll (like Europe's "mood") was then equated with a person's individual opinion. But since this opinion was really an aggregate of hundreds of different statements (animistically enlarged to the whole state through the magic of polling statistics), no single opinion had actually emerged. So this lack of any one opinion was then read as ambivalence—which is what it would be in an individual.

Then, "New York," the concept that with which all this discursive trouble began, was repluralized into "New Yorkers," and the ambivalence was literally assigned to them as individuals. (Of course, all this happened at once in the writer's mind, where New Yorkers remained a single glop.) And thus did *Newsweek* present the opposite of the truth. Instead of New Yorkers having *definite* opinions, some for and some against—as the poll made clear they did—the magazine reported that they hadn't made up their minds.

Of course journalists rely on this innocuous sort of animism all the time; it is what allows them to tell us that that we're "food crazy" or that "we have all become a lot more selfish" or, most bizarrely, "We tailgate. We cut in. We run red lights. We shout and snarl and shake our fists. We have even been known to shoot one another."[30] On a more elegant note, mild animism provides Shakespeare with some poetic images: England is "a mourning widow of her nobles" (I.ii.158), and its union with France a kind of "marriage" analogous to Henry's marriage to Katherine (V.ii.351ff.).

But for Shakespeare these are still literary devices, even if used to obscure uncomfortable political truths (like the fact that France hadn't consented to this marriage).[31] In Shakespeare's time, the steps were still being learned. The character who compares French cities to maids, for instance, makes clear that he knows he is drawing an analogy. But where political discourse of 1599 was crawling, that of today flat-out runs. Today the devices are more or less mistaken for reality. No one thinks it strange when NBC News reports that a large number of air-traffic deaths meant "1987 was a terrible year for air travelers."[32] Yet look at the bizarre theory of human experience this encodes: that air travelers somehow individually experience whatever happens to *them* (as a body), so that a rash of deaths is like an attack of flu—or for that matter, like a rash. Actually all the air travelers watching this report had lived, meaning that in terms of survival 1987 had been, for them, an excellent year.

But something else had died—the animistic metaphor that made this report possible. A metaphor dies when people forget it is a metaphor, when it becomes a way of speaking literally. And unfortunately metaphors, unlike people, don't leave life by dying; they leave language and enter life. Dead metaphors are mistaken for realities and, hence, are liable to be acted on. Even Shakespeare makes clear that it is not so long a step from mere analogy to unconscious metaphor to animistic action—from poetically describing a city as "a maid . . . that war hath never entered" (V.ii.316–17), to Henry's reference to Harfleur as "her," to his more or less guiltless threat to Harfleur's literal, physically real maids.

Ominously, that step has been taken. Animism has erected a true body politic; the modern state is actually treated as if it were a bodily being. This thoroughgoing triumph of animism in modern thinking gives us warfare as an assault on a body. If airline deaths are like flu, nuclear combat becomes a kind of spanking (a comparison I have actually heard made). And thus arises the possibility of a statement like, "My fellow Americans, I am pleased to tell you that I've signed legislation that will outlaw Russia forever. We begin bombing in five minutes." President Reagan's infamous microphone-test joke of 1984 inscribes whole volumes of modern political discourse. There is the issue of legality and the state: both the recognition of the state as defined by its power to authorize and legitimize, and the wish that our state's power somehow included the power to deligitimize others (something it does include under conditions of total war). And between the first and second sentences there is the grand, animistic conflation of the state as legal abstraction with the physical homeland (hence the people) it rules. A kind of physical reality has been accorded to the legal entity, and a kind of unreality or arbitrariness to the physical entity, so that outlawing logically leads to bombing. Bombing is no longer seen (once the state is removed) as the destruction of anything real or important. Most of all, there is the fact that Reagan got into political hot water with this remark, but *not* over these points; instead because the statement was needlessly provocative at that moment and seemed to hint at an overeagerness to see these theories put into effect.

The theories themselves, though, are widely granted, even accepted as simply natural. Though there will always be disputes over tactics, the basic notion of bombing an "outlawed" state hardly strikes people as puzzling or logically incoherent. When the Reagan Administration did bomb Libya in 1986, one member of the British Parliament, supporting the action while speaking to the concern about civilian deaths, said, "The Sermon on the Mount undoubtedly sets the highest standards of individual behavior that anyone could require, but it does not apply to those of us in this House who are responsible for the interests of millions of people."[33] Here, in one sentence, are the two key, related claims—that the state incorporates the people, and that it therefore rises above everyday moral censure.

The relevance to political actions of the Sermon on the Mount has never been crystal clear (though "does not apply" is a somewhat extreme way of putting this). Augustine, who laid down the essential points of just-war doctrine, acknowledged that "It is the wickedness of the opposing group which compels the wise man to wage just wars." But Augustine added a second clause: "and this wickedness, even if it led to no war, would still be lamented by a human being, because *human beings* do it."[34] This sense of the enemy's humanness is what seems to have been lost. Today, a moral philosopher like Edward R. Norman appears nominally to be in line with just-war thinking when he argues that

> the preservation of values by armed conflict against militant opposition is not murder. . . . The saintly man may acquire virtue by turning the other cheek in a personal matter, where he forfeits the opportunity of revenge or gain by doing so; but in the collective defense of essential values he cannot behave in that way, for the result would be not personal but social. The defenseless and the children would lose the opportunity of practicing or being nurtured in values whose eternal importance transcends the value of individual human lives.[35]

But the problem is that this is written in an era that has lost sight of the premise that made Augustine's (and Aquinas's and Mézières's) version of this viewpoint coherent—the premise that eternal and transcendent values really are ordained by God. Without God, the right to decide which values are transcendent (and the sole power thought capable of protecting them) falls to the highest human political authority, which in our world is the state. Augustine meant to affirm values that stand outside the state, that transcend it, instead of existing only by or through it. Hence, he would scarcely recognize the abstract and terrible meaning which moderns (including some who think they speak for his tradition) have given to notions like "the wickedness of the opposing group." Confronted with the notion of bombing in five minutes, I think he would more likely agree with theologian Richard John Neuhaus, who calls the politics of the modern state "idolatry": the raising up of a false god.[36]

It is argued that the twentieth century has seen an important movement in war limitation comparable to (and borrowing from) the old just-war ideas.[37] And it may be that there are practical changes afoot that the discourses of our culture have yet to catch up with. But where Henry's threats to Harfleur were laced with apologies, and where the *real* Henry V, back in 1415, had to observe all sorts of time-consuming rituals and courtesies while besieging the real Harfleur, leaders of today's states rely on threats that they hardly think of as threats at all, to precisely the same extent that they hardly think of the threatened people as people. During the Solidarity uprising in Poland of 1980–81, I wondered if any of Solidarity's supporters in the West, especially the many on the political right, had given any thought to the fact that the United States no doubt had nuclear missiles targeted on the Gdansk shipyards at the very moment Solidarity was taking shape there. Fired at the wrong moment, these missiles would have killed Lech Walesa. (He was, after all, one of the Warsaw Pact's economic recovery support personnel.) Did anyone stop to consider this? If that seems a strange question, the strangeness itself is no doubt the answer. Not thinking this way is structured into modern discourse itself.

True, the U.S. Catholic Bishops used just-war doctrine as the basis of their 1983 Pastoral Letter on War and Peace. But this was the exception that proved the rule. For it was evidence, first, of how lost to view that doctrine had been—the bishops seemed to be reminding people that it even exists. Second, in applying the doctrine to the nuclear question, the bishops were indeed moved to substantially critique current nuclear policy. And third, the whole effort had no discernible effect on electoral politics. A year later Reagan spoke of bombing in five minutes, and within a few months he was reelected by majorities in forty-nine states.

War and Technology
VI.

So, in modern thinking the state becomes the superior of nature, perhaps even a substitute for it. The state is regarded as the primary phenomenon, and the naturally existing world, including people, as its object, instead of vice-versa. Hence there is no higher standard for judging the state's actions, and the sovereign power becomes morally inculpable, beyond reproach in those things it does "for reasons of state." This especially applies to the state's right to use violence, which now expands virtually without limit. Violence is essentially the exercise of power over nature, and by transcending (in fact, authorizing) the natural order, the state gains the right to exercise this power at will. The state's prime prerogative, its monopoly of violence, is a corollary of its new position vis-à-vis nature.

Of course, authority over nature can mean something else besides sheer violence. The state exercises the same basic authority anytime it uses technology to further its ends. Intensive technological manipulation of nature is also a characteristic of the modern state. In fact, it is possible to view the state itself as a kind of technology, and this to precisely the extent that animism (viewing the state as a body) has come to increase. This curious fact further supports the existence of nuclear weapons, and so its history needs to be briefly traced.

Intuitively it seems that the democratic reforms of the last 300 years would have tended to diminish the mystique that sovereignty possessed when it was attached to kings. But in fact, crucial elements of that mystique have actually been enhanced. Even the Declaration of Independence, which strongly argues for subordinating governments to the greater sovereignty of nature and persons, can be seen as part of a general strengthening of modern animism by contrast with the more primitive version we see in Shakespeare. Since 1599 freer reign has been given for the erecting into historical reality of what in Shakespeare are still, in part, literary conceits.

We can see why this would be so if we turn again to the early theories of sovereignty articulated by Bodin and Hobbes. The absolutist quality of the sovereign—including his right to be his own moral arbiter—has been credited to (or blamed on) both those theorists. But significantly, Bodin and Hobbes argue for the self-justifying, self-legalizing sovereign from strikingly different premises. Bodin's derivation of kingly power is quasi-mystical and top-down (God makes the king); Hobbes's is pragmatic and bottom-up (the people make him).[38] Bodin stresses that the sovereign's quasi-divine authority gives him the right to make law—which is to say, to escape being held accountable under the law.[39] Hobbes has a very different notion of law—that it is "but rules authorized." People obey these rules for essentially the same reason they follow the rules of a game (a comparison Hobbes himself makes), the difference being that the prize in this particular game is a secure, civilized existence. But the upshot of Hobbes's theory is the same as Bodin's: the sovereign's immunity from censure. "Because every subject is . . . author of all the actions and judgments of the sovereign," says Hobbes, "it follows that whatsoever he does, it can be no injury to any of his subjects; nor ought he to be by any of them accused of injustice."[40]

Nonetheless, the difference between the theories is historically important. It is the chronologically later, more modern Hobbesian way of thinking that Shakespeare's Henry presents himself as progressive for having grasped. And it was this same theory, or its direct successors, that would eventually overthrow absolutist monarchy—yet in a way that ironically exacerbated many of its problems. The old hierarchical order demands to be reformed; initially, this is done by elevating the people as a whole over lords and dukes. This in turn involves elevating one individual, that mortal God who, as Hobbes puts it, bears all persons within himself.[41] "A multitude of men are made *one* person when they are by one man, or one person, represented."[42] And this is where animism in its distinctively modern form, as a structuring outlook rather than merely a literary device, begins to tighten its hold. The personal quality of the sovereign is at first looked to as compensation for the lost personhood of individuals. People made increasingly equal in society are also made increasingly anonymous, interchangeable, atomized; but this matters less if their persons are borne by what Hobbes calls the artificial man—the state whose soul is the sovereign.[43] And it matters still less if that artificial man also happens to be embodied in a real man, namely the king.

But how can the equality of people be achieved through their complete subjugation? This is the logical conundrum that Hobbes's theory (and before that, Henry's) has to face. Animism actually serves as one possible solution: by equating the king and the people, it suggests that the power flowing to the king will not be power subtracted from the people (that sovereignty, in other words, will not be a zero-sum game). Hobbes puts forward precisely this argument, hoping to show that the power granted the sovereign to rule the people is really the truest expression of the people's own wills. The argument launches him into flights of Shakespearian-style sophistry: "It is a weak sovereign that has weak subjects, and a weak people whose sovereign wanteth power to rule them at his will."[44]

The problem is that there is little chance of this being believed. (Indeed, it is not so much Shakespeare this formula recalls as Orwell: "Slavery is Freedom.") And there is another problem. *Mortal God* is a contradiction in terms. How many individuals can credibly play God, except in myth (or in a Shakespeare play)? Absolutism is seldom offset by the quality of the person bearing it; it is more likely to distort or undermine that quality. Once you've agreed, as Shakespeare claims, that a king like Henry gains his title to rule from his "virtue,"[45] you're stuck having to answer for the fact that most kings, like most people, leave some virtue to be desired.

So finally a different, more radical solution is needed in the form of new political institutions. First goes the king's quasi-divinity (Hobbes already has abandoned this), then the king himself. In Shakespeare's time, it was not the king as such who was sovereign anyway, but the "king in Parliament," and even Hobbes grants that the sovereign could be a popular assembly instead of a single man. Hobbes's own theory, in the long run, encourages faith in legislatures, not dictators. His admission that the soul can "depart" the body politic theoretically clears the way for a right of revolution against bad governments that don't serve their true ends. And his notion of law as "rules authorized" is precisely the spirit of constitutionalism, of "no taxation without representation." Seeing sovereignty as justified by the service it performs, Hobbes looks forward to the Declaration of Independence a century and a quarter later, as well as to the whole apparatus of checks on power to which it would give rise.

The solution of constitutional republicanism, though, creates a new problem—or aggravates the one with which this all began. Representative government leaves sovereignty intact, only less visibly "embodied." Previously it at least had a human focus; now it becomes an abstraction that is all the easier to take for granted, all the easier not to see. And along with this—in fact, inherent in such government—comes a metaphor even more relentlessly animistic than kingship could ever have been. Governments abstractly constituted as assemblies of many individuals can only function by adopting the fundamental rule of representation, as brought to our attention by Hobbes:

> If the representative consist of many men, the voice of the greater number must be considered as the voice of them all. . . . Every one, as well he that *voted for it* as he that *voted against it*, shall *authorize* all the actions and judgments of that man or assembly of men in the same manner as if they were his own.[46]

In other words, unless it walks out (with the result being civil war and the breakdown of the state), the minority agrees to subsume itself within the assembly as a whole, to join in the fiction that all speak with one voice. In Hobbes's analogy, it agrees to abide by the rules of the game and not cry foul even if it loses.

Republican government is thoroughly imbued with this fiction of unity. The congressman from Texas who voted against the housing bill remains an officer of the house that passed it. He is in the same spot I am in as I write this, represented before the world as an American citizen by a president I voted against. This is what makes it possible to say that "Congress today changed course on housing policy," or "*We* voted for Reagan because we shared his view of the world." Part of why these animistic metaphors have died is precisely the fact that there is no personal monarch whose "title" the people, like Shakespeare's soldiers, might be in some position to question.

VII.

To put the matter in terms that the founders of our system might actually have used, Western states replaced the king, a person, with governments consciously conceived to be *machines*. The advance made beyond Hobbes (though built upon his way of thinking) is the idea that the people, not government, remain sovereign. Government, therefore, is merely ad hoc, a trustee of the people. Like a machine, it is a device built to achieve certain purposes, or what Jefferson called ends.

In theory, Americans (and most of the modern West) have substituted this mechanistic view of government for the older idea that the state has a soul. But culturally the two views exist side by side. And far from canceling each other out, on the crucial issues of war and technology they actually reinforce each other. First, the mechanistic view is diluted with traces of the older, animistic view. What distinguishes machines from people, says Theodore Roszak, is that machines have functions but never a purpose.[47] The modern theory of government holds that the same is true of society: it is simply the arena of competing individual purposes. But because people have purposes, they want to believe that their society does too. (Indeed, they want to believe this even of their literal machines, which they constantly anthropomorphize—that is, treat as having souls.) Moreover, people wish to believe that the society bears *their* purposes into the world, as Hobbes said the sovereign bears our persons. And since the government is their trustee and our society's most visible, active agent, they transfer these beliefs to it, interpreting its acts as expressions of purpose. They look at the vote on the housing bill as a unitary, willed act, analogous to, say, one's personal decision to fix the roof or take out a mortgage.

But this means imputing will, hence purpose, hence a soul, to the state. And because people do the same to other states (with all the possibilities this implies for characterizing those states as good or evil), they easily stop thinking about those states as concatenations of many individual souls. This is how "enemy" peoples become soulless, nonentities. They are effaced in much the same way (and for the same reason) as the losers in a game, or the outvoted minority in our own legislatures.[48]

Second, even the undiluted mechanistic view itself pushes in different ways toward much the same outcome. When Herman Kahn frets that vengeance must sometimes be visited on people for the actions of their governments (see chapter 1), he is arguing not from animistic principles (though it sounds similar) but from mechanistic. He is appealing to the machinelike value of *technique* as a standard for social action. The true immorality, says Kahn, would be

> to jeopardize our national security interests and the values of most of the world on the basis of a strongly held but *emotional* evaluation of basically *technical* and *strategic* issues . . . . *spiritual* and *moral* values certainly inform *practical* and secular ones, but they cannot substitute for them.[49]

As this makes clear, cultural discourse in our era is constructed of certain oppositions—*practical* against *spiritual, technical* against *emotional.* Like Kahn, most people structure such oppositions into their moral thinking. Thus they agree, in effect, to evaluate social action the same way one evaluates the action of a machine: by whether it *works* in the *circumstances,* to use two more of Kahn's terms.

What Kahn means by *circumstance* is "that which is unavoidably rooted in nature," but what he uses the term to refer to is the modern system of state goals and interests, which he (like most people) mistakes for a natural fact. (*Circumstance* is a vacant word, like *state*—it can name and, thus, implicitly authorize almost anything.) Hence when Kahn uses the term *practical*, thinking it means "concording with nature," it really means "serving the interests of the powers that enforce present circumstances." Through such a series of discursive moves, certain questions—What about the Gdansk shipyard?—are made not to arise; for raising them, or imagining that "the values of most of the world" necessarily include "no mass destruction," places one outside the discourse—or worse, within it but in a category marked "emotional."

And finally, *spiritual* and *moral* are brought into proximity with *emotional*—Kahn's conjoining of these terms sounds, again, perfectly straightforward. So by now whole swatches of human experience have been disvalued, whole analytical approaches ruled out of account. And conversely, *technical* in all this has come to refer to whatever procedures take the circumstances (the state and its purposes) for granted, and do not try to introduce new standards for judging those circumstances from outside (whether "spiritual" standards, from higher realms of being, or "emotional," from within the individual). Technique becomes whatever procedure flows from the interests of the state—right up to, and including, the bombing of Leningrad.

One is tempted to say "mere" technique, for in a way this definition makes any such procedure seem not really an action at all—makes it seem, rather, like mere fidelity to the nature of things. Kahn, like Henry, speaks as if we are "bootless" and must do what we do. Characterizing an action as technical removes from those who undertake it the stigma of having done something, of having laid down an undertaking that might be measured against some preexisting standard and, perhaps, found wanting. It allows one to claim to be merely responding to circumstance, which is always justified. *Technical* and *practical* are, in short, additional ways of naming actions that it is thought to be pointless or impossible to criticize in moral terms.

All this is so familiar to us today that it may seem an odd issue to raise. Perhaps Kahn is wrong to conflate the state with "circumstance"; perhaps that mistake is peculiarly characteristic of the modern age.[50] But surely the notion of technique is universal? Surely it does make sense to see certain actions as concordant to nature, hence as "practical" in a way that others aren't? And isn't this especially true in warfare, where the purpose is, after all, to win?

In chapter 6 I will argue that there is such a thing as nature and, hence, concordance to nature (and, thus, a way of being moral). But Kahn's (and most other people's) overriding preference for actions that "work" in the "practical" circumstances is as historically novel as any of the other major ideas we have here been exploring. As obvious and inescapable as his oppositions of terms seem to be, they are still oppositions within discourse, and people did not always talk in ways that assumed or enforced them in the past. Nor did they view even warfare in terms of "circumstance," with the overriding goal being to find technical means to win. War becomes a pragmatic undertaking—an outgrowth of policy, a way of getting something done—in a culture that has also accepted machines and modern representative assemblies as ways of getting things done. But without the successful raising of the state as an ultimate value, people would not have accepted the idea of using virtually any technological means available for winning war. They would not have accepted the modern, pragmatic sense of war as fundamentally a kind of technology, designed according to the ends to be achieved—the continuation of politics by other means, in von Clausewitz's definitive modern definition.[51]

War in this mechanistic sense would have seemed a completely alien and possibly demonic institution to Augustine, with his fretfulness over the beating up of fellow Christians. It certainly is alien to Shakespeare's Captain Fluellen, with his fussy concern to maintain the "disciplines of war." Fluellen is the officer of Henry's army mildly satirized in *Henry V* for worrying that warfare be seemly. He is proof that the modern view is modern and, thus, he is another source of anxiety in the play, an embodiment of a medieval discourse which, like so many others, is pressing for recognition, and which Shakespeare both acknowledges and respectfully sets aside. An expert on the ancient Roman wars, Fluellen (in his Welsh accent) defends the "aunchient disciplines" in a way that Henry admires but admits is "a little out of fashion." Berating his troops for what we might call lowbrow behavior, Fluellen defends "the true and aunchient prerogatifes and laws of the wars . . . the ceremonies of the wars, and the cares of it, and the forms of it, and the sobriety of it, and the modesty of it" (IV.i.65–83). For him, war is a noble and chivalric contest among (necessarily) noble participants, and those participating ought to conduct themselves accordingly.

In Fluellen's discourse, *disciplines* therefore means what we might call rituals, and refers to forms of conduct that ought to be observed regardless of their practical usefulness to the war effort. Fluellen values preservation of the ancient rituals over innovation of new fighting techniques, an outlook that puts him light-years from any military thinker of today. But that outlook is in line with the general emphasis on social class over national ties that *Henry V* is at pains to reject. (Fluellen argues that nobility makes for favorable outcomes; Henry, that favorable outcomes make one noble.) Henry's whole idea of class leveling, such as would make his soldiers "friends" and "brothers," can only be based on a technological, pragmatic, utilitarian view of war, since observing Fluellen's more formal "disciplines" would tend instead to *reinforce* the old social structure.

But *disciplines*, like other concepts of the passing age, contain the seeds of its own destruction. For Fluellen's use of the word hints at a second meaning, one more consistent with the new emphasis in warfare; it ensnares him, we might say, in another discourse that happened to be crossing the one he favored at just that moment in history. When Fluellen speaks of the "discipline" of laying mines at a certain depth (III.ii.56ff.), the word has shifted to mean not ritualistic propriety but what we would now call tactics, or even military science: proven ways of getting the job done. It looks toward the modern concern with war as technique, as a method (for accomplishing state purposes) that is itself dependent on other methods. We might say that Henry takes up this pragmatic meaning and lets it take precedence in the managing of his war—just as Shakespeare lets it take precedence in his dramatic discourse.[52]

Although Shakespeare is not a historian, the oppositions he raises through the character of Fluellen do capture certain truths. The real Hundred Years' War had indeed marked the transition from Fluellen-like chivalry to warfare based on those new terror methods that were used mainly to win, and whose frightfulness had once made them almost unthinkable. One manual on gunmaking—known as the German Fireworkbook, written about the time of Agincourt and still influential until nearly Shakespeare's own—lamented the damage done to towns and princely estates, bulwarks of the medieval social order, when the new weapons of "shot, projectile and assault" were met with the older, Fluellenesque disciplines instead of with "adroit skill." Quite literally, the manual recommended fighting fire with fire, urging even the "pious" nobleman to hire himself a good gunsmith.[53]

Like Fluellen, the Fireworkbook foreshadows the dominance of war by technology. And thus it, too, voices the theme of social leveling. For sound strategy and the longbow were making it possible for unpolished foot soldiers to win the day over chivalric knights on horseback; and the cannon (as Henry says at Harfleur) was to involve all citizens in war in a way that earlier sieges, relying on what the Fireworkbook called "mischievous skirmishes [outside] the castles," did not.[54]

Shakespeare's play about knights in shining armor remarkably predicts the coming triumph of a new, pragmatic kind of war, war characterized by "the rational and disciplined application of existing technology to battle," as Gwynne Dyer has described it. Such "purposive," as opposed to ritualistic or Fluellenesque, war is taken for granted today, but it is really a particular style that only emerged in the period in question. (Part of what distinguished European conquistadors from the colonial peoples they overran was that the Europeans "fought dirty and (what was worse) fought to kill.")[55] And total or "mass" war, requiring enthusiastic support from the people as a whole while also laying the people at risk, is a further development still, an artifact entirely of the modern era.[56] Modern war does not just uphold the modern state but has grown up historically along with it, supported by some of the same popular attitudes. Dwight Macdonald's description of World War II—"the horror of vast technological power exerted in warmaking by nations with no positive aims and little social consciousness"[57]—needs to be supplemented; for there *is* a positive aim, namely enacting the prerogatives of the sovereign state.

So a number of modern themes here come together. One of those state prerogatives is violence, particularly the right to de-authorize whole other countries and peoples and so attack them wholesale. The new, pragmatic view of war furthers and supports this sovereign right. As with machines or representative assemblies, war is now regarded as an institution in which failures or nonresults are mere nothing, a kind of nonexistence. Nonfunctioning machines are not really machines at all, but scrap metal; the outvoted minority in a legislature is subsumed into its single voice; and by the same logic, the losers in a war are not people who still hold basic human rights, but mere debris (or booty), their physical reality ready to be effaced along with their ruined state. The mechanistic view of that state combines toward the same result as the animistic view.

And thus it becomes possible, for the first time, to conceive of actual devices whose purpose would be the literal, physical annihilation of those unfortunate nonentities. If machines are really ideas, here I think we have found one of the key ideas that nuclear weapons really are. Modern, mechanistic, purposive views of war and the state are essential to the existence of technology as the institution we take it for today: a dynamic, relentless, innovative system that will eventually produce anything it is possible to produce. Actually, it is important to recognize that technology does not produce just anything (which is why we are not forced to live with any particular invention). But it does produce virtually anything demanded by "circumstances." And we have already established what count as circumstances today.

If nuclear weapons follow from a new concept of enemies as nonpersons, perhaps they also embody, or literalize, the mechanistic quality that war itself had taken on from a certain point in history—the quality captured in our modern phrase *war machine*. Perhaps, besides being machines themselves, nuclear weapons are also independent products of the whole modern program that machines represent, along with wars and states: a program that placed new value on getting the job done, no matter how diabolical that job might have seemed to an earlier way of thinking.

VIII.

As coldly utilitarian as the new emphasis on results in war might sound, it would not have won support if it had been seen as entirely lacking humanity or romance. It could not present itself as too sharp a break from

Christian and chivalric views. If it had, it would have proven far too shaky a ground on which to construct a popular, heroic icon like Shakespeare's Henry. Hence, we must assume that Henry, and the whole attitude he stands for, embodies a spirit somehow more continuous with older attitudes, and that when he is shown to acknowledge these it is not just some empty courtesy.

To put it another way, we must assume that the cultural drive toward methodical statecraft and purposive warfare came from somewhere. For we cannot assume it came from the technology. Presumably cannons, like any other destructive means, could have lain ignored or unexploited. Presumably the medieval church's ban on longbows could have been heeded while the Fluellens went on forever skirmishing with lance and shield. To ask why these things didn't happen is to ask, What aspects of the older values were contained in the new?

To answer, we must analyze another term which, like *disciplines*, underwent a crucial shift in meaning in early modern times: the term *virtue*. Ultimately, to understand our modern ethics—the project with which this chapter began—we must understand what happened to virtue, the commodity that often seems so puzzlingly absent from the thinking that gives us the bomb.

Just as *good* and *better* could refer to social standing as well as qualities of character, and *disciplines* to either rituals or methods, so *virtue* has had dual, shifting meanings. In Shakespeare's time it could be used to mean both goodness *and* strength or effectiveness. In our era the latter meanings have largely been lost. There are echoes of them only in a few stock phrases, as when we say "by virtue of" something. And maybe, in some vague way, we also still believe that the outcome of one's labors depends on the quality of one's character. But while we would probably agree with the German Fireworkbook that knowing how to read makes one a better gunsmith, we would reject the same book's argument that modesty, honesty, and piety are equally crucial to such work.[58] If anything, we might believe today that the gunsmith's craft requires none of these qualities, and that his business—or any business—is actually hindered by them.

So here is an example of older values contained in the new. Guns are socially leveling: It doesn't take a nobleman to aim one and shoot. This is why they lend themselves to the new disciplines—fighting to win. But there is still a romantic desire to believe that success in these disciplines owes to one's qualities of soul—that the one kind of virtue depends on the other. And that desire lingers on in the modern era.

Shakespeare's pragmatism simultaneously reflected the socially leveling tendencies of the new methods and certain older, wholly different assumptions. Shakespeare was able to posit that the different classes of society were equally fit to the job of warmaking not only because he saw it as just that—a job—but also because of an archaic psychology that saw in the common life a character-building nurture. Thus Henry calls upon his "good yeomen/ Whose limbs were made in England" to show the "mettle of [their] pasture" (III.i.25–27). The English, supposedly, are better warriors because they are better than the French as a society. Francis Bacon says exactly the same thing in 1621 when he praises England for having discovered that "to make good infantry, it requireth men bred, not in a servile or indigent fashion, but in some free and plentiful manner." Said Bacon, "The middle people of England make good soldiers, which the peasants of France do not."[59]

Bacon is looked back upon today as an architect of the modern techno-scientific establishment.[60] He is famous for his defense of "learning" (science) against the intellectual "idols" that hindered it. But when we examine his arguments closely we see that they were not a call for value neutrality, such as we today associate with science, but rather for a full *realization* of values, which Bacon assumed would yield direct political and military benefits. "Neither hath learning an influence and operation only upon civil merit and moral virtue, and the arts or temperature of peace and peaceable government," said Bacon, "but likewise it hath no less power and efficacy in enablement towards martial and military virtue and prowess."[61] In this statement, science is seen as linked to two related kinds of virtue, moral and military. The assumption that human effort gets things done, and that the quality of the effort therefore depends on the quality of human character, softens what might otherwise be a harder and more thoroughly modern insistence on the sheer power to be gained through science. It is the assumption that leads Bacon, whose motives at bottom were ethical—"the relief of man's estate"—to raise a vision which, in our own time, gives us science that discounts ethics and threatens to destroy man's estate.

In terms of the state, this same assumption also supported what was at first a relatively enlightened belief—namely that personal integrity was a prerequisite of good rulership, since the good and the effective are inseparable. "Virtue he had, deserving to command," as his courtiers say of Shakespeare's Henry (in *Henry VI, Part I*). This enlightened view, rather more alien to the Middle Ages,[62] nonetheless grew logically out of the traditional belief that political unrest, the loss of good rulership, and even disorder in the heavens are all mystically linked, in what today we would call an astrological fashion—for virtue simultaneously governed the person, the society, and the whole cosmic order.

The ability of all these concepts to find a home in the single word *virtue* is less surprising if we remember the long period during which so much in European society was thought about theologically. The ultimate source and example of all goodness was God. *Divine power* meant both the most power possible and the best. Virtue and power were the two qualities that the spirit infused into the body, said the alchemist Paracelsus; they were also the names of two of the several orders of God's angels. Angels were thought to be responsible for the motions of the heavenly bodies, so angelic virtue became the prototype for what we would today call the forces of nature. In

1600 one would not have spoken of the *force* which, say, keeps the planets orbiting the sun; but a word one might have used was *virtue*, as Shakespeare's contemporary, the great cosmologist Johannes Kepler, in fact did.[63]

Moreover, Western thinking, including theological thinking, still showed, until Shakespeare's time, the imprint of classical Greek beliefs in which something's virtue was what we would today call its nature—its fullest realization, that which it was meant to be. This notion of virtue implied that the movements of a thing were its efforts to reach that fully realized state. In this sense, virtue was simultaneously a term of both physical or scientific discourse and of ethical: these two discourses were not clearly separate.

So when the idea of abstract, impersonal "forces" of nature and "functions" of the body finally established itself, over the course of the seventeenth century, it was not a sharp break from the older mystical and astrological view, but a surprisingly gradual evolution of it. In line with this continuity, the new, impersonal, value-free science preserved the basic assumption of unity in the cosmos. But the new cosmic unity was not that of astrology, in which events in the heavens directly influenced human well-being. Instead it was an impersonal unity based on the mechanistic operation of uniform "laws," like the law of gravity. (Such laws are what make it possible for nuclear scientists in our century even to conceive of harnessing on earth the same forces that fuel the sun.) This is how the new view eventually came to drain the cosmos of virtue, and to point in the direction of the bloodless pragmatism we take for granted today—a pragmatism based on the metaphysical assumption that effectiveness does not imply integrity or goodness, but sometimes the very opposite.

Even in doing this, though, the new view, at least initially, also re-emphasized the *issue* of virtue, and the problem of where, if at all, it was to be located. Precisely by causing intellectual confusion, it seemed to support the feeling—what I have called the traditional Augustinian tenet[64]—that everything was in decay, as John Donne put it in his "Anatomy of the World" of 1611. Donne's poem, with its famous lament that "new philosophy calls all in doubt," expresses the anxiety that bloodless material relationships and interests are, in social as much as in scientific affairs, beginning to take precedence over traditional order and hierarchy:

And freely men confess that this world's spent,
When in the planets, and the firmament
They seek so many new; they see that this
Is crumbled out again to his atomies.
'Tis all in pieces, all coherence gone;
All just supply, and all relation:
Prince, subject, father, son, are things forgot. . . .[65]

But we could well say that while Donne predicted the eventual supposed loss of coherence in modern thinking, he inaccurately gauged the science of his own time (or the popular conception of it) by failing to see that it was itself a kind of ethical theory rooted in the coherence of virtue. Indeed, as I argued of the pragmatic outlook in general, it would not have been embraced had it not initially been perceived in this ethical light. Donne's contemporaries, like Shakespeare, would have had little use for our more modern notion of "forces" pure and simple.

IX.

In all, the early modern outlook was an attempt to extract, and to put to serious use, an assumption about the power of virtue in the world which came down to the seventeenth century from the Middle Ages (and hence bore some credibility), but which, until that point, had served to rigidify existing institutions and hierarchies. Freed of these, the assumption was used to underwrite a new kind of pragmatism, and the older institutions and authorities, once its custodians, now became its victims. Moreover, the intellectual attack on these received authorities, conducted simultaneously on the two distinct but not yet isolated fronts that Bacon called natural and human philosophy, followed an agenda that also had been drawn up in the medieval world. This was the view, Augustinian in its analysis of things (though residually Pelagian in its belief about human capability), that both nature and humankind were sinful and in need of "command," understood as an exercise of power owing to virtue. "As mankind, so is the world's whole frame/Quite out of joint," as Donne put it, for "the world did in her cradle take a fall."

The "governing" of both nature and society are, to the new way of thinking, equally needed and closely related. Everywhere we see the same terms used in reference to the two kinds of "method." Bacon, for instance, speaks of science as enhancing a kind of sovereignty of man over the natural world.[66] Shakespeare, too, shifts with ease from the one concept to the other. Tensions among human beings, needing political methods, and tensions between humanity and nature, needing scientific ones, are no more distinct than is the fallenness of man and the fallenness of nature. There is one single phenomenon in the world that ensures both that there is less of everything than people want, and that they will fight over what little there is.[67]

So we see in the early modern period an interpenetration of scientific and political thinking that we are still influenced by but that has been lost to consciousness. There were scientific thinkers like Bacon who were everywhere concerned with politics, and political thinkers like Hobbes who tried to mimic the methods of physicists.[68] The new theory of sovereignty must be seen not just as supporting a new technology, but as a kind of technological theory in itself—hence the machinelike vision of the state it came to promote. And the new theory of science must be seen as a kind of political program, another way (along with good kingship) of granting society a "largess universal." That the two kinds of governing are so close to each other from the start makes it logical that they would come to fuse in the modern notion that the state rules nature itself.

Formally, virtue dropped out of this discourse; technology and the state, both concerned with doing things (and hence originally bound up with ethics) increasingly came to be regarded as self-justifying ends in themselves. But informally, the assumption that power depends on virtue lingered on. It has underwritten both science and the modern state ever since, as predecessor notions of virtue had underwritten the divinely sanctioned authorities of centuries past. Technology is still, in part, an ethical theory; machines are not just ideas, but moral ideas. People look with favor today on a world of more or less relentless technology both because they see technology as the value neutral servant of the valued state, and because, following older traditions, they see technology as not value neutral at all, but value laden.

In fact, people today are at one and the same time heirs of the early modern outlook, of the separate elements comprising it, and of what it eventually came to evolve (or degenerate) into. They are inclined to believe, more or less all at once, that goodness determines whether things work; that goodness, rather, has nothing to do with whether things work; and that in any case, the whole issue is overcome and subsumed in great institutions that are no longer seen, that manifestly work, and that must be intrinsically good.

I have already noted that as the state came increasingly to be defined in utilitarian or mechanistic terms, the tendency to think of it as a person was, ironically, intensified. By the preceding analysis, so too was intensified the tendency to see the state as a repository of virtue. It is not much of a step from the idea that things must have virtue in order to work, to the idea that things that work must have virtue. Nuclear weapons gain legitimacy from this assumption, obviously, yet at the same time they also benefit from the more thoroughly technologistic view that virtue has nothing to do with it, that results justify the effort in and of themselves.

In short, we see once again that nuclear weapons stand at the shared apex of dialectically opposed—that is, both complementary and contradictory—cultural traditions. The ancient idea of military success as dependent on and expressive of virtue may seem at odds with the modern, pragmatic view, in which war, like any other state policy, is simply a means to an end, and its effects automatic, like a machine's. (The idea that the sovereign's "vain command" is "bootless" seems an especially sharp rejection of the chivalric ideal.) But what both views do is lend war the legitimacy of coherence. Under the older view, war is justified as a kind of playing out of the moral hierarchies in the human world; it is the arena in which the virtuous get their just reward.[69] Under the modern view, war is justified because it serves an overriding purpose—namely, promoting the policies of the transcendentally important state. And because that which works must have virtue, success in war will tend to be seen as confirming that this overriding purpose, the state, really deserves its transcendent status. Both views, superficially opposed though they are, combine in reinforcing the sovereign state.

X.

I hope I have made clear that when we talk about sovereignty, we are concerned with much more than an abstract legal doctrine. The point at issue is the vital question of how people in our world think about power, and what power they are willing to grant as ultimate. I also hope I have made clear that *our* world's thinking on this is not *the* world's thinking. Sovereignty, as one theory of ultimate power, arose within history. So while one can understand the common belief that, as David P. Barash and Judith Eve Lipton put it, "there has been only one era of human history so far, the one dominated by Neanderthal urgings and primitive gene-based strivings, overlain in varying degrees by little more than a patina of civilization," this sort of claim clearly lacks a crucial dimension.[70] Those urgings and strivings are far more historically contingent than any analysis based on the assumption of a uniform "human nature" can hope to discover. Our dilemmas are rooted in political society, and the particular type of political society we call the sovereign state is historically a very special case. If we are to get anywhere in resolving our dilemmas, this peculiarly modern form of the state (along with its concomitants, modern war and technology) must be, as I put it earlier, problematized. Problematizing the sovereign state, we should now understand, is the opposite of equating it with history, as Barash's and Lipton's "one era" thinking (and many equivalents) tends to do.

As long as any human institution claims ultimate power and ultimate allegiance, there will be serious moral embarrassments involved in aligning oneself with it. As Jonathan Schell says, there will be a fissure between our political selves and our moral selves.[71] Schell's mistake lies in assuming that nuclear weapons created this fissure rather than resulted from it. But the fissure itself not only exists, it is the essence of sovereignty, or of any other totalizing ideology. What my argument has attempted to do is to develop, with Shakespeare's text as example and guide, the historical linkage of ideas that has led modern Westerners to build a whole society precariously atop the fissure. Schell is on firm historical ground in finding a definitional link between sovereignty and war. But if we then say that war is legal because the sovereign makes it so, when the sovereign is definable as that power which can legalize war, we are arguing in circles. People at large are smart enough to see through such an argument unless the whole construction is held up by some other sort of prop. The question arises, what makes this edifice of ideas seem solid to people, seem morally acceptable?

My answer has been that the metaphysics of virtue is that prop. Grounded on this notion, the idea of sovereignty presents itself as a moral innovation to societies at a certain point in their development. And the new sovereign regime emotionally justifies itself by way of the personal connectedness it establishes between the people and the person who bears their power, or between them and their collective, personified self. Politics since Shakespeare's time has been largely a question of shifts in the image of who bears the power, with the personhood of the state evolving from mere analogy, which it is in Shakespeare's literary images, into a controlling but still visible metaphor, and finally into an accepted reality—the structuring principle of Western popular thinking on politics and war. And through all these shifts, key assumptions underlying the existence of nuclear weapons have remained constant, or have actually been strengthened. It is possible, in fact, to say that one important goal of developments both then and since has been the leveling of social differences and constraints, and that in that sense, nuclear weapons derive in roundabout ways from a grand effort to promote human equality.

We might note in passing that this metaphysics of virtue is slowly being challenged in our own time. For what none of the cultural traditions just discussed allows for is the entirely modern and deeply pessimistic view that war is really, finally, irrational and meaningless. Neither by way of medieval nor early modern assumptions could a Shakespeare, for instance, have endorsed this recent argument by Thomas Powers: "History suggests that war is something else [besides a rational act of aggrandizement]—a characteristic and habitual form of human behavior, a thing men do—sometimes for one reason, sometimes for another." It is, Powers adds, "something which happens to us without reason or purpose," and whose root causes we don't really know.[72]

Powers's outlook is the exception that proves the rule: To the extent that people today accept and even, sometimes, grow enthusiastic at the prospect of war, they clearly are not under the influence of any view like Powers's. Apart from the occasional theorist or critic, people today by and large agree in taking the state for granted; they agree about the state's relation to science, technology, and warfare; and they agree, finally, that technology itself, the essential means of modern war, is morally coherent. Nuclear weapons are borne up on the belief that methods are virtues, and the world a field of error penned around by interlinked technologies—the state a technology for governing men, war a technology to serve the state, and "technology," as such, a search for improvements in waging war. Each term serves the others, not just in the practical and material sense but, at least as importantly, as an expression of the same metaphysics: the belief that the order of things is underwritten by virtue. This new metaphysics may not be grounded on God or custom, but it is just as metaphysical, just as committed to certain rather rigid views of the ultimate nature of things.

And once we understand that metaphysics, we do know the root causes of war, at least modern war. We know, in fact, why it seems irrational and habitual (in Powers's terms), and why certain of its methods—like the nuclear threat—seem from some perspectives positively insane. It seems irrational because we no longer "see" the premises that make it rational, premises like the moral transcendence of the state. Or, we sense the truth that those premises are themselves not rational, but are, rather, a program of commitments whose power to bind culture together derives from precisely this unreasoned quality. (If metaphysical views were thought through they would largely cease to be metaphysical.)

Powers is right: When its premises are holding most firm, war does take on a puzzlingly autonomous quality; it seems almost able to "happen" all by itself, as Henry threatened it would at Harfleur. And the same for its weapons: with the metaphysics behind them hidden, they seem intractably omnipresent, like something we can't imagine being rid of.

But those very feelings are rooted in a certain discursive history. The metaphysics of a culture itself, as I have tried to show, arises and changes within history. The next chapter will explore the further evolution of the modern metaphysics in a specifically American context, and will examine how its assumptions actually make their way into contemporary policy. If the powerful confluence of Pelagian and Augustinian views was one turning point in our cultural history, and the growth of animism and the morally transcendent state another, a third will turn out to be a specifically American conjoining of discourses to whose examination we now turn.

FIVE

<hr>

Nostalgia for Industry:
SDI and American Metaphysics

Yankee doodle guard your coast
Yankee doodle dandy,
Fear not then nor threat nor boast
Yankee doodle dandy.
  —"Yankee Doodle Dandy" (1799 version)

I.

Often in this book I have spoken of the ironies of cultural history. In America, one ironic episode has recently come to an end—though its consequences and its legacy demand that we continue trying to understand it. Ronald Reagan fought his 1980 presidential campaign in part on the issue of whether he was a warmonger. Early on his administration aroused public nuclear anxieties comparable to those of the first fifteen years of the nuclear era. And Reagan did accelerate several programs to build offensive nuclear systems.

Yet ironically, even as the anxieties and the weapon-building peaked, Reagan dreamed that his principal legacy to history would be a solution to the nuclear problem: an internationally shared technological defense against the threat of nuclear attack. So unorthodox was this dream, at least by comparison with the *public* policies of earlier presidents, that it took most of Reagan's eight years in office to get the pundits (and even some of his friends) first to listen to the idea and then to believe he was serious about it. Besides being subtly disparaged as a gimmick, "Reagan's so-called Star Wars scheme" (a name that stuck), the Strategic Defense Initiative was variously regarded as anything but what Reagan said it was. For some it was "temporary political plumbing" and even "bungling," for others a deliberate, systematic effort to attain U.S. strategic superiority. For some it spoke of well-intentioned naivete, for others of "psychopathology" and "ideological delirium." Most simply, SDI was widely dismissed as "myth."[1]

But myths, as we have learned in this sophisticated age, are not to be dismissed. The word has a double reference: "falsehoods" on the one hand, but on the other, "deep, culturally vital systems of shared belief": the essence of a culture's metaphysics. This second meaning is as relevant to

SDI as the first. Yet when Reagan kept refusing to trade Star Wars away, even rejecting "an agreement on literally total nuclear disarmament" at the 1986 Reykjavik summit solely to preserve it, commentators could only describe this as paradoxical and wonder aloud what Reagan "really" meant. David Broder said with a verbal shrug that the question would have to be left to historians.[2] Behind it all, many observers' approach to Reagan seemed to be the one articulated by Martin Gardner: "It is always hard, of course, to know when Reagan is expressing actual beliefs, or just skillfully choosing words to win votes."[3]

That view is quite wrong; with few presidents has it been *easier* to know this. Above all is this true of SDI, which Reagan was clear and emphatic about for a longer time than we have come to believe is possible for a politician. There is plenty of evidence of his sincerity about it and his own active role in incorporating the idea into policy. It is popular on the left to assume that SDI was the simple result of those entrenched military-industrial interests too often invoked to explain the arms race in general (see chapter 1). Physicist Edward Teller's role in formulating the project is frequently noted in this regard. But not only do such analyses overlook the likelihood that Teller and other scientists and policymakers are, like Reagan, also driven by deeper cultural beliefs; the interest analyses also overlook what we know about Star Wars' actual genesis. The fact is that Reagan bypassed his own advisers when he proposed SDI on 23 March 1983, and reportedly he drafted the SDI section of his speech on national defense (the "Star Wars" speech) in his own longhand.[4] At the very least, even if other authorities did sketch the strategic defense concept first, Reagan took it up in a way that made it his own and a force to be reckoned with. He is the true "author" of Star Wars as public policy. To borrow an analogy from the preceding chapter, Reagan was the Shakespeare to Teller's Holinshed.

Most importantly, that speech was simply the culmination of a pattern of thinking that remained consistent both before and thereafter. The puzzle is not that Reagan meant what he said, but that anyone should ever have doubted it. But maybe these facts explain each other. People didn't believe Reagan precisely because sincerity isn't what politics is thought to be about. Even the clearest statement sounds senseless if you're unprepared for it. What we need to do is stop filtering Reagan through those assumptions, and instead do the reverse: belatedly grant him his consistency and allow it to alter our interpretations as needed. For SDI did stand normal politics on its head, and in the process revealed that American politics contains forces we wouldn't otherwise be aware of. Reagan's SDI statements become consistent when seen as part of a web spun from the discourses on virtue, human power, and the state that we have been untangling throughout this book—plus, in this case, another discourse whose key term is *America*. By taking Reagan seriously (if only in retrospect) we uncover this web of discourse, and thus learn much about how these concepts function in specifically American popular thinking, not just on SDI but on the nuclear issue and global relations in general.

We have in SDI a case study in how popular thinking manifests itself in public policy. In fact, the gap Martin Gardner assumes between actual beliefs and winning votes did not really exist in Reagan's case. Reagan was "simply saturated in the American identity" (as *Time* magazine put it) and won votes *by* expressing beliefs.[5] He is the best proof that ordinary people's thinking does shape and support policy, for his own thinking was nothing if not ordinary. Here was a man whose policies were condemned by many churches' leaders (including his own), and who was capable of misattributing Biblical quotes. Yet he ran for the presidency as the candidate of true believers, was embraced by the bloc of voters most vocal in bringing "spiritual" concerns to politics, and with the help of these voters defeated a born-again Sunday School teacher and, later, the son of a prairie preacher.[6] It is time to figure out exactly what faith Reagan *was* speaking for, since it is still there to be contended with; fundamental public beliefs do not follow a leader out of office.

In addition, SDI is worth understanding in and of itself. It has become a major new factor in superpower relations and perhaps "the Pentagon's biggest weapons project ever."[7] The project absorbs the nation's technical elite; "no single project," says John Tirman, "is [as] likely to dominate our discourse and deliberations about defense policy in the rest of this century."[8] This will be all the more true to the extent that the project does resonate with deeper themes in American cultural history. Indeed, it has been so firmly embraced by the political right, so imbued with Reagan's "prestige" and so integrated into a whole worldview, that some Republican presidential candidates in 1988 acted as if it behooved them to be regarded as the truest heir of the Star Wars dream.[9]

II.

To say that SDI resonates with deeper American cultural themes is to say it accords with a certain American metaphysics. Reagan typically spoke of SDI in metaphysical terms. For him it was not just another policy, to be politically positioned and cost-benefit-analyzed like any other. It was, rather, a worldview, a statement of how things just are. This is important, for the news media, Reagan's critics, and even some SDI supporters were misled all along by the superficially *innovative* character of the program. If there's one thing SDI seems undisputably to be, it's technologically forward-looking. As the Star Wars sobriquet suggests, the program is thought of as a "high-tech dream," and also, of course, as "warlike."[10]

But the sleek, shiny chrome and futuristic body can distract us from what's powering things under the hood. If the program *had* been an effort to give the world something new—the "total change in policy" it was inaccurately called[11]—it would have been vulnerable to scientific critique, and pushing it as Reagan did could indeed have been considered politically aggressive. It would also have been, maybe even for Reagan, just another political card to be played in Reykjavik or at some other propitious moment—for the world can presumably do without something it doesn't yet have.

But as his repeated statements made clear (or would have if anyone had paid attention), Reagan found such a view of SDI not just wrong, but inconceivable. SDI could not be bargained away any more than could the physical laws of the universe. That is because it was a mere expression of those laws—an attempt, which in Reagan's view would inevitably succeed, to re-create a natural equilibrium that had temporarily been skewed. Star Wars was a purely passive and restorative (or, as Reagan always put it, defensive) effort to go not forward but *back*: back to the way things used to be and the way they are in nature. The language of Reagan's 1983 Star Wars speech was the language of "turning back." For all its particle beams and imaging radars, Star Wars embodied a hope that was not future oriented at all but radically nostalgic, even Luddite.

This language was never completely assimilated even by Reagan's own lieutenants, who faced the problem of having to make sustainable programs out of what their chief considered not policy but cosmology. Defense Secretary Caspar Weinberger took up the notion that Star Wars couldn't be traded, but he was unable to explain this in Reagan's own internally consistent way. "Moscow would like nothing better than to get us to trade away SDI," Weinberger wrote in 1987. "We must never do that. SDI already is paying off by keeping the Soviets at the bargaining table."[12] Weinberger failed to notice his own self-contradiction. We must refuse to trade something because of its usefulness in trading? Perhaps Weinberger also kept a ten-dollar bill in his wallet that he swore never to spend so it would always be there for buying things.

But this is less bad faith (though it must look that way in Soviet eyes) than an attempt by a seasoned bureaucratic bargainer to speak to an issue that arose outside the realm of politics altogether. SDI embodies a metaphysics that goes back quite a long way. It is not just a backward-looking but also an old dream in American cultural history. And it was an old dream even for Ronald Reagan himself. Largely unnoticed by the press, Reagan was talking about strategic defense long before launching SDI in 1983. Indeed, he was talking about it even before becoming president. His SDI statements were simply extensions of a general philosophy of defense that can be traced through remarks on a variety of issues over a surprising number of years.

For instance, while Reagan's comparison between Star Wars and radar (a purely defensive technology, he claimed) made headlines after Reykjavik, there was nothing remotely new in his making such a comparison.[13] One year earlier, Reagan had compared SDI to an antiaircraft gun, and also to a gas mask—and he had just repeated the latter analogy in his speech to the nation the day after leaving Iceland: "I likened [SDI, at Reykjavik] to our keeping our gas masks even though the nations of the world had outlawed poison gas in the years after World War I."[14] Really he had been making the same general points at least since 1980, if not 1976. Worrying publicly over U.S. vulnerability to bomber attack, Reagan in 1980 explained in an interview what he had learned from experts at NORAD, the North American Air Defense Command:

> At NORAD, you know, we can track the missiles if they were fired, we can track them all the way from firing to know their time of arrival at their targets, and we couldn't do anything to stop the missiles. NORAD is an amazing place—that's out in Colorado, you know, under the mountain there. They actually are tracking several thousand objects in space, meaning satellites of ours and everyone else's, even down to the point that they are tracking a glove lost by an astronaut that is still circling the earth up there. I think the thing that struck me was the irony that here, with this great technology of ours, we can do all of this yet we cannot stop any of the weapons that are coming at us. I don't think there's been a time in history when there wasn't a defense against some kind of thrust, even back in the old-fashioned days when we had coast artillery that would stop invading ships if they came.[15]

This anticipates what Reagan would say in announcing SDI three years later, when he would speak again of "coastal forts and artillery batteries." In fact, speaking off the cuff, Reagan in this 1980 interview found almost the very words he would later use in his Star Wars speech, right down to that key word *turn*:

> I do think that it is time to turn the expertise that we have in that field—I'm not one—but to turn it loose on what do we need in the line of defense against their weaponry, and defend our population, because we can't be sitting here. . . . one of the first things I would do would be to turn to those who are knowledgeable in military affairs, knowledgeable in the weaponry that would be coming at us, and so forth, to find out what we could do.[16]

Strategic defense was the correlate all along to Reagan's then much more famous "window of vulnerability." In fact the window of vulnerability, in Reagan's mind, was not just the particular and recent problem others meant by that term (and assumed he meant, too), but the whole nuclear-age axiom of total reliance on offensive deterrence. It was a window that had arguably opened wider under Jimmy Carter but really had been put in place to begin with some twenty years earlier.

In fact, strategic defense was in a sense the grand theme of Reagan's whole career in national politics, making sense of any number of otherwise disparate concerns and statements. It tied in, for instance, to his foreign-policy focus on Central America (the Panama Canal in his 1976 campaign, Nicaragua during most of his presidency). For Reagan, securing Central

America was of a piece with building SDI. This was clear in his post-Grenada speech to the nation, which in language much like the above speaks of a lost era of coastal defense (even though critics would say the only serious issue of coastal defense raised by that action was the fact that Grenada didn't have any).[17] And his early statements as president about "limited" and winnable nuclear wars also had links to SDI.[18] In fact we could say that SDI even makes sense of some of Reagan's gaffes, including the costly and dramatic one in which the new president seemed to endorse the idea of a limited nuclear war in Europe. What Reagan was really doing in that case was pressing the case for strategic defense. Asked in 1981 if he thought a nuclear war could remain limited or would inevitably escalate, Reagan said,

> I don't honestly know. I think, again, until someplace—all over the world there is being research going on to try to find the defensive weapons. There never has been a weapon that someone hasn't come up with a defense. But it could—and the only defense is, you shoot yours and we'll shoot ours. And if you still have that kind of stalemate, I could see where you could have the exchange of tactical weapons in the field without it bringing either one of the major powers to pushing the button.[19]

Just as they had seized on a narrower "window of vulnerability" and overlooked strategic defense, so journalists (and tens of thousands of protesters) seized here on limited nuclear war, the subordinate idea, and overlooked defense, which was actually the main idea. Had they not done so, it would have been harder for nearly everyone to agree that Reagan's "surpise unveiling" of SDI had "astonished the world" nearly two years later.[20]

III.

Whatever gave Reagan such unshakeable faith in an idea long left aside by experts? It would seem to be that characteristic appeal to history: "There has never been a weapon in the history of man which has not led to a defensive, a counter-weapon," as he said again in debate with Walter Mondale in 1984.[21] Reagan's repeated allusions to the weaponry of the world wars were all attempts at proving this point about "history." Coastal and antiaircraft batteries, gas masks, radar, Gatling guns—war technologies of the industrial but prenuclear era—these were the weapons relied on during the impressionable years of people Reagan's age. They were the weapons glorified by the movies made in Reagan's Hollywood, at a time when coastal defense literally included the beach at Pacific Palisades.

By *history*, Reagan really meant something like "nature." What belonged to history was in the nature of things, and so could not help but be realized. Far from posing "technical uncertainties" that at best would have been "difficult to assess," SDI was not just possible, but inevitable, unless we somehow failed to do right by history.[22] Reagan always refused to answer either the strategic objection to SDI—that it would be too easily overwhelmed by offensive forces—or the political objection—that it would be destabilizing—with corresponding technical or political arguments. While others were happy to point out on SDI's behalf that, for example, "one-ounce particles of space shrapnel would have to be traveling at nine miles per second (not nine miles per hour) in order to pierce satellite surface shielding," Reagan never rebuffed critics with this sort of talk—talk of countermeasures or software or tests of electromagnetic rail guns.[23] All such niggling details were subsumed by a theory of technology's inherent nature itself.

But as is true for the modern state (see chapter 4), the seeming naturalness and inherency of something is also a subtle *justification* of it. Truth to nature (Reagan's "history") is the essence of right behavior. When Reagan spoke of earlier wars and weapons, the nostalgia one heard was no coincidence. In Japan during his first term, Reagan said, "Once upon a time we had rules of warfare . . . in which we made sure that soldiers fought soldiers, but they did not victimize civilians. Today, we've lost something of civilization. . . . Let us, at least, get back to where we once were."[24] Reagan was apt to thus recur to the two world wars when arguing all sorts of points. He loved those wars' terminology and strategic concepts: "frontiers," "choke points," "corridors," "beachheads."[25] "We can't help but look back and think: Life was so vivid then," Reagan once told the European Parliament.[26] Soldiers fighting soldiers, civilians all snug in the rear behind their radar shield, a day when you suddenly heard that it was over, over there: that's how wars were meant to be. So when done that way they were actually moral (or "civilized"), just as any other tale beginning "Once upon a time" has its "moral." (There is evidence that the Star Wars speech came when it did because of Reagan's desire not to be morally preempted by the U.S. Catholic bishops' pastoral letter on war and peace.[27]) Hence, too, those were the kinds of wars—and weapons—to be relied on when trying to generalize about history.

Of course, in reality there is no reason for generalizing about history from the early 1900s but not the late. In fact, Reagan's theory arguably contradicted itself, for if it were true that the characteristic fact of history is innovation (rather than vulnerability), then any Star Wars system would inevitably be overwhelmed by some new offense, and yet more defenses would have to be developed in turn, presumably forever.[28] Nonetheless, Reagan insisted on seeing our current, threatened situation as atypical, an example of historical *dis*continuity. Nuclear weapons were an aberration, not the norm. Believing this, Reagan was no doubt sincere when he claimed to be appalled by them, even while his own administration was deploying them in huge numbers. For it follows that if the old ways were moral, then the new ways are immoral, specifically to the extent that they make self-defense impossible. When discussing nuclear issues Reagan seldom failed to mention his abhorrence of MAD (Mutual Assured Destruction), the doctrine whereby each side lays its own citizens defenseless while holding the other side's hostage. MAD was the bogey Reagan invoked in that 1980 "coastal defense" interview and in many statements as president.[29] It was, as I mentioned, the true window of vulnerability, the problem for which strategic defense was the solution. Reagan called MAD "our real defense" and even "the only program we have," and almost pleadingly asked if there weren't a better way—and what possible harm there could be in developing some kind of alternative.

It is to the everlasting discredit of journalists worldwide that while they were busy "gaffing" Reagan's limited nuclear wars (and many more trivial errors), they never brought to public attention this tremendous and obstinate gaffe regarding MAD. Reagan's views notwithstanding, MAD was not America's policy—let alone its "only" policy—at any time during his presidency. His own Strategic Air Commander said as much to Congress in 1982.[30] For decades, and increasingly so since the 1970s, official U.S. nuclear policy has been to prepare for nuclear war-fighting in some form. The correct name for the policy is not MAD, but deterrence by denial, counterforce, damage limitation, flexible response, force-matching, proportionate retaliation, or some combination of these terms. Reagan spoke as if he had never heard any of them. He was no doubt honestly stumped, therefore, when critics more familiar with them pointed out that SDI would simply further rather than supersede the nation's existing defense posture.

But here is where the method of listening closely and finding coherence in Reagan's statements becomes particularly important. Recognizing the mistake, we could simply dismiss it: Reagan was misinformed, detached, maybe even stupid. But that would be an even bigger mistake. Reagan's misstatements were a lode that such dismissiveness leaves unmined. His very persistence in them reveals their resonance with something deepseated, psychologically satisfying, and, presumably, widely shared, and we must try to grasp what that is. Reagan was wrong to present his anti-MADness as some sort of strategic iconoclasm, for it had already won the day before he came to office. But he was right to rhetorically position himself against MAD. For in doing so Reagan was reflecting a truth about the debates that have given rise to U.S. policy: they have partly been a prolonged argument over the claim that this nation must accept being vulnerable to nuclear attack.[31] Despite his ignorance of the details, Reagan was taking themes from the strategists' sometimes arcane debates and making them publicly resonant by connecting them with long-standing themes and anxieties of the culture. SDI partly spanned the gulf between elite policy analysts and the millions of people who felt enough kinship with Reagan to sustain his tenure in office.

IV.

Reagan's view of things was an outgrowth, but also an interesting variant, of a peculiarly American romanticism that has a long cultural history. To European settlers America was once unspoiled nature, and thus potentially an unassailable garden. But in the industrial era, the continent fell under the shadow of advancing technology, superficially a threat to its pastoral perfection—until, by a clever synthesis, the images of garden and technology were reconciled and made to complement each other. This synthesis constitutes the popular American view of America today. But it, in turn, has been threatened in our own age by nuclear weapons—a new shadow. Reagan's outlook, and its concrete embodiment in SDI, is an attempt at a new synthesis that would achieve the same purpose as the old synthesis of technology and garden. It is an attempt to recover the *virtue* that once was felt to inhere in technology, and, under the old synthesis, in America too.

Literary historian Leo Marx calls the enduring American attitude pastoralism, and in his classic *Machine in the Garden* he traces its complex evolution throughout the course of American history.[32] The machine here is industrial technology, and the garden the American landscape that for generations has been suffused with nostalgia (a feeling it did not take Reagan to remind us of, though he often did so). Now, pastoralism of what Marx calls the popular and sentimental type provided the Rockwellian tint so often noted in Reagan's musings. The early part of Reagan's *Where's the Rest of Me?* is a description of "Huck Finn-Tom Sawyer idylls" more bucolic than anything in Twain: roaming, sledding, "woods and mysteries," swimming holes, crystal radio sets, a "climb into the sleigh with hot bricks at our feet," and a "drive off with the bells jingling." (Included in the idyll, if uneasily, are parades marking the end of World War I.)[33]

As one in a long line of New World propagandists, Reagan encouraged belief in American uniqueness: there is something in the land that makes the people good, and something in what the good people can then do that promises to blaze a trail of redemption for all of humankind. The "innate openness and good character of our people," whose hard work built the world's greatest democracy, bodes well for the whole world, for "history has shown that democratic nations do not start wars. . . . It's in the nature of Americans to hate war and its destructiveness . . . . Americans always yearn for peace. They have a passion for life. They carry in their hearts a deep capacity for reconciliation."[34] Reagan spoke these lines (during a UN speech) to the people of the world, to whom they are directed both as justification and as promise. Similar promises have been made for generations. "The idea that the United States was a pure, high-minded nation and a model of virtue among sinners went back to the early nineteenth century, and even further—to the Protestant notion of an elected people," says Frances Fitzgerald, who traces the long pedigree such ideas have in American schoolbooks. In U.S. history texts over the years, the United States "always acted in a disinterested fashion, always from the highest of motives; it gave, never took."35

Since school texts aim to be noncontroversial, they are always a good index of the lowest common denominator of national thinking, the basic beliefs that few people are likely to question. "In countless ways Americans know in their gut—the only place myths can live—that we have been Chosen to lead the world in public morality and instruct it in political virtue," says Loren Baritz. "Domestic goodness" equals "strength" that can project itself into the world.36 When the United States began to fully realize its power, the word *imperialism*, briefly used to describe the country's policies, was conveniently banished from public discussion.37 In its place, adventures like Reagan's own invasion of Grenada are today described in terms not of power but of virtue: Grenada, said one typical observer, was "the measured use of force in the pursuit and defense of values for which history has made us trustee."38

No doubt almost anyone who has ever used force has imagined it to be an exercise in virtue, whether expressed as defending territory, upholding international law, or carrying out the will of God or Allah. It just happens that the United States is powerful enough to avoid having this view contradicted by obvious limitations on how far its power can project. (The Soviets are almost as powerful, but they labor under the belief that their state represents an avant-garde whose values have not yet been realized by the march of history.39)

And in one respect, the "garden" view of American uniqueness seemed absolutely confirmed by objective fact, until quite recently. To an extent almost unique in the history of civilization, America possessed a virtual immunity from outside attack. It could contemplate a role of pure virtue in the world because it had been blessedly released from the normal, grubby give-and-take of political conquest. If Reagan insisted on seeing the nuclear threat as an aberration, that is consistent with the fact that external threats *are* historically a new thing for the United States.

Generations grow up used to such threats today, but until recently the starting point of American political thinking was the very different assumption expressed, for example, in 1837 by a twenty-eight-year-old student of law who, as a member of the Illinois state legislature, had been asked to speak before a local club on America's political future. Since we Americans "find ourselves in the peaceful possession of the fairest portion of the earth," asked this aspiring young politician,

> shall we expect some transatlantic military giant to step the ocean and crush us at a blow? Never! All the armies of Europe, Asia, and Africa combined, with all the treasure of the earth (our own excepted) in their military chest, with a Bonaparte for a commander, could not by force take a drink from the Ohio or make a track on the Blue Ridge in a trial of a thousand years.40

State Representative Abraham Lincoln was here simply stating what were widely considered givens. His point was that the true danger to Americans was *internal* disorder.[41] (Unwittingly he was gesturing toward the dark vortex of his own political destiny.) But whatever this threat of internal strife, the United States was first and foremost "unprofaned by the foot of an invader" and thus could serve as "the fondest hope of the lovers of freedom throughout the world"—the same hope so often invoked by Reagan.

Lincoln could not foresee a Bonaparte with ballistic missiles. But no sooner had he said the above than something else entered the scene and began making tracks (or laying them) on the Blue Ridge: the railroad, prime symbol of technological incursion into the pastoral idyll. The technology represented by the railroad was a centrifugal force breaking down rural styles of life and merging them with the city. It was a force for urbanizing the whole landscape and was perceived as such immediately, even while the country remained far less urban than we are used to today.[42]

Reactions to this development take us beyond the simple sentimentalism of the garden image, though in the sense of complicating rather than negating it. The new, industrial conditions were deplored by some, but in general, technology was assimilated in nineteenth-century America through a slight adjustment in cultural symbolism. Americans already had a tradition of identifying themselves by their industriousness—as against, for instance, the allegedly lackadaisical native tribes.[43] So it was possible to redeem the threatening new technology, to rescue industry for the beautiful, human, and moral, by treating it as a kind of art form. John F. Kasson says that nineteenth-century Americans developed an "aesthetic of the technological sublime" that "glorified machines not simply as functional objects but as signs and symbols of the future":

> To many historians [Americans'] refusal to recognize a moral and aesthetic conflict between this passionate embrace of the machine and their professed love of nature appears maddeningly perverse . . . but the great bulk of Americans believed that the progress of American civilization contained its own controls. To be both Nature's nation and a rapidly developing industrial power was to them not a contradiction, but the fulfillment of America's destiny.

Americans started by identifying national unity, hence successful republicanism, with technology (for it did "join" the dispersed towns of America); then they began to measure national success by prosperity; and from the time of the railroads they "increasingly identified the progress of the nation with the progress of technology."[44]

Until recently this synthesis kept technology safe for virtue (with which it had long been equated—see chapter 4). It held up technology as not simply a neutral force, which *people* use for both good and evil. Rather, technology and progress were so closely linked that the phrase *technological progress* could be considered redundant. Technical advances made the world a better place, and by leading the way in them, *America* made the world a better place. Competence was goodness, or, as Lincoln also said, America could prove that "right makes might." A few years ago, a Midwestern professor who showed an Australian documentary on Vietnam in his history class discovered that students "were generally willing to place the blame for the war on the misconceptions and errant views of civilian and military policy-makers," but they couldn't "stomach" the film's "implication of U.S. military ineptitude. . . . Several students simply refused to believe this description of the U.S. military."45 This seems typical of many Americans' belief in their own technical prowess. It is as if, for Americans, policy becomes the merely technical issue, and *technique* the moral issue on which no compromise is permitted.

The strength of this feeling allows minor failures often to just go unnoticed, even if they are taken note of by others. A British correspondent, reporting on the 1986 bombing of Tripoli, pointed out that

> whereas in Britain, the inaccuracy of the bombing is the subject of ribald mirth, comforting and complacent proof that the Yanks can never get it right, here [in the U.S.] the attack is seen as a flawless military operation, comforting and complacent proof that America almost always does get it right.46

Of course, some failures can't be ignored or easily reinterpreted. For these there are other reactions, which in their own ways affirm the basic equation of right and might. When the space shuttle Challenger exploded, there was a flourishing of theories that put the disaster down to sabotage. "You could see why people wanted to believe that," said columnist Roger Simon. "How could America build a bad machine?" What worried people was badness in both senses: the fact that the machine failed, and the fact that it caused suffering and death. Incompetence *and* a kind of evil: to most Americans, these concepts are related. Even nonsabotage theorists saw in the event something more than mere machine failure—something transcendentally meaningful, "almost a biblical quality."47 For a major American machine to fail is for basic questions of good, evil, and cosmic order to arise in a more than ordinarily troubling way.

In the case of the shuttle Reagan compromised. His public reactions combined elements of this "biblical" view with the less extreme course of wrapping the event in the blood-soaked flag of hardship from which virtuous American uniqueness has supposedly emerged. But the synthesis of technology and virtue was never less important in his thinking than in anyone else's. Industrial prenuclear technology remained, essentially, the unspoiled reality—the garden. Reagan called the period from 1790 to 1875 the era "when we were becoming the great economic power that we are in the world today."48 Industrial growth, that is, was no encroachment on the country's simple, natural endowment, but the fullest realization of it.49

"Here in this land," said his first inaugural address, "we unleashed the energy and individual genius of man to a greater extent than has ever been done before." Industrial productivity in America expresses the inner "genius"—virtue—of individuals nurtured in this great garden. Success is a kind of American heroism: "You can see heroes every day going in and out of factory gates. Others, a handful in number, produce enough food to feed all of us and then the world beyond. You meet heroes across a counter."[50] It is interesting that in this address Americans are categorized by occupational groups, that is, by their contributions to national productivity. If Martin Luther King, Jr.'s famous dream was of *reconciliation* among "God's children" regardless of what they are—"black men and white men, Jews and Gentiles, Protestants and Catholics"—Reagan's was of *recognition* for "this breed called Americans . . . professionals, industrialists, shopkeepers, clerks, cabbies, and truckdrivers"—regardless, in other words, of what they do.

SDI was part of the same Reagan dream. The Star Wars speech was a call to heroism on the part of a certain profession—science—to prove that "the human spirit must be capable of rising above" that one work of American genius that calls the whole complex of beliefs into question. For that is the heart of the problem Reagan perceived: the "very strengths in technology that spawned our great industrial base and that have given us the quality of life we enjoy today" had produced a nonminor failure. It had eventuated in something as seemingly dangerous to the world as America's industrial power was seemingly helpful to it. And, Reagan appeared to think, those technological strengths were not being "turned to" for a solution—until he himself spoke up.

V.

Put another way, the old synthesis seemed close to breaking apart. Nuclear weapons threw the equation America = virtue = technology = power at least temporarily into question. They, too, raised the question, How could America build a bad machine? Nuclear weapons suggested that technical progress could be moral *regress*. The old wars and weapons hadn't "assured mutual destruction," they had assured eventual V-days with church bells and ticker tape. They had left American civilians at home (in their garden) while the fighting went on in Europe or on the seas. But just as the railroad had dumped the city everywhere, obscuring the difference between urban and rural, so strategic bombing, enhanced by nuclear weapons, dumped war (or threats of it) all over the impregnable U.S. heartland, obscuring the "old-fashioned" distinction between front and rear. The "paranoiac" fears of the external world that had long been another American cultural theme were enlarged and made concrete, and arguably by America's own technical magnificence. To one brought up on the old synthesis, this was the most cognitively dissonant problem of all. For here was technology going haywire: Yankee know-how learning to track astronauts' gloves but unable to stop hundreds of millions of people from dying. Worse, *Russian* know-how seemed now to have a chance at beating us to that secret.

America as "trustee" of the "values of history" had once seemed final proof of the whole modern theory of the state and its technology as projections of virtue. Nuclear weapons threatened to knock that line of dominoes over. If America's war technology was suspect, then perhaps the world's most successful state wasn't simply and sublimely virtuous. And in that case perhaps the modern state as an institution wasn't virtuous either.

Reagan led the crusade for SDI because on the one hand he was so deeply imbued with the old cultural assumptions as to be genuinely revolted by all this.[51] Yet on the other hand he was not deeply imbued enough. An even truer believer might have simply not allowed the bomb to call his ingrained beliefs into serious question. Alan Brinkley has described the postwar situation as follows:

> The existence of the bomb was troubling, but far less troubling, apparently, than the idea that science and technology and knowledge might be dangerous and destructive things. And so, for most Americans, the real challenge of the nuclear age was not to repudiate the new atomic discoveries, but to find a rationale for them that would fit comfortably within the larger framework of the belief in progress.

Most Americans were remarkably quick to meet this challenge.[52] Essentially what they discovered was the Pelagian-Augustinian synthesis I described in chapter 3, or at least an application of that synthesis to the nuclear issue: the bomb could, after all, be viewed as affirming both human power and the transcendent. But it stands to reason that some people lagged behind, perhaps precisely to the extent they were genuinely, *personally* committed to the old, threatened vision of the world, and so unable to rescue it by mere reflex.

We have already seen the depth of Ronald Reagan's commitment to the terms and concepts of past wars, and it is easy therefore to imagine him as one of those people. Reagan appears to have shared in the shock that Thomas Powers reports atomic scientist I. I. Rabi feeling in the late forties:

> "During the war I heard a lot of people say, 'Our next war will be with Russia,'" Rabi told me. "I'd always say, 'Who'll rent us a battlefield?'" Gradually he realized that aircraft meant the whole planet might serve as a battlefield.[53]

To one as fond of the very idea of precisely confined battlefields as Reagan, these twentieth-century revolutions in strategic thinking would have been a major upset—like a Ptolemaic astronomer's being asked to throw out his epicycles.

And apparently they did upset Reagan. He indicated as much in several ways. There was his spontaneous raising of the issue of vulnerability, narrowly read as a slam at President Carter but, as I have shown, really a questioning of the long-settled axiom of defense through offensive deterrence. There was his uncalculated and even naive-sounding tone in describing our situation: "Someone pushes a button, and, within thirty minutes, there is devastation and horror in our country, or, if we've done it to them, in their country."54 And there was his general belief that things really were objectively different in the world from what they had been in those Tom Sawyer days. Life wasn't as vivid as it had been; history had taken a turn, and therefore needed "turning back."55

Star Wars looked backward in two senses. First, it reflected nostalgia for an earlier, seemingly less problematic industrial order—the one thrown into question by nuclear technology. E. P. Thompson has argued that SDI was an effort by Americans to crawl back into the comforting "womb" of American world dominance of the post–World War II years.56 But in fact, to a Reaganesque romantic, those years aren't a womb at all. They are the source of all our troubles. Of course, to a still earlier or "purer" type of romanticist, nostalgia for industry would seem absurd: industry was the *problem*, and nostalgia was reserved at most for the cultivated but still clean landscape. But such are the ironies of cultural history. Ideas and movements take the forms of their predecessors but with the contents exactly reversed. In this case, within the same basic orientation, the sign attached to early industry had changed from minus to plus.

Nor is this as surprising as it sounds. Pastoralism and the cult of industry had always had something in common. Both were anti-intellectual movements, in Richard Hofstadter's sense—reactions against Enlightenment-era, republican rationalism.57 And on reflection we can see why a romantic philosophy that once fostered a cult of medieval heroism and chivalry would today foster a cult of early modern warfare. Both chivalric and early modern wars offer a vision of warfare that makes sense—and hence of a world that makes sense.

But Star Wars also represented a more radical backward look. It was not just an attempt to recover a lost past—that too—but also an attempt to recover history itself. History for Reagan was a metaphysical term, and with SDI he was insisting on a metaphysical solution to the nuclear threat: a restoration of the natural pattern of history. This insistence had important practical consequences. Because the problem was, as Reagan so often said, moral—having to do with violations of the nature of things—the solution to it had to be qualitative, not quantitive. "Mere" numbers were relatively meaningless, as Reagan often pointed out: "This [SDI] is too important to the world to have us be willing to trade that off for a different number of nuclear missiles."58 Numerically subtracting weapons even to zero (as Reagan apparently had a chance to do in Iceland) could not by itself restore the credibility of a worldview.

Similarly meaningless to Reagan were niggling details and trivial issues, such as what U.S. policy happens to be. At worst, even discussing such issues can force one into the dreaded ways of thinking of the present age. Entering the mainstream technical or strategic SDI debates meant, in many ways, accepting the basic axiom Reagan rejects.[59] So it was no more possible for Reagan to enter them, even in defense of SDI, than it would be possible for our epicyclical Ptolemist to ask NASA for the best route to the moon. Reagan's refusal to get things straight in those mainstream terms was far more than some simple mistake. The issue for him was not "selling" SDI, as though he were dealing with something less than cosmic. The issue was the threat to that worldview. SDI was offered as a way of retrieving science for human purposes and of turning us back to its "very strengths," which are also "our" most characteristically American strengths. If even nuclear weapons could be fit into the classic pattern of history (for every offense there is a defense), then their defeat would be possible through further innovation itself. Technology would turn out after all to provide, as Reagan put it, "ever greater safety, not ever greater fear."[60] So both technology and, hence, America would remain fundamentally benign.

SDI sought to save technology's virtue from, as it were, violation by the nuclear monster. It was often criticized as a technological "fix," meaning a belief that technology can fix things; but in fact it was meant to *fix technology* itself. As Reagan told high school students in Fallston, Maryland, in a post-Geneva summit speech that linked together and summarized many of his favorite themes:

> I told [Gorbachev] that SDI was a reason to hope, not to fear; that the advance of technology, which originally gave us ballistic missiles, may soon be able to make them obsolete. I told him that with SDI, history had taken a positive turn. I told him that men of good will should be rejoicing that our deliverance from the awful threat of nuclear weapons may be on the horizon, and I suggested to him that I saw the hand of Providence in that. What could be more moral than a system based on protecting human life rather than destroying it? I could no more negotiate SDI than I could barter with your future.[61]

VI.

I have spoken of nuclear weapons as the disruption that Star Wars responded to, but this now needs to be qualified. To say SDI meant to set right the nature of things is to say that it was addressed not to particular, real-life devices, but to what was perceived as a new force in the world—a force we don't really have a name for. Reagan's anxiety was directed against a *quality* of a certain technology, a world-threatening, history-disrupting quality that transcended the specific capabilities of particular bombs or missiles. Reagan tended to get the actual devices confused; it was their "nuclearistic" quality that worried him, posing as it did the threat to technology's virtue.

The confusion of devices, like the confusion about MAD, was another unnoticed gaffe—though one that ended up causing a good deal more trouble than MAD. It had not yet become a problem when Reagan spoke at Fallston High School, and if we look again at the quotation above, we see that Reagan slides easily from the word *missiles* to the word *weapons* two sentences later in naming what SDI would combat. This was a liberty he had for a long time. *Weapons* it would be one week, *missiles* the next, in prepared speeches as in impromptu remarks. Once he even switched within a single sentence: "What would be safer than if the two great superpowers—the two that have the great arsenals—both of us sat there with defensive weapons that insured our safety against the nuclear weapons and both of us eliminated our nuclear missiles?"[62]

Even the Star Wars speech caught this confusion. It spoke of "rendering these nuclear weapons impotent and obsolete," but when the White House published the policy (still over Reagan's own signature) the line was changed, without explanation, to "rendering ballistic missiles impotent and obsolete."[63]

Missiles are not, as such, weapons, nor do the two necessarily go together. (Apollo 11 was a missile.) But thanks again to the press corps's complete failure to point it out, Reagan was allowed to carry this confusion all the way to Reykjavik, where it suddenly exploded into an international crisis. By all reports, notably Gorbachev's and Reagan's own, Reagan and the Soviet leader worked on a scenario for total bilateral nuclear disarmament—elimination of all *weapons*. So Reagan told members of Congress at a later briefing. In the ensuing uproar administration officials were forced to clarify and reclarify, suggesting first that Reagan hadn't meant "weapons" and, later, that he *had* talked at Reykjavik of abolishing weapons but that this had been merely "discussed," whereas what had been "proposed" was the far more limited possibility of abolishing ballistic missiles. The *Chicago Tribune* put the whole confusion down to "the careless use of key words by officials," politely obscuring the fact that "proposed/discussed" was really a *careful* distinction designed to cover for the only official whose grasp of things was in question—the president of the United States.[64]

If there is any further doubt about what Reagan meant, it is settled by still another unremarked-upon muddle, the "madman" theory Reagan so often invoked. To defend the seeming inconsistency of proceeding with SDI even while seeking arms reductions, Reagan for years invoked the spectre of a madman, a hypothetical Idi Amin or (as he was more likely thinking) Colonel Qaddafi of the future who might build a bomb and use it to threaten the disarmed nations. The madman is why you have to keep your "gas masks." "I explained [to Gorbachev] that even though we would have done away with our offensive ballistic missiles, having the defense would protect against cheating or the possibility of a madman sometime deciding to create nuclear missiles. After all, the world now knows how to make them," said Reagan in his post-Iceland televised speech, echoing many other nearly identical remarks before and afterwards.

Though on other occasions Reagan had imagined a madman with "weapons," here he strangely postulated one with missiles.[65] After Reykjavik, Reagan's speeches were checked more carefully for semantics. (They were brought, that is, into closer conformity with his administration's formal policy.) But this shift in terminology just obscured Reagan's real thinking more. In fact, it proved that he had meant what he had been saying all along. For given their size and cost, ballistic missiles, which are one means of *delivering* nuclear weapons, are hardly likely to be available—especially in "secret"—to some lone international outlaw, who would much more likely just use a truck or a ticking suitcase. Reagan therefore could not have meant "missiles" in speaking of madmen, even if he did succumb to pressure to use that word. To have thought SDI capable of stopping a madman, Reagan must have believed that SDI envisioned a defense against *weapons*. (An idea absolutely no one else endorsed: for how could particle beams stop a suitcase?)

Perhaps noticing this, the White House added yet another notion late in the game—that the residual threat wasn't just madmen but nuclear accidents, "a Chernobyl of the sky," which it is at least somewhat more sensible to see SDI helping to avert.[66] But by then the madman theory had exposed the truth: that contrary to his staff's absurd "clarifications," Reagan's thinking really had fused missiles completely with weapons. (So, it is perfectly reasonable to conclude, eliminating weapons was what he was aiming for at Reykjavik.) Now, it is frightening to imagine the president discussing nuclear issues at a summit without a basic grasp of the facts. But knowing that Reagan did just that, it is also tempting to see the Reykjavik episode as evidence for Bernard Brodie's hypothesis that national policies are as likely to be shaped by stupidity as by anything else. Tempting, but unhelpful, for *stupidity* (like *carelessness* and *mistake*) lacks positive content and so is not a useful term of analysis.

Instead let us find a reason for this particular "stupidity." Within his system of metaphysics, Reagan's confusion made a kind of sense. Seeing the evil of the nuclear age as the new vulnerability of the American homeland, and seeing ballistic missiles as the most obvious bearers of that danger in practice, it is natural to confuse the missiles with the actual nuclear devices themselves, the bombs that ushered in the age and gave it its name. (It is arguably just as much the "ballistic missile age" as the nuclear age, but no one ever speaks of it that way.) This easy confusion accords well with what one *wishes* an SDI could do. Since Reagan's aim was to restore the lost order of nature, he had to imagine his program being effective against a *concept*: that new, unnamed but evil force in the world, nuclearism as such, a quality embodied in *all* nuclear-related devices. SDI could not be this if it were aimed against one or two kinds of device, for then it would be just one finite machine pitted against a bunch of other machines. Reagan fumbled in those situations that called for him to acknowledge the harsh truth everyone else already knew—that no SDI imaginable can ensure "we would all be safe" once again, period.[67]

VII.

But the need to make ultimate claims for Star Wars grew out of the ultimacy of the purpose for which it was conceived. I have called this purpose moral and metaphysical. As such, its roots were religious—bound up with the essentially religious quests that drove a great deal of New World settlement in the first place, and that have only gradually and imperfectly been secularized. Given prevailing cultural beliefs, Reagan clearly played some sort of quasi-religious, priestly role in this national drama (or, perhaps, liturgy). He was asked by millions to play it not because he knew Scripture better—his opponents did—but because he better grasped the particular needs of the secular ministry demanded by this age. (Though, of course, he also had been raised pietistically, by a mother who was a devoted Disciple of Christ.[68]) Reagan was deemed most adept at the ritualistic aspects of the president's national secular televangelism, perhaps because that side drew on his acting talents. He had less success with the ethical side, which drew on the skills of his other prepolitical work—as spokesman for the wonders of industrial technology (he had done PR work for General Electric). Building SDI was Reagan's idea of an ethic, something he tried to get his congregants to believe they had an obligation to do. Like the ethics proffered by a parish priest, it was not as firmly embraced as the mysteries and metaphysics from which it grew. (By some it was rejected outright, as was the metaphysics.) But Reagan's zeal for it, like the fervency of a skillful priest's sermon, helped reinforce faith in the mysteries even among some who overlooked what he actually was saying. The mysteries clearly had power for him, and in turn, his responsiveness to that power reinforced people's feeling that he was committed and credible: a serious conservator (*not* innovator, despite high-tech appearances) of things which, as best many people could tell, they valued too.[69]

Looming large among mysteries is the mystery of evil. It obliges any faith in the Judeo-Christian genus to construct some sort of credible demonology. Reagan's sense of the radical evil of nuclear weapons—their disruption of the order of the cosmos itself—is part of the demonology he offered to Americans, the part usually overlooked in favor of his early demonizing of the Russians. But the Russians do figure in, and if we put the two together, we get an explanation for the strange paradox that a Reagan who supposedly so hated and feared nuclear weapons spent several years adding mightily to the U.S. stockpile of them.

It is another of those cultural-historical ironies. If you think of a particular device as evil, you will naturally expect it to serve the devil better than it serves you. Reagan followed a long tradition in so conceiving of a frightful new weapon; as long ago as Henry V's time the devil had been seen as comfortably ensconced in weapons of terror (though the weapons in that case happened to be gunpowder and the cannon).[70]

And if, in addition, you have decided that your *earthly* adversary is the devil—in Reagan's case, Russia, "the focus of evil in the modern world"[71]—then you will naturally see yourself at a disadvantage. It is one thing for two human parties to be equally handicapped by the devilishness of their weapons, but another thing if *you* have to fight the *devil* with them: you are bound to lose. The devil will cause his weapons to work and yours to fail.

And thus, no number of the weapons will ever make you feel secure. Though you have no choice but to acquire as many as you can, each one falls down this bottomless well of Manichean pessimism.

Professional nuclear strategy, as we know, rests on pessimistic worst-case analyses, and what Reagan usefully revealed—perhaps beyond what the professionals were comfortable with—was the emotional and spiritual anxiety driving such analyses beneath their seeming rationality. Some of Reagan's stranger hyperboles (all Soviet industry is hardened against nuclear attack; "the United States is still well behind the Soviet Union in literally every kind of offensive weapon") make sense in terms of the long history of American devil theories to which Reagan was heir.[72] These theories have depended on a belief in adversaries who are "free, active . . . not caught in the toils of the vast mechanism of history" (as Richard Hofstadter has put it). What was wrong with Communists, for Reagan, was that they tried to make history, not follow it. Their philosophy had already changed history in his lifetime. In that sense it had done what nuclear weapons, the "only weapon with no defense," also had done.

It was this metaphysically "unbound" quality that made the Russians moral "monsters," as unprotective of human life as, again, nuclear weapons.[73] The Russians, Reagan seemed to think, had a diabolical cleverness with machines that was the reverse of Americans' ability to project virtue technologically, at least so long as history is on track.[74] This gave them an advantage over us, since we "carry a special *burden*" of believing in God and the dignity of man.[75]

We saw in the last chapter that "governing" a recalcitrant nature was the political goal served when virtue was projected in the form of the state's power. It follows from the deep American belief in America's virtuous power that any sphere ungovernable by that power is a sphere bereft of virtue—in plainest terms, hell. If our power cannot reach it, it is as if God could not reach it. This attitude has crept into popular imagery of Vietnam, a place that Americans found ungovernable. Oliver Stone's movie *Platoon* begins with a line that equates Vietnam with hell. It then paints a visual picture of Vietnam as a garden, lovely in its way but also *sublime*, meaning caught up in visual traditions that link attractiveness with a sense of threat and foreboding. Also, Vietnam is depicted as a garden of snakes; to be sent there is like being driven back into the Garden of Eden after the fall. It entails a struggle for sanity itself, as all recognizable values have been demonically suspended. Reagan's kind of nemesis—adversaries able to make history as they will—is captured in *Platoon* in the evil Sergeant Barnes, who declares "I am reality" and who gets to "go on making up the rules" any way he wants. This stylized film, so saturated in a very traditional American metaphysics, took the Academy Award for Best Picture in recognition of its "gritty realism."[76]

Of course *Platoon was* realistic in the sense that it looked at Vietnam as many Americans had already come to; its metaphysics was transparent to most viewers for that reason. (*Realism* is another term for "transparent metaphysics.") The film recalled the defense of some real-life GI's during their trial for the rape and murder of a Vietnamese woman. "There were some," said their counsel, "that would say [the crime] did not even occur in civilization."[77]

Reagan's dream was to confound the forces of hell. If technology were restored to its proper functioning, consistent with the moral laws of the universe, we good guys would be able to live safely and sanely. Few seemed to believe Reagan's repeated promise to share Star Wars technology with Russia, yet it was consistent with a dream of technology recalled to its true purpose. The U.S. would have nothing to fear from such sharing, for just as "bad" (nuclear) technology can only work to the bad guys' advantage, so "good" technology, technology recalled by SDI to its true purpose, can only work to ours. So long as history is in force, we, the trustees of history, are safe. It is surely significant that SDI envisioned weapons in space, and that even Reagan, in the end, was willing to call it Star Wars. SDI was about the cosmos (figuratively speaking), and space literally is the cosmos. Space is not only "up there" where heaven was traditionally thought to be; it is also a pristine garden of the future into which we are just beginning to project our virtuous machine. (That machine being, of course, the spaceship. The shuttle disaster was not just any technological failure; it was the crashing of our era's heroic equivalent of the railroad.)

It also followed that Reagan could never grasp the seriousness of anti-Star Wars opposition, even from Gorbachev. In fact, by Reagan's own reports, he spent valuable summit time bizarrely trying to *sell* the idea to this Soviet leader, who really had no choice but to oppose it. Understandably he couldn't see how anyone failed to share his logic, inasmuch as it seemed to him the very logic of history and natural law. Whatever his early rhetoric, Reagan gave the Soviet leaders credit for being at least as rational as that. He seemed sincerely befuddled when they didn't seem to get it: "I don't know why the guy believes this." Similarly, when he deflected offers to trade Star Wars, it was not so much with some strong-jawed "No deals"; rather it was more in a tone of bewilderment, as if to say, "Gee, what's the big fuss? It's just a kind of radar. What could be wrong with that?"[78]

VIII.

This discussion points toward several specific lessons. First, it argues for dismissing any lingering idea that SDI was just "a lunatic fraud designed to place money in the hands of arms contractors and supported only by greed-maddened boffins slavering for research funds," as Alexander Cockburn put it.[79] And we also have to throw out more sophisticated analyses:

> The administration's dream of prevailing in a nuclear exchange is a function of its primitive hatred of the Soviet Union. In the president's mind the Soviet Union—or, as he prefers to say, since he sees the contest in theological terms, Marxist-Leninism—is lusting "to conquer the world." Since, in religious wars, a sense of human reality gives way before doctrinal fury, and zeal overrules all qualms, the true crusader may feel tempted to use even nuclear warheads to frustrate the Soviets' evil ambition. In spite of the president's pious—or at least political—denials that he believes in nuclear superiority or regards nuclear war as an instrument of policy, the logic of his twilight struggle against the "evil empire" calls into question those disclaimers.[80]

This analysis, by George W. Ball, is far from the simplistic interest theory of Cockburn's, and it sums up a number of ideas that became commonplaces among critics of the Reagan administration—most of them, we can now see, incorrect. There was indeed something religious in Reagan's outlook, but nothing "primitive"; the religion in question was entirely modern, even subtle. It involved an abhorrence of nuclear weapons that suggested they could *not* serve as instruments in some final battle with the forces of darkness.

And Reagan's "disclaimers" were never just political. It is more accurate to say that while at first he attached his theology to the policy arguments of the Herman Kahn school of strategists—arguments designed in their own way to rehabilitate nuclear technology by making it "useful"—later he hit upon SDI as a more publicly palatable vehicle for the same basic set of values.

Indeed, Reagan's sincerity, certainly as much as economics, was the driving force of SDI and its point of contact with larger cultural traditions that gave at least the impetus for it some public grounding. As an advisor to Walter Mondale aptly put it, "I have learned to ask when Reagan does something: What does he know about the American people that I don't?"[81]

My analysis also suggests that even Reagan's mistakes and confusions are coherent, in the sense that they flow from a consistent underlying point of view. They cannot be discussed in a historical vacuum.[82] This leads us to a specific lesson regarding journalistic coverage of the presidency. It is sometimes said that mainstream American journalists pay too much attention to the president, but with regard to Reagan they clearly weren't paying enough. Nor did they give Reagan enough credit for having a settled view. Where SDI was concerned the news media persisted in assuming incoherence on his part, if not even political subterfuge. Instead of analyzing the ideas he had emphatically and repeatedly put on record, they were ever in pursuit of yet one more quote, as if that would finally have revealed what was "really" happening. (Yet of course it couldn't have, for yet another would have been sought the next day.) But when they got such quotes, and Reagan gave them many, they consistently failed to analyze or put them into any context, including the context of similar statements by Reagan himself.

What generally happens is: each presidential remark is conveyed as isolated "news," no matter how like past statements it is. Lacking the context of history (the current administration's, let alone that of American culture), journalists treat presidential policy as if it were continually just made up on the spur of the moment.

Perhaps this has something to do with the idea that what a president says is "just politics." As noted, any such idea was especially untrue of Reagan. What Reagan said on SDI was metaphysics, and metaphysics is virtually the opposite of politics; it is that which one believes to be nonnegotiable and embedded in nature. In line with another long-standing American tradition—political idealism and isolationism—Reagan seemed only grudgingly willing to manage U.S. foreign policy in political terms (as opposed to moral and symbolic terms). At Fallston High School he reflected that

> when you stop to think that we're all God's children, wherever we may live in the world, I couldn't help but say to [Gorbachev], just think how easy his task and mine might be in these meetings that we held if suddenly there was a threat to this world from some other species from another planet outside in the universe.

One wonders what Gorbachev's reaction to this was. Perhaps it was to feel pinched by the irony of a politician disliking and distrusting politics so much that he wished to be saved from it by little green men from space.[83]

But we should be most surprised if that were the only irony, for irony figures into almost all complex cultural belief systems of the kind that we have here been exploring. Central to such systems are discursive events; discourse attaches meanings to things in ways that conflict with the reality of those things. Actions are therefore taken that undercut their own intended goals.

That is how SDI could give us high-tech innovation driven by nostalgia and technological skepticism; a nuclear-war-fighting philosophy embraced from a Manichean sense of nuclear evil; and the piling up of yet more nuclear weapons based on a dim understanding that nuclear weapons are a tragic historical mistake.

But we must not just write "Here Be Dragons" and give up exploring these murky depths. It is not enough, as E. P. Thompson has done, to hear Star Wars sounding the "worst chords of American right-wing populism" (albeit this is at least an attempt to grasp the project's cultural appeal). The project and the beliefs underlying it can never be fully explained by

Thompson's purely negative terms (*psychopathology, delirium, palpable insanity*). We need, rather, the kinds of terms used by SDI supporters themselves, positive terms like *vision* and *dream*. And we need to recognize that there is no guarantee that the ironies will always be negative.[84] Even SDI, it has been pointed out, is part of a general undermining of deterrence theory whereby "the whole structure of American political predominance [in Europe] is unbolted and starts to disintegrate"—in other words, whereby history as we have grown used to it might well be made to change.[85]

The next and final chapter will conclude my discussion of how to go about taking Thompson's terms seriously, how to use them in addressing the nuclear problem, and what we might look for in the way of further positive ironies—if such be our best hope. What I have tried to show here is that we *must* do all this if we're to understand SDI's ideological momentum, as well as its greatest dangers. It would not be so bad if, as Thompson says, SDI merely stood for our "worst" American traditions. A people can rise above its worst traditions—but how will it ever rise above its best?

SIX

Breaking the Wall of Virtue:
1984 and the Hope of Politics

> The attributes of a person, his wit and
> his moral energy, will exercise, under
> any law or extinguishing tyranny, their
> proper force . . . . All public ends look
> vague and quixotic beside private ones.
> —Ralph Waldo Emerson

> Winston woke up with the word
> "Shakespeare" on his lips.
> —George Orwell

I.

In the preceding chapter I criticized journalists for endlessly seeking yet one more quote, instead of making something of the many revealing quotes a figure like Ronald Reagan so often provided. I also pointed out the ironies we discover when we do make something of Reagan's quotes. There is more to be said on both counts. A basic reason journalists behave in the ways I've described is that they fail to credit cultural history, fail to see events as embedded in any significant context broader than that of the last few months or years. (It could be said that journalists don't know enough about such history to use it, but clearly that is an effect of the problem as much as a cause: For they would learn what they needed to if they thought it significant.)

This fact about the mainstream American media is itself a product of cultural history, partly the history I've outlined and partly a history this book has not explored. Mainstream journalists accept the axioms of modernity, like technological "progress" and the sovereign state. They regard these institutions as unproblematic, fail on the whole to "see" them—and, as sources of public information, the journalists help obscure them for the rest of us, too. They are inclined to view affairs of state in administrative and management terms, rather than in terms of basic principle or purpose.[1] To mainstream journalists, how the state is *run*, or how technology is *used*, are legitimate matters of controversy, but truly fundamental questioning—by Marxists, say, or by true Christian fundamentalists who believe that even the state must bow before God's will and plan—this kind of questioning of modern axioms is "ideology" and is thought to be entitled to very little space in the public debate.

As to Reagan, he was one influential figure who at least on paper argued for holding the state to higher values than its own—values of God's will and of history—just as Augustine or Philippe de Mézières might have done, back before the state came to be taken for granted. But here was the greatest Reagan irony of all. For by associating the divine plan with a certain nation, and by defining history as the heroic march of that nation's achievements, this supposedly critical assessment of the state in fact helped to further aggrandize it. Reagan's banner of higher values always looked suspiciously like the Stars and Stripes. At best, Reagan acknowledged that it was possible for us to be more or less faithful to the role that America and its technology were destined to play—nuclear weapons, for example, he saw as a stain on the banner, to be washed away by SDI. But then, SDI was in the nature of things, and was therefore, in a way, inevitable. We had to build it, and the stress was on *had* to—for that was how history was destined to go. And we knew this, Reagan preached, because that was how American technology had gone so far.

So to this way of thinking—and it has not left us even though Reagan has—the definitions are all circular: American know-how needs to be brought to bear today to do those same things which American know-how has done in the past and which, by so doing, it has proven to be the way of nature. Our state and technology can be tested against God, history, or what have you, but they can never, by definition, ultimately fail such a test.

Contrary to mainstream thinking (such as that which we get from the media, but also, unfortunately, from both nuclear policymakers and most antinuclearists as well), we need to write true history. True history would be truer assessments of the sources and significance of the conditions under which we live. And contrary to the Reagan rhetoric, we need to *make* true history. We need to acknowledge and join in the contest of opposed wills (and opposed *theories* of will—see chapter 3) that constitutes our culture, and that creates such problems as a nuclear threat. Nuclear weapons need to be, in the theoretical parlance, "demystified," taken off their metaphysical pedestal and brought back into the realm of history and, hence, politics. They need to be seen as produced things, hence as conceived things—as precipitates of discourse and of ideology, against which other ways of thinking and acting might reasonably contend.

Recovering true history in the one sense, the sense of knowledge, is intimately tied to re-creating it in the other, the sense of politics. For failure to do one entails failure of the other: if we misunderstand the conditions that produced our world or, worse, if we fail to see that it *was* produced in the first place, we will have no idea how best to act. This is the lesson of one of the great parables of modern history and politics, George Orwell's *1984*, a text written in the shadow of the first atomic weapons.[2] I believe it is, coincidentally, also the lesson of the real 1984, the year in which Reagan and his view of things won their most decisive electoral victory (in a way that is still instructive for the Bush era and beyond).

1984 is all about what becomes of the state and the media when true history, in both senses, is obliterated. The party that rules Oceania, Orwell's imagined Anglo-American state of the future, acts on the premise that "Who controls the past controls the future; who controls the present controls the past." Hence history rewriting becomes thought control and, thus, political control, in an eternally self-sustaining loop.

Now, *1984* is usually read as a warning raised against one sort of totalitarian political system or other. Commentators across the political spectrum have been able to point to their opponents as incipient examples of what Orwell was writing about, or, contrarily, to look about and smugly conclude that the warning was misplaced: 1984 came and went chronologically but not politically. But in fact Orwell's vision is not of any particular political system so much as it is a defense of politics itself. It is also a polemic against totalitarianism, but mainly because totalitarianism is a system devoted to annihilating politics as such, to erasing the possibility that private concerns or interests will insert themselves contentiously into the public sphere. (This is how the state and its interests become "total".) Orwell is widely regarded as a conservative and an anti-Marxist, but what is most important in *1984*, anti-Marxist or not, is its view that the eventual end of politics would be not utopian but dystopian. What Orwell recognized is that the totalizing of the state is, unfortunately, one logical eventual outcome of our cultural history so far.

In a world where all human meanings have been replaced by the state's (London, for instance, is Airstrip One, no longer a polis but a strategist's cipher), the Party of *1984* chases down Winston Smith, one of its own history rewriters who has gone off in search of true history and—though he didn't know the two were connected—true love. But they *are* connected, and this is the theme of *1984* that has tended to be overlooked. Just as knowledge of history raises a vision of values prior to and larger than the state, love gives rise to private relations and private interests which the individual may experience as prior to the state. It creates "ownlife," individualism, against which the Party must be eternally vigilant. ("A Party member is expected to have no private emotions . . . mere impulses, mere feelings, were of no account.") As we have seen, the realm of emotions, like the spiritual realm, must be suppressed by a state that wishes to set up its existence as mere "circumstance," and to persuade people that actions taken on its behalf are mere "practicality."[3] For the spiritual and emotional realms both offer other values, potentially "higher" ones, that could become standards for judging the state's activities and so could drive the individual toward political contention with others whose interests differ— toward, that is, genuine politics. They could give people "the power of grasping that the world could be other than it is," hence the power of making history. So to prevent this, the Party lifts people "clean out of the stream of history" and instead makes history as it wills (173–74, 136).

Winston Smith embodies the qualities of character that support such higher visions and drives. He revives for himself the lost value system of earlier times (i.e., our own), when things like friendship, family, "an embrace, a tear," had value in themselves. He exults in pleasures of the body, from sex to better quality chocolate. ("The sex instinct created a world of its own which was outside the Party's control and which therefore had to be destroyed if possible," 136, 110.)

He refuses unqualified love to Big Brother and instead is choosy, testing declarations against feelings and so declaring that his real love is for a woman named Julia. And he is intellectually skeptical, which is to say, choosy also about what he believes; he tests belief against observed reality and so, in a word, thinks—an undertaking criminalized by the Party and its Thought Police. The state is not concerned to destroy Winston or even to stop his activities, but just to eradicate this insistence on private choice (and with it, the implication that state activities are inherently political, that they are "about" anything besides their own perpetuation). The story therefore ends not with Winston's victory or death, but with his being forced to redirect his belief and his love, to adopt a strange love focused on the state and its works. And this redirection requires, first, that he do two things, one emotional and one intellectual: betray Julia, and betray his own reason and senses—agreeing finally that two plus two equals five.

II.

There are no Thought Police in present-day America. But the logic of the modern state is essentially the same, even if not yet fully able to operate. On cultural-historical grounds we might even argue that this is more true of the American state than of others. Politics is on the defensive in America, and this was never more clear than in the very year of Orwell's title. Reagan's massive reelection victory was partly a denial and rejection of politics itself by millions of voters. Christopher Hitchens, reporting on the antiapartheid demonstrations that year, spoke with one counterprotester at the South African embassy in Washington. "I'm completely unpolitical," said the man, and "a very strong Reagan supporter." Hitchens was correct to point out that "these two statements are perhaps not as ill-matched as they sound at first."[4] The man was carrying a picket sign, but apparently as an act of protest *against* politics. Reagan got this man's vote, and many others, partly by playing like an idiot savant to this deep-rooted American antipathy toward politics—an antipathy that traces to the utopian visions of the country discussed in the last chapter and, beyond them, to the Founders, who had hoped to build a political system that would somehow rise above parties and "entanglements," a governmental machine driven (like a mechanical machine) by the laws of nature itself.

Partly through Reagan, the right has in recent years become the party of hope for an apolitical social order, as the left has been in other periods (particularly the 1960s). In the right's case, this hope is embodied in dreams of a Christian commonwealth where everyone follows the same rules, while for the left it takes the form of another dream—a land of total equality and brotherhood, perhaps. But the principle is the same. Reagan adroitly aligned himself in 1984 with the cries of "USA!" at the Los Angeles Olympics, and the unspoken assumption in these cries that "USA" denotes a unitary, unproblematic entity whose meaning and direction are not the subject of debate. He was thus able to paint even his mild-mannered, consensus-oriented opponent, Walter Mondale, as the candidate of division, disagreement, and special interests: "politics" in the pejorative sense. Of course, incumbents always wish to seem above politics, but Reagan's effort to persuade the country that "we" were "feeling good" was a particularly successful example of this strategy, an example drawing more deeply than usual on cultural tendencies of much longer standing. It took particular advantage of the left opposition's problem today, which is that it has been (politically) maneuvered into arguing for more politics in a culture that for many reasons has long yearned for less.

The desire to see politics come to an end leads to the kind of self-reinforcement at the ballot box that obviously helped along Reagan's victory. Once it seemed his reelection was likely anyway, people indulged the belief that no other president was possible. Reagan became self-confirming. After the election I heard this attitude expressed in a remark that was phrased different ways by different speakers, but that always amounted to the same idea: "Fifty million people can't be wrong." (Reagan's 1984 vote total was 54,281,858.) "If Reagan got all those votes," people asked, "doesn't that show he must be *right*?" Of course, the question is an example of what chapter 4 called modern animism, effacing as it does the more than 37,450,000 people who voted against him. (That's a lot of people too. Were they wrong?) In that sense, this bizarre idea—that numbers make truth—doesn't even stand up in its own terms. But it fits very well within the American antipolitical calculus. It is analogous to an idea put forward by several black leaders after Reagan's big win—the idea that blacks ought to start turning Republican so as not to be "left out." (As though there had not been some reason they had declined to do this in the first place.) Blacks, who voted heavily against Reagan, had been "proven" especially "wrong." But such a proposed solution—join the Inner Party, since that's where the action is, and never mind what that party *stands* for—is obviously very convenient for those already in power. It is a solution that would obviously tend to reinforce the very problem against which it is supposedly offered.

Hence, something like this notion is just what ruling elites would like people to think: that since there are no great political struggles left, not just politics but, really, history itself has ended. And despite all the injustices that have irrupted into public concern and political action in just the past thirty years, there are large numbers of people, even well-informed ones, who are ready to embrace essentially this view. (In an affluent culture, after all, large numbers of people belong more or less to the ruling elite.) Maybe union or civil-rights movements were once worthwhile and necessary, but today, it is thought, everyone finally has "opportunity"—a Reagan buzz-word. Today things have at last arrived at their cosmically preordained places; the nature of things has at last been fully realized, and no further political work really needs to be done. The world as we find it today is grounded not politically, but metaphysically.

In fact, as I have heard it argued, it is "insulting" to, say, the pink-collar, low-wage workforce to offer a vision of a better lot in life. That workforce and its current circumstances did not arise out of political decisions in favor of certain economic arrangements and against others. If they exist today, here at the end of history, then they just *are*. They represent the inevitable nature of such things. So let it be; don't torment the people concerned with reminders of how unfulfilling it is to spend one's days keypunching or slinging french fries. Indeed, do not even formulate the judgment that it *is* unfulfilling, for that is unprovable, and to claim the unprovable is arrogant.

History-has-ended thinking of this kind is closely related to an attitude that has been called relativism. Relativism is the belief that no view of things is more persuasive than or preferable to any other, and that therefore the legitimacy of any given claim is relative to who makes it (instead of to the nature of things). Relativism, as various commentators have said, is very much "in" in our culture today. It seems to reflect impulses both self-disciplined (do not have strong feelings about anything, including evil or injustice) and hedonistic (leave me and everyone else alone to "do our own things"). In other words, like other outlooks we have seen becoming domi-nant over the course of history, relativism draws upon *opposed* discourses and synthesizes two *opposed* views at once, and this persuades many people that it is the only reasonable way to think.

Certainly relativism is fashionable in, for instance, academia, where one sometimes has trouble telling whether students who espouse it are echoing their professors or vice versa. There is great fear in academia of seeming dogmatic, on the one hand, or intellectually or politically naive, on the other. Relativistic acceptance of all views equally is the simple way to avoid both. Plus, students (in their characteristic "conservatism") want to fit in, which means avoiding disagreement even with each other as well as with the powers that be; and many professors (in their left liberalism) want to appear nonjudgmental and open to the views of others, particularly the disadvantaged—including the intellectually disadvantaged, which is to say, those less prepared than themselves to reason soundly. Relativism, again, superficially meets both concerns.

But in this clamor of confused ideas it is, if anything, the students' and not the professors' view that makes the most sense, for in the end there is nothing left-wing about a relativist. Relativism cuts away the grounds for criticizing power, for holding power to any higher values than itself. Relativism leads not just to numbers-make-truth, but finally to might-makes-right. Extreme relativism declares it unimportant whether we affirm that two plus two is four or that it is five. Therefore there's no reason to disagree when those in power say it's five. In *1984* relativism is the position of the establishment, not of the antiauthoritarian rebel Winston Smith. Smith's view, like that of our own Founding Fathers, is that the truly liberating philosophy is *empiricism*—belief in real, knowable, self-evident truths.

Of course, university people do not seriously argue about what two plus two equals. But I have heard students in class claim, with wide assent, that (for instance) there are no rational reasons for condemning the enslavement of blacks, so long as such a social policy has majority support. (These students, let me emphasize, were not racists but simply relativists. They were nonpartisanly willing to excuse the oppression of all different kinds of minorities besides ethnic.) And I have heard professors claim that they couldn't, and didn't care to, defend the value even of their own life's work—let alone judge students' work, as the students themselves are expecting[5]—for that would be dogmatically to "privilege" one value system over others.

These bizarre attitudes are worrisome because there is some evidence that they are endemic in American education—though perhaps most proudly put forward at higher levels and especially in humanities fields whose objects of study, like literature and art, were long ago declared to have nothing to do with the real world anyway.[6] History-has-ended thinking in a sense comes to the rescue of what otherwise would seem—even to the people who hold them—the ethical obtuseness of the views I have quoted. For by pointing out that history has ended, we can declare ourselves (luckily) released from having to worry about such problems as human oppression at all. Slavery, after all, was abolished before our lifetimes; ours is not to reason why over this. Everything *today* is just "the way things are" (even if that wasn't true in the past, when history was still in progress), so in fact there's no point in discussing how the world ought to be. To paraphrase a *Los Angeles Times* ad campaign, the world is just there for us, every day. We don't support its being a certain way by dint of our own activity, whether conscious and active or unwitting and passive. It does not occur to relativists that, for instance, we are quietly deciding every day not to *reintroduce* slavery, and that implicitly we must have reasons for *that*. No, the world is not constituted by our actions or lack thereof. It is simply the accretion of history—a history happily done with. It is what it is. And therefore it should be what it is: You can't argue with history.

We might well notice in all this that history-has-ended thinking tends to be paternalistic. It holds everyone to be meant to do what he or she is doing (or aspires to do, within the boundaries of "opportunity" helpfully laid down by history). Hence some people are meant to run things, some to be taken care of. This paternalism is another point of contact with *1984*, where the state is embodied in a figure called Big Brother. Orwell saw that totalitarianism is the reductio ad absurdum of the very common tendency to think of society as a family. What characterizes the family is that its hierarchies are rooted in nature, or at least more so than the hierarchies established in society.[7] The family seems the one social institution that follows most directly from the inherent way things are. You submit to authority in the family for obvious reasons—because you're younger or smaller—and, in turn, the family both shelters you and names you (gives you an identity and sets you a place in the scheme of things). Families seem God-given, and the drive to give an impersonal society the appearance of familial bonding, as totalitarian regimes and, to some extent, all states try to do, is part of a drive to make the existing social and economic order seem equally God-given, equally not the product of history and political choice.

But—and here again is where the Winston Smiths of the world become a problem—such a drive depends on hindering people's tendency to form *real* families, and generally to express their wishes and desires and to contend against each other in achieving those wishes and desires. Such contention is politics, and it must be defeated by making Big Brother the focus of all desire. One's public loves and loyalties must become as absolute as they are in the family—hence not the *basis* of one's political claims on the rest of society, but rather something extracted by society from the individual. In the terms of certain contemporary social theories, totalitarianism is a grand project in the reconstructing of desire, hence of culture itself. And, as Orwell makes clear, it goes about this task by constituting a whole new human "subject" at the deepest level of thought and belief.

Indeed, the concepts of *1984* that have passed most readily into collective wisdom are Newspeak and doublethink, names for the Party's efforts to reconstitute reality through language. If the Party can create reality (which it does by making disbelief in *its* tawdry version of reality impossible), then in this way, too, it can make itself seem natural and God-given. It can remove itself from history and begin to create history as it wills, starting with the construction of a bogus history that rationalizes the state's power instead of opening it to question. (In *1984*, history as a chronicle of various wars and five-year plans has degenerated into one unceasing war and one unending five-year plan.) It is no coincidence that *1984* is the classic satire of intellectual dishonesty, for totalitarianism is at root a vast exercise in circular self-justification and state-centered metaphysics. It is one logical end result of the modern state's self-serving redefinition of virtue, and it is the ultimate, fully institutionalized answer to the cultural anxieties about the state that were unwittingly revealed, but less thoroughly answered, in some of the more dubious arguments of Shakespeare's Henry. The state as depicted in *1984* is simply an extreme parody or literalization of what I have argued all modern states are. It defines itself *wholly* by its technologies and its wars. It erects itself as the font of value by draining the world of all other goods. It attempts not just rhetorically to construct an animistic "we," but literally to turn the people into a faceless, indistinguishable mass. And instead of covering up its own historical contingency, it simply expropriates history itself. Oceania demonstrates the implicit interconnectedness of all these characteristically modern state projects.

If our problem stems from the fact that all modern states have basically these same tendencies, then the solution lies in wider adoption of the values of Winston Smith. Genuine virtue must be cultivated in place of the state's bogus virtue. Extending a notion of Winston Smith's, we should want to "break down the wall of virtue" and replace it with qualities like his: honesty of feeling and intellectual honesty. There is much public talk these days about restoring lost cultural values, but what seems more to the point is restoring a lost *ability to value* in the first place. Intellectually dishonest relativism is both such a loss and its rationalization, the declaring of valuing itself as passé by people who don't know anymore what to value. It is the easy way out: just declare that all things are equally valuable—hence equally worthless. Perhaps there is actually a glimmer of hope in the fact that important public figures, who in many complex ways are part of the problem, nonetheless win a sympathetic hearing by at least *seeming* to model some sort of public process of valuing. That is what Ronald Reagan did, even if on closer inspection his values really turned into state-as-virtue and hence were at bottom relativistic. It is also what the news media do by at least laying claim to "truth" and to an adversarial role with respect to power (a role that doesn't even survive as a pretense in the world of *1984*). The question is whether these elements of true valuing can or will be brought to bear in the reconstruction of some better metaphysics—some sense of nature and of higher truth that will replace belief in the state and its wars and weapons as the "natural" way of things. To answer this, we need to look more closely at what such reconstruction would entail.

III.

Intellectual dishonesty, the concept I think more pertinent to our dilemma than stupidity or vileness, arises when serious, well-intentioned people adopt the rational irrationality discussed in chapter 1. It involves judging a thing's rationality purely at the level of ongoing function—does it work as it was designed to?—rather than in terms of whether its fundamental reason for existing is sound to begin with. Henry V's threat to Harfleur is rational given his goals (after all, it works), but irrational if one asks why he's there in the first place. Similarly, nuclear deterrence theorists are rational in their analysis of geopolitical "realities," but irrational in failing to investigate and criticize those realities in turn. It is the unspoken first principles that present the problem and that must be brought into full view. In chapter 2 I spoke of the misplaced criticism of *leaders* by many antinuclearists, who often seem to ask in bewilderment, "Can they honestly believe what they're saying?" Yes, they can, but the trick is in the word *honestly*. Today's nuclear policymakers and strategists are honest by their own lights, but where they start to sound like Henry at Harfleur, as some come close to doing, it is because they have not honestly reexamined basic premises. They are "honest" in the everyday sense, yet intellectually dishonest.

This intellectual dishonesty is the seemingly intractable element in nuclear discourse, the thing that keeps the debate from ever being resolved. It is akin to "the terrible thing" Winston Smith sees in O'Brien, the Party official who tortures him:

> The terrible thing was that when O'Brien said this he would believe it. You could see it in his face. O'Brien knew everything. A thousand times better than Winston, he knew what the world was really like, in what degradation the mass of human beings lived and by what lies and barbarities the Party kept them there. He had understood it all, weighed it all, and it made no difference: all was justified by the ultimate purpose. What can you do, thought Winston, against the lunatic who is more intelligent than yourself, who gives your arguments a fair hearing and then simply persists in his lunacy? (216)

The only additional question I have posed is whether in *our* situation there is really such a difference between policy elites and that "mass of human beings," who, after all, still have the democratic power to stop underwriting this sort of thinking on the part of the leadership. The dynamic relationship of policy to popular opinion is complex, but finally it is one of mutual support. Intellectual dishonesty on the part of leaders requires intellectual dishonesty on the part of very many people. But, importantly, not all people. It is not a simple case of leaders as perpetrators and the people as victim, not only because citizens still do have some power, but because there is no "the people" to be victimized. There are only those who actively support the dominant view, those who passively acquiesce in it, those who might be pried loose from it, and those who sense its wrongness and oppose it but who, unfortunately, are at as much risk from it as anyone else.

By contrast with all this, intellectual honesty consists in the willingness to reexamine institutions and practices in terms of first principles. Winston Smith's way of intellectually honestly probing first principles is to search for true history. This is also what ought generally to happen in our world. That doesn't mean that people in general must all become historians. For true history is all around us: this phrase means, simply, truth about how our present situation came to be (starting with the fact that it did come to be, that it isn't just in the nature of things). Not every citizen need probe for this truth directly, à la Winston Smith, but serious citizenship would seem to require being *fair* toward it, allowing in principle that it is there to be found. In practice, this would mean that when particular policies, like nuclear-weapons deployments, proffer themselves as rational, one neither dismisses the claim as mere pretense nor accepts surface rationality as true rationality.

First principles that remain *un*examined beneath a surface of rational activity are ideology in the worst sense. In common political and journalistic use, the term *ideology* is applied to so-called extreme views that advertise their own systematic and nonmainstream character. As Terry Eagleton puts it, " 'Ideology' is always a way of describing other people's interests rather than one's own."[8] But there is another possible definition, the one that Eagleton prefers: ideology not as the refusal to accept mainstream views, but instead as those premises which constitute the mainstream in the first place. Such premises, as I have tried to show, can also be remarkably systematic, though as mainstream assumptions they may not be recognized as even existing. But they will be all the more widely held and firmly rooted for just that reason. The most thoroughly ideological position is that which holds certain social and political arrangements, albeit ones with majority support, to be simply the nature of things, and which thus sacrifices the chance to measure those arrangements against the real nature of things. Ideology in the deepest sense is the mistaking of history and politics for metaphysics.

By this subtler, nonmainstream definition, the strength of ideology is better measured not by the presence but by the lack of organized political activity in a given society, or by the lack of overt political position taking. A society where everyone seems to agree—and, hence, where people forget that other views are possible—would be the most ideological society of all. Total agreement, after all, is what the Party ideology of *1984*, Ingsoc, is all about. We would scarcely grant that Ingsoc is unideological, yet that is how it presents itself to its society, and that is essentially what it tortures Winston Smith into believing about it.

If ideology in the deepest sense is a function of seeming *non*commitment to any given view, then apolitical politics and pervasive relativism, supposedly rejections of ideology, are in fact good candidates for the ideological. The premise on which relativism rests, that history has ended, would in fact *be* an ideology, with all that the term implies about its serviceability to particular interest groups (in this case, comfortable, middle-class white Americans—the only serious relativists I've ever met). It would be what those groups self-servingly *wished* to believe and what they clung to against all the evidence.

It might be objected that the people I'm referring to also provide substantial opposition to some government policies, that political debate in America is partly debate *within* those privileged groups. That is true, and it is one reason for not confusing "the people" with a mystical "we" that subsumes all differences; the ideology is not omnipotent. But the debate in question basically occurs atop an unexamined structure of beliefs which themselves are not subject to debate. Ronald Reagan is again a good example here. He is a politician who built his career on attacks on "government," yet who breathed the dominant ideology in every sentence: that the life of Western nations is the highest kind, the standard to which other cultures aspire; that America is both shining example and agent in helping these other cultures achieve this life; that history is the story of all this becoming apparent; that what America does, "we all" do. And assumptions like this are hardly confined to Reagan: I have heard it said that "America has never invaded another country" and, apropos of foreign aid, "Americans [meaning the nation] are the most generous people on the face of the earth." The speakers in both cases were college professors.

That shows that ideology has nothing to do with intelligence or even being well informed, since it persists quite apart from information: as though facts and ultimate beliefs had separate compartments in the mind. Thus it can affect seemingly nonrelativist policy intellectuals just as easily; in fact, some argue, it is what makes one a policy intellectual—a Herman Kahn who pursues only "practical" matters, that is, those that regard the state's interests as givens. As such intellectuals demonstrate, it is possible to affirm higher values, like freedom or democracy, but also—because history has ended—stop seeing these as goals to be won through Jefferson's "eternal vigilance" and instead regard them as names for the existing arrangements themselves. David Rieff points to an interesting example when he says that the question that came out of the televised Iran-contra hearings in 1987 was "why so many people shared [Colonel] North's notion of democracy as being neither an idea nor a system, but, instead, simply an appellation for the American side."[9] Or, we might ask how it is possible for a journalist to say, "[Secretary of Education] Bennett continues to endorse reading the basic works of Western democratic thought: Shakespeare, the Federalist Papers, the Bible"—arguably none of which is a work of "democratic" thought.[10] It would seem that *democratic* here encodes the idea: "having contributed in some way to the creation of a society that we have long since agreed is democratic." This shift in meaning—from democracy (or other such terms) as a certain state of things to an unexamined presumption—is the precondition for doublethink. In doublethink, words lose all reference to any testable condition, and it becomes possible to say things like "slavery is freedom."

The public nuclear debate is largely waged between policy intellectuals or their allies, who believe like Colonel North that higher values are best served by serving the institutions that supposedly embody them, and "ideological" critics who do think in terms of the values themselves and either support or resist the particular actions of particular institutions accordingly. Most members of the public side with these ideologues in polls, because there the value questions are put in isolation. But they vote (if at all) with policy intellectuals at the ballot box, where the issue is managing the state. And they don't regard this as a contradiction. Like John Foster Dulles, they have come to "identify . . . the values of the United States with moral rightness itself."[11]

IV.

The bridge between that intellectual debate and the public is the news media. Media are another agency of the dominant ideology. The "objective" mainstream press is essentially a line of access to the discourse of specialists who ordinary readers or viewers don't come into contact with on their own. Medical news tends to be fragments of the discourse of doctors and researchers; sports news, of coaches and bookies; political news, of politicians, insider analysts, and, to a lesser degree, self-identified policy opponents. (In other words, policy intellectuals plus a smattering of ideologues.) The press calls these specialists "sources," implying that they each just provide information, but of course they also convey the *style* of their respective discourses, and thus the values those discourses presume: tacit "instructions about what to attend to, and how to attend, within the going concern of American political life."[12] To journalists, "objectivity" involves sticking close to what some source has said, instead of raising questions about it or critiquing it. Hence, objectivity means allowing the underlying assumptions, the ideology, of the source to come across to the reader unimpeded. Of course, multiple sources will be used and even set against one another. But to the extent that the sources are part of common discourse communities—and this is usually true even of policymakers and their vocal critics (who are often, though not always, other policymakers)—they tend to share the same fundamental assumptions, and their surface disagreements therefore cover the wholesale importation of their ideology, all the more enhanced by the credibility lent the report by its "balance."

The media's instructions about what to attend to come in the form of certain ways of contextualizing and defining events and in a certain language which, in our culture, not only conveys the dominant ideology but is itself an aspect of it. The media don't tell us what to think, it has been said, but what to think *about*. An ideology of state-as-virtue, authorizing the state to be its own moral arbiter, is going to tend to remove something like nuclear weapons from discussion. Journalists (following the policy community) will in effect instruct us only to think about them in certain narrow ways, because there is (the ideology holds) no point to doing otherwise. They will tend to make an issue of serious calls for change in the situation, but not of the maintenance of the situation itself. (Actually the most serious calls, questioning state-as-virtue itself, would probably be ignored altogether. Opposition will tend to shape itself to fit this fact, meaning such calls won't even be raised.) And of course, by narrowing the focus of its reports to yesterday or last week, the very structure of mainstream media discourse all but declares that history in any broader sense is, indeed, over.

All these moves are encoded in the very words that public discourse makes available. "There is no term 'warnik'," says Noam Chomsky. "Advocacy of militarism is . . . the norm, so no term for this stance is required."[13] This fact of popular usage is the sort of thing Orwell is famous for pointing out, and which *1984*'s Newspeak is an attempt to systematically enforce. It is an effacement of certain viewpoints, complementary to the effacement of minorities by majorities under conditions of modern animism (see chapter 4). Erecting an animistic ideology requires effacing the fact that the majority view isn't total, a given. This means both overlooking minority views altogether and conveniently noting them—naming them in ways that position them somewhere, hence leave the mainstream view positioned nowhere. If peacenikery can be named, then it must be a thing, not a part of the structure of the universe itself. By implication, non-peacenikery *is* structured into the universe. The fact that minority views exist can, thus, be selectively cited to ratify the norm, which is all the clearer if it is defined *against* something. To the extent that the media participate in this naming process they convey ideology in multiple ways at once. Besides *being* animistic, busily constructing "we"s who are assumed (thus, tacitly, instructed) to be interested in this or that, they help establish animism in particular as an aspect of the nature of things.

Less ideologically loaded objectivity could well start with some creative thinking about who gets quoted—specifically, about which potential sources are speaking the truth. But that is precisely what mainstream journalists consider unobjective. Of course, mainstream journalists make all sorts of judgments about who counts as a source. But since they want to believe that truth emerges from the sources (rather than determines who they are), who gets quoted often becomes a function of how powerful and vocal the potential source is. This, again, is relativism, and it has consequences, as we have seen, not unlike might-makes-right: the media were forced to lend credence even to President Reagan's mistakes (like weapons/missiles) because his power made him an "authoritative" source.[14]

At bottom, who gets quoted and what gets covered—in other words, which discourses help shape our common, public discourse—is left up to "common sense," which is what is thought to drive most news judgments. And that is the problem. If there is a dominant ideology to begin with, and if it holds, for instance, that the American state is uniquely free of self-interest, then no judgment will seem like common sense if it doesn't incorporate this assumption. Hence to follow common sense will be to unconsciously put forward that ideology.

Whether in the media or in popular thinking generally, resisting this sort of ideology requires looking for the foundation of it—the aspects of the world that are taken to be natural and inevitable—and seeing their historical contingency. This is what Winston Smith haplessly tries to do. War, for example, has stopped making even limited sense in the world of *1984*. It has become "a purely internal affair" designed to maintain the Party's denial of reality and "keep the structure of society intact" (162–64), rather as it did for Shakespeare's Henry except more thoroughly, and without all the apologies and rationalizations. (In fact, war has come full circle: Orwell interestingly suggests that because it is waged for ultimately arbitrary purposes of state, even "purposive" war at its logical extreme becomes once again a kind of Fluellenesque ritual, though far more inhumanly destructive.) Winston tries to convince Julia that Oceania had switched alliances four years earlier and before that had been fighting Eastasia, not Eurasia. Enmity toward Eurasia, he tries to insist, is historically contingent—as is dramatically confirmed when the sides switch once again, "actually in mid-sentence" in the middle of a war rally (127–28, 150). The Party knows that if this contingency were recognized the whole structure of things would start to unravel. Its own goals would be revealed as arbitrary too, and its ability to control the past, and, thereby, reality, would be lost. Eventually people would demand human meaning from the state, and would overthrow the state if it failed to justify itself in terms of humanly meaningful values. So Winston himself must in the end be forced to believe that "Oceania has always been at war with Eastasia."

The same sort of insight Winston Smith tries to insist on would pose a similar peril to the ideologies of nuclear threat. If our own state is unable to say it has "always been at war" with anyone, it is nonetheless committed to maintaining people's belief that its conflict with the Eastern bloc is so rooted in basic values as to lie outside the flux of time, hence in a way to be "always." And it is also committed to obscuring that commitment, which is one reason President Reagan had to stop actually calling Russia a metaphysical "focus of evil in the modern world." Lacking recourse to torture or the power to impose Newspeak (though the latter is sometimes tried), our state cannot enforce such a view if people start to question it—and posing it bluntly as Reagan did, instead of encoding it as unquestioned premise, is inviting people to question it. If it became widely believed that (in true Augustinian terms) evil has no particular social or geographical focus, then popular support for massive nuclear deployments would be called into question, since they depend at present on something close to Reagan's view being widely, if vaguely, supported. And calling these deployments into question, in turn, would undermine the less wild-eyed, more "rational" scenarios of justification put forward by elite strategists. For once a major national policy had been thrown open to question on first principles, political factions would develop not only which opposed the policy but which, newly aware of the possibility of moral error by the state, refused to grant the state a monopoly on virtue and began to question the supremacy of national goals in general. So crucial axioms of policy like that supremacy would become points of political contention.

Hence, they would no longer *be* axioms. Citizens would still have to make decisions about the goals, structure, and security of their common life, but they would no longer be locked into essentially one line of reasoning on these points.[15] And in the end they might even begin to question (or "problematize") the whole animistic notion of there being *national* goals or interests in the first place, as opposed to millions of individual, local, or community interests and rights—the kind "secured" under Jeffersonian liberalism, obscured by the animistic state, and systematically abolished by the masters of Oceania.

Depending as it does on a diversity, and even, if one happens to arise, on a competition of differing interests, politics ultimately presupposes that fatal quality of Winston Smith's, skepticism. Allowing a contention among different claims to truth, it rests on our willingness to let metaphysical ultimates be debated and discovered. But skepticism, as Winston Smith demonstrates, is as different from the relativism I have described, which denies metaphysics altogether—there is no "truth," only what's *true for you*—as it is from the state's imposed metaphysics—"whatever the Party holds to be truth *is* truth," as O'Brien tells Winston Smith (205). Intellectually honest skepticism underwrites, like relativism, an ongoing conflict of different views, but it ultimately believes in truth and therefore holds those views to tests of their truth. It demands that we continually seek to discover and live by the truest possible views, and it rejects the notion that any view with support from the vocal or the powerful is equally as valid or worthwhile as any other. Therefore it must also reject the idea that fifty million voters can't be wrong. For this idea expresses a desire for some flexibility in the nature of things. It bespeaks a wish for truths that can be enacted, instead of having to be painstakingly discovered.

V.

Ultimately *1984*, and through it our current situation, can be interpreted in terms of the Augustinian-Pelagian analytical schema discussed in chapter 3. The political health of a culture depends on Pelagian and Augustinian tendencies not slipping out of balance. Ideally one's philosophy, or reading of the nature of things, needs to be rather more Augustinian: All people share a basic and sadly sinful nature; corruption is ever-present and ceaselessly demands a response from us. But one's *policies*, meanwhile, need a certain tinge of the Pelagian: The world is capable of improvement; our personal actions are meaningful and can contribute to that improvement. What happens in *1984* is that the state gets this backwards. To support a *Pelagian* view of the nature of things (reality is open to human definition; the state's actions are exempt from sin) it practices policies whose animus is *Augustinian* ("the object of power is power"). Its misplaced Pelagian philosophy gives us the Party's belief that "men are infinitely malleable" and that history can be legislated; hence there is no nature of things in which to ground policy. And with policy no longer grounded in nature, there is no "good" to be sought, so the Augustinian emotions of "fear, rage, triumph, and self-abasement"—which make some limited sense as *reactions* to a world of sin—fly loose and become autonomous goals in their own right. If *controlling* sin is no longer a rationale for the state, since nature is not seen as sinful nor as anything else in particular, then sinning itself will do as an object: "Progress in our world will be progress toward more pain," says O'Brien (217, 220).

Put another way, the problem is Pelagian metaphysics giving rise to perverse Augustinian ethics, instead of Augustinian metaphysics giving rise to Pelagian ethics. At the root of our modern dilemma is this basic confusion—a kind of relativistic skepticism toward nature combined with an insistence that human works have some certain, fixed quality, instead of vice versa. We can see how this situation would have arisen historically. Nuclear weapons complete a process of abstraction inherent in both the modern state and modern technology. Technology manipulates the world by treating it as an abstraction, and the state extends its sovereign domain by enclosing more and more areas of wilderness (the "heath," as it was called in Shakespeare).[16] Both processes tend to cast doubt on the world's concreteness apart from human formulations of it. And people uncertain how to formulate the world are inclined to accept the state's formulation of it as the one backed by the most power (hence what I am calling Pelagian metaphysics).

Reagan's bombing-in-five-minutes joke, in which Russia's physical reality is conceived of as *owing to* its legal status, relies on both this inclination *and* a counterposed anxiety: the fact that the international sphere still looks frighteningly like an untamed and unformulated heath, which seems to demand an Augustinian ethic of sheer control—precisely what *our* state, grown absolute within its own territory, would now be entrusted to provide. In general the more shocking remarks of relativists can be read as examples of this perverse Augustinian ethic. "Slavery isn't right for us, but maybe it was right for them"; "*They* [the powers that be] will always do what they want, so of course might makes right"; "Why *shouldn't* we blow up Leningrad if they blow up New York?" All such remarks express a kind of shrugging at evil, as if it were never shocking even when preventable.

Plus, there is still that residual Augustinian view of more ancient vintage, the view that nuclear weapons are justified by the fact that there *is* objective evil in the world (not here, of course, but over there) and that the threat this evil poses demands use of our ultimate means of control and restraint. This more traditional view is vaguely present in popular thinking, explicitly avowed by certain groups (like some Christian fundamentalists) and turned into a system by the professional strategists (Herman Kahn, for example, appeals to it). It is not the same as, but it allies itself with, the crasser relativistic willingness to excuse even mass murder if we decide it's "right for us." In short, two forms or interpretations of Augustinianism combine to produce the same end result. And as I have already indicated, where nuclear weapons are concerned Augustinian beliefs also combine with Pelagian to produce a common end result.[17] Massive nuclear deployments (again, like any other firmly entrenched cultural policy) answer simultaneously to different, even conflicting ideas within individual people, and to potentially conflicting ideas and pressures in society. They represent a policy "we" positively want and accept and not just one foisted on "us"; but with the qualification that the "we" and "us" are constituted *by* this convergence of actions and aims, and are not mystically (animistically) preexisting.

That last point needs emphasis. In the modern world society tends to be thought of as a "we" that is represented *as a whole* by the state. In getting rid of kings, moderns did not get rid of the notion (so useful to kingship, and vice versa) that they could stand and act as a single body, a single personality. In this political environment, in which it is always this "we" that is acting, it becomes very difficult to entertain the idea that "our" actions could be evil and wrong. They are, after all, seen not as mere actions or mere policies, but as expressions of what "we" fundamentally are. Maybe "they," our enemies, are basically evil—that is still considered possible, and would be used to justify punishing them as individuals (for instance, by blowing up their cities) when "they" have expressed *their* fundamental nature by doing some evil. But "we" cannot see our own collectivity, expressed through the state, as doing evil without seeing our *individual* selves as evil, since if this "we" means anything we are all part of it. And evil is not what we see in ourselves at any given moment.

But if there is no "we," except the useful fiction we construct for essentially narrative purposes (to make it easier to describe the things that happen in the world), then society instead becomes a loose structure of differing parties and interests—policy intellectuals and the apolitical, Pelagians and Augustinians, relativists who accept whatever is done by power and absolutists who confuse the state with their cherished higher values. At present, these various parties *happen* to have joined together in a broad coalition of support for the modern state and its technology. That state and technology (including massive nuclear deployments) are not straightforward expressions of "our" common will, but rather are particular interests in their own right, interests that this coalition happens at the moment to patronize. Once this is understood, it should become possible to restore particular actions to the status of mere policy and thus to begin seriously to assess who in fact *is* responsible for them—who, on any given issue, is inside the coalition and who is outside it.

Hence it should become possible to criticize the policies, to allow that even some with overwhelming majority support are simply wrong. For the policies are no longer "us," so the wrongness is not intrinsic to "us." They are factional positions (even when the faction is huge) that can be evaluated: some are better, some worse. And they can be politically altered or abandoned; the coalition can re-form itself away from them.

In all, it becomes possible to believe that "we" are sometimes evil, and yet to maintain our perception that as individuals we are not being or meaning evil. Above all, it becomes possible to see the current system as arising from "our" desires *without its thereby being validated* just because we feel those desires to be good.

But to speak of good and evil brings us back to the need for an Augustinian metaphysics, for under Pelagian-relativist metaphysics these terms have no meaning; "good" becomes merely whatever is desired by those with privilege or power. The question is whether there *is* something absolute besides power, something that would objectively ground our judgments of good and evil *and* cry out from our souls for the making of such judgments (for if there is no cry, it will not matter if such an absolute exists). This is the question posed by the real-life parallels I have been drawing to *1984*. The political process is dispirited today by the pressures of an antipolitical tendency that points in the direction of all politically contending forces, having already joined the coalition that constitutes the state, being further aligned beneath the banner of a single agency or party within the state—and perhaps, most chillingly, in the end being abolished altogether. The nuclear issue is, perhaps, simply moving further along in this direction than other issues; certainly debate on it is dispirited, and it is viewed from all sides as more an arena of tragedy or cosmic fate than of politics. The question is, How dispirited will things get? Is it possible for the political process simply to break down under the cultural pressures already at work, with each step in its disintegration encouraging the next in a dynamic that spirals downward—if not toward *1984*, then toward something else as bad in its own way? Or does the process brake itself? Is the great modern coalition genuinely able to be undone? Perhaps we cannot trust (as relativists would) that the world people choose to build for themselves is necessarily the right one; but can we at least hope that pockets of opposition to the Party will always exist?[18]

Winston Smith believes we can. He dreams of a continuity of humanness that cuts across geography, time, and hence politics:

> It was curious to think that the sky was the same for everybody, in Eurasia or Eastasia as well as here. And the people under the sky were also very much the same—everywhere, all over the world, hundreds or thousands or millions of people just like this. . . .
>
> . . . one can imagine little knots of resistance springing up here and there— small groups of people banding themselves together, and gradually growing, and even leaving a few records behind, so that the next generation can carry on where we leave off. [181, 129]

That is Winston's dream, and the horror of *1984* is that it turns out to be wrong. The Party's Pelagian view of human nature is, in the novel, the factually correct one. "You must get rid of those nineteenth-century ideas about the laws of nature" and about human nature, O'Brien tells him (218). "You are imagining that there is something called human nature which will be outraged by what we do and will turn against us. But we create human nature. Men are infinitely malleable" (222). Winston's destruction is then offered as proof of this claim. In *1984* the human condition is terminal. Global nuclear destruction, in fact, would almost be redundant.

Here is where one would like to say, *1984* is just a novel. In real life, its conclusions are not proven. Of course, if they were, there might still be ways of grounding a useful ethics, despite what O'Brien thinks. But there would be little use in calling for a new metaphysics. There would be no way of declaring that the Party's view, or its real-life counterparts in our world, were objectively wrong or contrary to nature.

But in real life there *is* reason to believe in a cross-cultural, cross-political human nature; indeed, there is even reason in *1984* to believe in one. The Party claims to create nature and human nature as it wills, but it must finally contend with the sheer physical reality of a Winston Smith. This is what causes it trouble all along: Winston Smith has a *body*. From this body can spring love, curiosity, and desire, hence a whole value system, a "mute protest in your own bones" (63) that empowers him, ultimately, to distinguish good from evil. It is interesting that to break Winston, O'Brien not only inflicts him with pain but shows him his own bodily emaciation. O'Brien must establish that all the state-sanctioned definitions of Winston— Winston as a "legal" entity—are more important than his physical reality. He must prove that Winston's bones are mere bones, bearers of no mute protest, and that their survival or destruction is arbitrary compared with the status accorded them by the state (just as Russia's existence becomes arbitrary once it is "outlawed," as in Reagan's joke).

But as always, the act contains the seeds of its own undoing. In laying waste the body, O'Brien proves its importance. None of the twisted logic at which O'Brien is so adept can finally do the job by itself; to break Winston the Party *must* attack him physically. It must play to Winston's nightmares, meaning it must acknowledge the body that can feel fear and thus have nightmares. And in granting these bodily experiences, it implicitly grants all the others. The Party cannot finally prove Winston wrong for believing that people store "in their hearts and bellies and muscles the power that would one day overturn the world" (181). It claims "we shall squeeze you empty, and then we shall fill you with ourselves" (211), but even by claiming this it allows that there was something to be squeezed out in the first place. (O'Brien himself is an enemy of his own argument, since his willingness to participate in a drive for "power, pure power" (217) must also have its origin in some bodily state.[19])

On this irreducible premise of the body the Party's whole metaphysics falters.[20] To create reality entirely "within" people is not to create it at all, for it grants that there is some separate reality within. And if this fundamental core of humanity exists, then so can everything else O'Brien denies: the earth, the past, facts, dinosaur bones. If there is a *human* nature then there is a nature, and if that, then a way of being true or adequate to nature—if only in the sense of respecting the irreducible fact of its existence.

If we believe in nothing else, we may believe in the "stuff" of the world, starting with the body. This is the starting point for a nonrelativism that is not simply fundamentalism—a metaphysics that does not just reinstate the rigid assumptions of earlier epochs (by contrast with which, modern animism and relativism are reforms). Rather, this metaphysics would allow for complexity and even disagreement in matters of fundamental cultural outlook, so long as there remained an underlying sense of a physically true reality of which each of us is a trustee. Trusteeship of physical creation must be a function of each creature, not of some abstract agency supposedly standing for "all of us." Beyond that basic sense of trusteeship, it would not be necessary nor even, possibly, desirable that everyone agree on how exactly to construe nature and human nature. Such agreement on specifics as there has been up to now has, as I will argue below, contributed to feelings of helplessness over nuclear weapons. Politics should not be mistaken for metaphysics, but in a sense neither should metaphysics. There is no use in simply moving from a denial that there is any fixed reality to an insistence that reality is everything we have been taught to believe it is. For in that direction lies a willingness to let the culture's most powerful institutions decide what reality is—exactly the problem from which we were just fleeing. To avoid this relativistic circle, we want neither to avoid questioning even very basic assumptions, nor to question them outside a framework of basic respect for human physical existence and the world that supports it.

VI.

So the most productive attitude at present would be one that respected basic reality and humanness even if there remains disagreement over what precisely these entail. Now, I can see three major objections to this thesis, all from intellectual traditions I have drawn upon in this book. First, some versions of the contemporary philosophy of discourse would argue that if we are serious about seeing history as discourse, we would have to give up on being "true to nature." They would hold, in other words, to a kind of relativism of their own: that truth is a quality of statements, not of the world, so that rather than "grounding" statements in "reality" all we can measure is how well they contribute to some discourse or other.[21] Thus, even if Winston Smith were correct for discursive reasons in preferring "two plus two equals four" to "two plus two equals five," he would not be correct in some absolute sense. Even mathematical discourses, it would be said, are reinvented all the time.

The second objection is that which might be raised by traditional Augustinians. It must sound strange to call respect for existence an Augustinian metaphysics, since Augustinianism in its original religious and theological form involved a condemnation of the physical realm—particularly the body and its (apparent) desires. What we are living with today is the original secularization of that idea, which stressed this condemnation and so has been used to underwrite harsh and dangerous policies.

But that is not the only way Augustinianism can be secularized, nor is it the right way where the nuclear-armed state is concerned. In fact, so far the one objection answers the other. The whole thrust of discursive theories of history is that the secular versions of Augustinianism that have prevailed so far —what I am calling fundamentalisms—have tried to overspecify what is natural and so have included too many things, so that eventually we ended up with even particular machines and particular political organizations coming to be believed in the way God was traditionally believed in. Against this, Augustinianism as a metaphysics (as I am calling for it) offsets discursive theory with the reminder that there is *something* real, something that isn't just discourse, that remains in any conceivable world, no matter how "demystified." As I just noted, we want to be very leery of trying to say that something has this particular content or that, this particular tendency or that. But if we still believe in history of any kind, then we must also believe in the basic reality of the creatures who inhabit that history and of the world in which it happens. Maybe history is just how people talk, but then there must be people talking, and some ground on which they meet in order to talk. The discursive view may teach us that history, like a modernist novel, has a meaningless plot and no theme at all. But it cannot deny that there are characters and settings. Even the most avant-garde fiction gives you that.

So the right way to secularize Augustinianism is *not*, "Our enemy is incorrigibly sinful; knowledge is irreversible; the power of our state is the only hope. Therefore, we must forever threaten nuclear destruction." The right way is, Humanness, at its most basic level of needs and desires, is undying, for good or ill. The desires may be warped or misguided, especially as they are given play in the world of historical circumstance. But finally they are real, and no policies or ideas can be rational at the level of first principles without taking account of them, starting with the right of the beings who embody them to exist.

Finally, there is a third counterargument to be brought against any view, including mine, that finds a solution to our problem in the values of the Western Enlightenment. Enlightenment principles are everywhere encoded in my claims for intellectual honesty and human rights based on human nature, and the counterargument would be simply that these are the principles that got us in trouble in the first place. They were, in fact, partly outgrowths of modern ways of thinking I have here been criticizing. Moreover, they have arguably displaced other important values, "organic" values of cooperation and community that go completely against my call for greater political contentiousness.[22]

This is a tougher objection to answer because I, too, believe in those organic values. They partly figure into my own idea of trusteeship, since what we would hold in trust is the organic reality of our worlds and our bodies. In the end, maybe pure community and some kind of "resacralization" should be the true goal for the world. But meanwhile we are bound to *believe* in something, to engage the world intellectually as well as spiritually or organically. I am proposing beliefs that make use of aspects of what most people currently think—beliefs that can be extracted from the same discourses that gave rise to the prevailing beliefs. I can only suggest that such beliefs would be historically easier to achieve than a new growth of community (though I know it has been argued otherwise), and that they would logically guide the movement of discourse from where we are now to where we would be in Utopia.

This is not a meaningless quarrel, since whether we make these interim moves or embrace the "organic" ideal directly makes a difference in terms of tactics. The organic ideal is usually held to be achievable locally: one builds up new forms of community wherever one lives, until the whole world is eventually changed from the ground up. My call for restoration of certain Enlightenment values suggests a program aimed directly at the top: one works through the media and through political organizing to reorient whole discourses of the culture. I believe what makes my goals achievable (and what the organicists have usually failed to see) is that the work at the top *is* conceived in terms of discourses—far more easily manipulable things than the grand economic forces and seemingly unmovable "interests" that have usually been thought the problem at that level.

VII.

But there is little use arguing that people should see things this way; the real question is whether they will. One cannot really speak of what "we should" do, having taken apart the whole notion that such a "we" exists to meet the obligation. However, having outlined what ideally ought to be happening, we have grounds for believing also that it will happen. For if some essence of humanness exists to be protected, it also exists to act, to assert itself on behalf of itself. It is a fault in the prevailing secularized Augustinianism that it assumes that the desires of a fallen humanity produce the same sorry result in all historical circumstances. In fact, as I have tried to show, cultural history is complex and full of ironies, and a given desire, once turned loose in history, can produce any number of effects, including the opposite of whatever it originally aimed to produce.

Failure to see this, and belief in too rigid and specific a notion of human nature, have led on the one hand to Jonathan Schell's impossible call for disarmament as a sheer existential act of will, and on the other to strategists' belief (and the public's, when it isn't just relativistic) that nuclear weapons are tragically rooted in a human nature that ensures eternal hostility and threat. Both these extreme views fail to grasp the complex truth about culture and history. Human nature cannot be canceled at will, but (apart from its basic bodily reality) it is also not some one thing that has the same orientation and effect no matter what. Culture may take different forms as human nature plays itself out historically, and there is no reason to suppose that the ironies that result from this can only hurt and never help us—that President Reagan's abhorrence of nuclear weapons can increase our danger from them, for instance, but that a similar anxiety, in other circumstances, might not with equal irony help produce some kind of safety. Our vices may be defects of our virtues, but the reverse may be true as well.

Some of the threatening political tendencies I have spoken of already hint at this truth, for like Shakespeare's monarchism and Reagan's moralism they dialectically undercut their own overt content. The antipolitical politics of today expresses not just hope but also, paradoxically, anxiety and frustration at the feeling that history has ended. Totalitarianism has been attributed in part to the complexity and confusion of modern life and to the apparent meaninglessness of the individual within it. People turn to the paternalistic and self-justifying state or Party when they feel they can't govern the forces that govern them, even if, ironically, the state is itself one of the main such forces. Much the same observation seems to apply to our own, nontotalitarian situation too. People today who say that might makes right are not so much committed to that view (relativists, after all, supposedly aren't committed to *any* view), but rather are afraid of not acknowledging the power of might and thus ending up, like Winston Smith, on its wrong side. The problem is that they have stopped distinguishing the factual situation—power often does prevail—from the way things *should* be; and they have rationalized this by concluding that there isn't any "way things should be" to begin with.

The same fear, that power will do what it will and that the danger is being left out altogether, would explain some of the other political peculiarities of our era. When black leaders said blacks should turn Republican after having their overwhelming electoral choices repudiated in 1984 by Republicans, they were expressing, in part, a desire that blacks go on being political. And this desire no doubt came in turn from frustration at the lingering racism still out there, racism that proves history isn't over and that demands political action, but that also is harder to put one's finger on than it was in the days of Birmingham and Selma (hence those black leaders' feeling that it was no longer obvious which political party represented opposition to it).

Similarly, those antiapartheid demonstrators bedeviled by "apolitical" counterprotesters are themselves acting out a form of apolitical politics driven partly by this same frustration. They take up apartheid as a safer and starker issue, an easier issue to get a grip on, than anything currently on offer in our own invisible, seemingly omnipotent state.[23] For history more obviously has not yet ended in South Africa, and the South African state more obviously is not omnipotent. South Africa is an arena where invoking higher values against power doesn't automatically seem senseless and naive.

One of the most common political attitudes today is the simple dismissal of politics as a charade. "Who cares?" says Julia in *1984*. "It's always one bloody war after another, and one knows the news is all lies anyway" (128). Reagan called ordinary people "heroes," and journalists show solicitude for those whom, supposedly, they admire for not being as obsessed with politics as the journalists themselves: "Most people, of course, are too busy waiting on tables, filling teeth, planting crops and raising children to follow the intricacies of government."[24] The John Does of the country are its back-bone precisely because they mind their own business; if they start getting "ideological" they cease to be John Does. (Of course, by the deeper defini-tion of ideology, they are never *more* ideological than when minding their own business.) This attitude is unquestionably dangerous. But, like the others I've been discussing, it too contains promising elements—elements of skepticism and respect for private interests. For even while it concedes the state a large sphere of action, privatism also refuses to yield it every value. In a sense, Julia plays into Big Brother's hands with her "Who cares?" but in another sense it is this attitude that frees her for the private concerns that Big Brother correctly views as a dire threat.

In short, the present situation rests on many factors that happen to reinforce each other at the moment but that could also break apart. In fact, the dynamics of discourse are such that they almost certainly will. Cultural beliefs give rise to their opposites—or, in the technical terms I have used in order to describe the dynamic more precisely, expressions within a dis-course encode the very anxieties they try to repress, and those anxieties, inevitably, become the basis of counterexpressions. Discourses, therefore, constantly shift and re-form; coalitions arise and eventually disperse. His-tory created the nuclear crisis, and history can end it—may be ending it even now.[25]

VIII.

The term *coalitions* suggests the possible role of political activity in all this. One reason I prefer discursive analysis over sociological and economic vocabularies that have sometimes pointed in similar directions is that the idea of discourse preserves a sense of the human role in making history (though this might be denied by some of the idea's stricter exponents). For unlike Marxist economic determinism, or even the psychoanalysts' "return of the repressed" (which comes a bit closer), discourse suggests how things can be *made* to change. Discourse can itself become an object of discourse; that which had seemed metaphysically given can become a point of debate and contention, and at last be argued away. The past is full of examples of this happening. That which precipitates out of discourse, especially if it is troublesome or evil, becomes something to talk about, and the talk changes history. At any historical moment, many different discourses are all crossing and recrossing—far more of these, even, than we find in a Shakespeare play. This is precisely why people in a given time and place are able to disagree with each other. And it is also why they are able to disagree with themselves: that is, change their minds.

So it matters how people are thinking, how they've made up their minds. If positive ironies are possible and if history doesn't just go one way, then there is no substitute for persistent, conscious political pressure designed to keep it moving in the way desired. Returning to politics may seem an anticlimactic proposal, but the politics will be different if it is based on true cultural history. It will be less likely to fall victim to the prevailing metaphysics. It will be based on a more profound understanding of people's interests and how these translate into events, how they arise and change.

Specifically, a new antinuclear politics would:

1) *Reflect a newly sophisticated understanding of the relationship between people's personal feelings about things and their political actions (or inactions)*. In a world where political discourse is saturated with animism, it is easy even for opponents of prevailing policy to confuse what happens between states with what happens between people. It is easy to overlook what Rousseau said long ago: "War is not a relation between man and man, but between State and State, and individuals are enemies accidentally."[26] The official U.S. posture toward the Soviet Union is not an expression of individual Americans' aggressiveness (at least not in any simple, one-to-one fashion). Thus, calls for people to "make friends with Russia," as Dr. Helen Caldicott has urged, risk irrelevance or, worse, risk becoming part of the problem they are aimed against.[27] (As John Lewis Gaddis has noted, nearly every major war of the past 150 years has involved nations whose citizens knew each other well—all too well.[28]) Relationships between the personal and the political are filtered through animism and other modern ways of thinking, and close attention needs to be paid to the social and historical dynamics that convert individual good will and good intentions into world-threatening crises and standoffs.

I am here rejecting the premises which I earlier described as functionalist: that particular conditions and policies persist because they serve some distinct needs. It may be that the beliefs that underlie policy serve such needs. But, first, the needs themselves are historical constructions that change over time. And second, the same needs, in a different discursive context, can produce wholly different policies and actions. There is no one-to-one correspondence between a human urge and a given form of behavior (let alone a particular outcome). This is one of the key lessons of depth psychology. People rarely, if ever, take a single action based on a single, static belief. Ronald Reagan did not inexplicably like nuclear weapons and so decide to build some. Rather, as I tried to show, he hated them in a certain way which, given the context of his actions, ironically led to his building them.

What ordinary people do arises out of similarly dynamic interplays of feelings and attitudes—attitudes which, in addition, reflect perceptions that are rooted in cultural ways of formulating and talking about things—that are, in other words, discursive. Hence there are numerous ways of explaining people's actions apart from dismissing them as sadistic or stupid. And—the really good news—there are numerous points of possible intervention in people's behavior. It is not necessarily the case that we must get people to "change" their "beliefs." What we need to encourage are discursive shifts. Discursive shifts are the restructurings of the discourses that give rise to beliefs, the smaller movements and recombinations of ideas that can neutralize an attitude just as effectively as a conscious change of position. Expecting bigger, more obvious changes is part of what makes a problem seem intractable. What ought to be looked for instead are transfers of given beliefs into new contexts in which they take on different colorations, have different outcomes, perhaps even ironically reverse themselves.

People's political behavior is especially vulnerable to discursive shifts because political attitudes are crossed by additional discourses beyond those that shape private attitudes. This means that in many cases, political behavior is not very deeply rooted; it is especially vulnerable to being literally talked away. The difficulty of correlating public action or inaction (frequently bad) with individual people's private desires and values (nearly always good) drives some antinuclearists to despair, but in fact, by this analysis, it is a main reason for hope.

2) *Show respect for, as well as attention to, people's personal and private feelings.* People's private concerns—homes, jobs, families, communities—are not simply enemies of public action. They are, rather, what make people value peace. Therefore they, in turn, should be valued. This recognition would lead to a different kind of agenda for the antinuclear opposition. It would lead to skepticism about certain antinuclear arguments—Jonathan Schell's belief that we should "let our daily business drop from our hands for a while," for example, or Helen Caldicott's call for people to "take the world on their shoulders like Atlas, forgetting all other priorities in their lives, and to say *I* will save the earth."[29] Since people presently do not perceive themselves to be acting badly or failing to value the valuable, such calls tend to fall on deaf ears—or, again, worse: they risk denying the value of private concerns and interests that can actually help to mitigate the problem.

Recognizing those interests, moreover, steers one away from the organic or lifestyle strategy, whereby new forms of community and personal life are cultivated as a seedbed for new national and international political arrangements. Changing people's fundamental ways of life is slow and difficult and runs counter to most people's everyday wishes. But the greater problem is that it might not even work. The notion that people project into politics the forms of their personal lives and interactions is as questionable as the notion that they plainly and simply act on their beliefs.

3) *Never rule out any human impulse as irredeemably bad.* If given outcomes do not follow in one-to-one fashion from willed intentions, then by the same token we never know which urges might, in the right context, prove politically helpful. Even the morally impermissible act of attacking the human body may arise from good motives that have been contextually warped. This is undoubtedly true for many individual soldiers in combat. It may also be true at the national level, in the sense that citizens' willingness to see other countries' attacks as aimed personally at them comes from an awareness of the body's value (combined with an animistic conflation of one's body and the state, so that an enemy nation's assault on one's state is felt as an assault on oneself and, unfortunately, as a license to strike back at the real people who make up that nation).

We need to remember that even major problems—like the animistic view of the state, or the shift from ritual combat to technologized modern war—began as reforms, as attempts to escape some earlier, overly rigid social order or metaphysics. And the modern attitudes continue to have credibility because of people's deep (though again, contextually warped) intuitions about the value of human life and safety. People accord absolute moral authority to the modern state, for example, to the same extent that they perceive it to represent a morally nonnegotiable good: their own collective physical existence and the naturalness of their goals and desires.

This principle will be easier to follow if we also remember two other things. One is that no tendency we discover at work in cultural history is total. Modern attitudes, as we have repeatedly seen, do not replace pre-modern ones but work underneath or alongside them. This is what leads to the irony of contradictory views contributing to the same grim result; but it also reveals some politically useful facts. It indicates that cultures are conservative and tend to maintain valued older traditions in some form somewhere. And it points toward the possibility of recovering those traditions, of making use of what is socially beneficial in them. We have, in a sense, the discourses of our whole culture's history available to work with all at once—Pelagian optimism, the just-war tradition, the belief that technology is bound up with virtue, and many others that might be used in constructing some new politics.

The second thing to remember is that the initial way an idea enters cultural discourse is often by being resisted or worried over. We saw many examples of this in Shakespeare: absolute kingship, for instance, recognized both through explicit arguments against it (as by the soldier Williams) and through its seeming to be abjured (as when Henry claims he is "bootless").[30] This, again, argues against taking the presence of any given idea in culture as a complete victory for that idea. It is true that some ideas carry the day, but almost always in the company of resistance to them (which indeed is inscribed in the winning ideas themselves). And it follows that when true reforms finally do take hold—for instance, when our world finally agrees that the state and its interests are not morally self-justifying—

we may not recognize them, for they will appear first in the guise of denials and counterclaims. Which means there may be reforms afoot at this very moment that simply haven't been understood as such.

4) *Do less moralizing and more analyzing.* Antinuclear discourse currently tends to limit and simplify the problems it deals with in the interest of moving more rapidly to exhortation. Yet precisely by trying to exhort, it ends up being struck speechless, unable to say much of anything about the problem's roots except by bad-mouthing political and military leaders or complaining that "we" are doing something wrong.

The approaches that make praising and blaming easiest also make analyzing hardest. Analysis is best served if we assume that people are well intentioned—so that if they are nonetheless producing bad policies then there is a dynamic to be explained. Real explanation involves theory, which is why theories of history and of the arms race are largely what this book has been about. But theory is not just some arid academic concern. Even (or especially) if not consciously articulated, theories structure everyone's thought and behavior all the time. The antinuclear debate in large part consists of a clashing of assumed theories, which often prove to be dramatically at cross-purposes to each other.

There are examples of this in Emile de Antonio's docudrama *In the King of Prussia,* about the trial of several antinuclear protesters convicted of breaking into a Pennsylvania nuclear weapons facility and symbolically attacking the warheads under construction there. At one point Daniel Berrigan, reenacting testimony he gave in his own defense, speaks to the jury in language full of we-they, leaders-versus-people fallacies. Don't side with these people who build the warheads, he says (though some of those people were the jurors' neighbors), or with this court that serves such people's interests (though the jurors had sworn to do that court's work). Berrigan is working from a wrong theory of popular attitudes: specifically, from a belief that ordinary people, including the jurors, considered themselves to be more at odds with their own society's leaders than with courageous but marginal figures like himself. No doubt believing he was acting from compassion, he spoke as if taking the jurors' side against those inexplicably ill-intentioned leaders.[31]

But crucial to compassion is assuming that people do think what they think and mean it, though they may not necessarily intend all of its consequences. (Traditional antinuclear exhortative writing gets this backwards. It assumes that people aren't already thinking something—that their beliefs have no positive content—but that somehow they *are* intending nuclear weapons and so need to be argued away from them.) In regard to the King of Prussia jurors, compassion involves assuming that such individuals, too, have their theories, that they are not just misinformed or manipulated. And political effectiveness requires grasping what those theories are: beliefs, for instance, about the legitimacy of the state and, in this case, the importance of protecting property. One juror interviewed for d'Antonio's film said the

King of Prussia jury was in agreement that nuclear weapons were a terrible threat, perhaps portending doom for the world. But the jurors could not see their way clear to disavowing the cultural institutions that built those weapons—institutions on which people perceive themselves to depend. Berrigan was asking them to abandon that dependence without offering them another way of grounding their lives that would be as coherent and sustaining. Perhaps he saw the jurors as lacking something, as experiencing an emptiness that his moral heroism could fill. But in their view, the situation was more likely the reverse: they already had something and were being asked to trade it for a kind of existential blankness—for a life of what must have struck them as sheer, willful, impractical courage.

5) *Work to change discourse so that people's good intentions are realized in actual practice.* This does not become possible until we have granted those good intentions and begun to analyze their peculiar outcomes, as discussed above. But once we do grant them, we again discover all kinds of useful material that history has given us to work with. In d'Antonio's film, one worker from the nuclear weapons plant argues that plant personnel did not understand themselves to be working on nuclear weapons. They didn't know, he says, what those nose cones actually were for. The worker seems simply to be lying—to himself, certainly, and perhaps to the jury and the filmmaker. But even such a lie is a positive sign, for it shows that this worker (and others too, if he really does speak for them) senses evil in the building of nuclear weapons and wants to distance himself from it. The job of politics is to get people like this to truly distance themselves from such efforts, instead of falsely or partially distancing themselves by doing (or supporting) the work but denying its real meaning. The job is to eliminate people's need for engaging in doublethink.

Here is an example that points to how this could happen. It is from a televised interview between Ted Koppel of ABC News and then-Secretary of State George Shultz, following ABC's 1983 screening of the nuclear war drama *The Day After*. Shultz had just reiterated that U.S. policy foresaw no necessity of nuclear war, and Koppel said:

> Mr. Shultz, that is an answer of the secretary of state to a reporter and that's fair enough, because that's what you and I respectively are. But what if you were answering the question to your son or to your granddaughter. What would a grandfather—what would a George Shultz who is talking to a member of his family say in response to the same question?

Shultz's reply was simple: "I would give the same answer."[32]

Now, those who strongly object to current policy hear that answer and either suspect leaders like Shultz of some kind of duplicity, of not acting on values they would act on as private citizens; or, they deplore those leaders' obtuseness in not seeing this gap between policy and values. Yet this exchange actually seems full of hopeful signs. First, Shultz and Koppel both agree that policy *ought* to make sense in terms of ordinary values that anyone could grasp and explain to his or her children. Second, Shultz values integrity—he needs to believe that he himself does not have two faces, one private and one official. Third, Koppel suspects (or voices for others a widely held suspicion) that current policy and officials can't possibly be so well integrated, since manifestly there is something very dangerous in the world. And while he may go about it clumsily, his question is intuitively aimed at uncovering this deformation of intentions that gives us kindly grandfathers participating in what seems to many a great danger. The question indicates some level of awareness that nuclear policy is something other than a simple outcome of willed decisions, with each official view A producing policy Q.

And finally, the whole exchange demonstrates what can happen in discourse, as people talk (and especially as they talk publicly) about these things. It may seem this particular question and answer changed nothing. But that is just because so much was agreed on by the principals going in. The secretary of state is not going to be interviewed on television saying things that leave the discourse altogether, that violate the basic premises of the questions. Hence he has already moved some distance toward the questioner, or has been picked for his job because he was already there. He is under a certain pressure from the discourse, in other words, pressure to say some things and not others. And if we believe that he really doesn't have two faces, then we must also assume that he believes those things and will not say anything substantially different in private, whether to his granddaughter or to the president. (There is every reason to think, as we saw in chapter 5, that a similar degree of personal integration characterized the president Shultz happened to serve.)

True, the question was mild; one might want the discourse to exert more pressure than that—and so to shift more quickly. But the tracks on which it might do so have already been laid. Even the mildest question inscribes crucial values. The shift from their precarious realization in the present discursive context to their fuller realization in some other is a process that happens gradually, as each answer gives rise to new, slightly different questions, which narrow the space for the old answer and open up spaces for new ones. But there is no reason to suppose that this process isn't occurring.

6) *Finally, always strive to keep cultural discourses going.* There is nothing left to work with if discourses are shut down, or if the urges they embody are left unacknowledged. In practice, this rule would require that peace groups stop doing things like organizing boycotts of TV movies, as the antinuclear group SANE/Freeze did over ABC-TV's *Amerika*. A text like *Amerika* either is or is not going to strike some responsive chord in people; if it doesn't, no harm done, and if it does, then that event, too, needs to be studied, needs to become part of the discourse. The discursive view of things argues for total commitment to the First Amendment. For we can

never be absolutely sure where a discourse is going. The working-through of a public anxiety can create problems, but in the long run it can also solve them. What is needed is to hear the anxieties while continuing to exert conscious, sustained political pressure on the George Shultzes and Ted Koppels of the world. For though the discourses ought to be kept going, there is nothing wrong with intervening in them to the greatest extent possible—the goal being to bring about shifts in discourse that will open up space for new ways of getting anxieties resolved.

All these principles boil down to the idea that people can be respected even while things they do are opposed. Antinuclearists have failed in subtle ways to practice this idea—thus ironically proving how easy it is for good intentions to be warped by circumstance. And since it is so easy, one can never fully assess intentions by looking at outcomes, which means there is no good substitute for assuming the best about people and, so, respecting their desires. In fact one must do so to accomplish anything, for those desires are the materials out of which new worlds are shaped. There is a temptation, once something like the bomb is no longer regarded as tragically eternal, to assume it has no roots at all outside the nation's leadership and so can be opposed directly—as if someone were willing it to exist and we could counter that will with our own. I have tried to show both that someone (indeed, nearly everyone) *is* willing the bomb to exist, but also that this willing is a very complex business, which means opposing it is a matter of thinking and analyzing as much as willing.

Put another way, cultural history demonstrates *both* the contingency and the rootedness of things. To be effective, a political program for change— on the nuclear question or, for that matter, any other—needs to recognize both. It needs to take the contingency as a reason not to despair (for change is possible), and the rootedness as a reason to be conservative and cautious. There are positive urges behind certain states' reliance on nuclear weapons and people's trust in the policies of those states. These "pronuclear" attitudes have their inner dimensions of health and so can wind up undercutting themselves, just as antinuclear urges sometimes do. The political task is to shift the favorable elements to the fore. The world needs people's intuitive respect for the physical self but not their attaching of this to the state. It needs the state's pursuit of collective goods but not the state as a fetish. It needs open-mindedness that is not mere relativism; it needs truth to nature that is not mere technique. But the point is that, somewhere, it already has these things.

IX.

I have dwelt in this book on literature and film mainly because they are part of cultural history and give us access to the discourses that ultimately concern us. But there is one further lesson we can learn from the narrative arts. Narrative can be viewed as an exercise in moralizing, analogous to the moralizing I criticized above. In a work of fiction, one does not have actual human beings, one has characters. And what distinguishes characters from people is that characters exist for particular purposes, purposes defined and limited by the narrative artist's moral vision. Characters' activities are meaningful to the extent that they help advance the plot. Even the most fully rounded main character's life derives its meaning from some narrative function; this is why it "must" follow the course it does. One could say that without its climax and eventual outcome, and without the theme these implicitly convey, even the protagonist's life, in any classically constructed story, is meaningless. (Modernist fiction has experimented with narratives that violate these rules, but the esoteric quality of such fictions, and their failure to catch hold with general readers—if they were ever intended to— make these experiments the exceptions that prove the rule.)

This principle of narrative has profound consequences when it becomes part of one's real-world outlook—as for most of us, most of the time, it does. We have all read stories or watched movies in which someone is killed without being mourned. Perhaps the character was a "bad guy," or perhaps he was a good guy whom we didn't know enough about to fully concern ourselves with. (Good narrative artists know exactly how much to tell us or not tell us about given characters, depending on how much we are meant to care about them.) Perhaps the character only existed to get shot or tomahawked or thrown overboard. It is all right for this to happen in a story; well-managed plots even require it.

But it is not all right in real life. In real life, there is no one who exists just to serve some purpose, let alone the purpose of getting killed. People just exist; they don't need to prove they deserve to.

Modern, state-sponsored violence and threats of violence presuppose otherwise, for they necessarily reduce people to characters or, more precisely, to types: the criminal, the enemy, the godless communist. To lash out at someone physically is to subsume that person's physical reality to the role played by the person as social being—a role to which, if we are attacking the person, we presumably object. Animism complements this basic dynamic of violence by reducing whole peoples to types: "we" good guys, "the allies," "the Warsaw Pact," "the Russians." It thus becomes possible to narratize the whole world, to cast (literally in the theatrical sense) whole peoples as characters in the drama that constitutes a culture's dominant worldview—in our case, the dramatic tale of American virtue saving the world. (Even the most moderate proponents of deterrence, those who avoid simplistically stereotyping the enemy, base their advocacy of nuclear threats on scenarios—which is to say, on imagined stories, stories they hope to see come out in certain ways.)

Luckily, since drama is a kind of discourse, people's narrative constructions of the world can shift and change too. The actors can switch roles (as Germany and Japan did after World War II) and, ultimately, the story itself can change, even evolve a different ending. History is a narrative that is still being written. And it is a narrative to whose writing we can all contribute.

But we fail to do this if we narratize the world ourselves, reducing our own political opposition to a story of, for instance, heroic martyrs rescuing innocent people at large from the clutches of an inexplicably evil national leadership (the scenario Daniel Berrigan seemed vaguely to want to convey to his jury). Ideally everyone, including antinuclearists, would give up trying to narratize experience altogether. While guided by moral insight, people would stop trying to fix other people or groups into rigid moral roles, as characters are fixed. They would recognize that history isn't really a story at all in the sense of following any particular moral course; it is more like the book in which all our stories are written. And they would recognize that those stories go beyond our own. Not only each human being, but the nonhuman creation as well, has the right to play (and to write) its own part. This is precisely what the deploying of nuclear weapons fails to acknowledge. Even if history is read as drama, it ought not be read as a specifically *human* drama.

So the last lesson we learn from studying literature is to recognize and avoid the literary tendencies in our own thinking. Literature distills real life and so gives us an important kind of access to it. But that doesn't mean we ought to treat life as if it were literature. Those who want nuclear policy to be different need to model this recognition. They need to stop moralizing and narratizing the world themselves, and instead acknowledge the complex reality that happens at present to keep their wishes from being realized but that could, under other circumstances, help those same wishes come to pass. They need to stop casting the various parties to the cultural debate as heroes, victims, or mustache-twirling villains. For just as there is no "we," there is also no "they." Just as there is no protagonist with some grand, ineluctable destiny, so there is no enemy with evil written on his heart. There is a world of individual, usually well-intended political choices; there are policies that represent the (often paradoxical) outcome of those choices; and there are possibilities for intervening in policy, for mobilizing what support one can on behalf of the safest and the best.

As discourses shift, new ideas do enter culture and old ones are, in effect, unthought. There is nothing mystical about getting this to happen, not even in the case of nuclear weapons. It is said that politics is the art of the possible, meaning resign yourself to what little is possible. But the same phrase can mean, Anything is possible if it's within the realm of politics. Ending the nuclear threat is within the realm of politics.

Notes

1. Ancient of Days

1. Oppenheimer and Truman are quoted in Paul Chilton, "Nukespeak: Nuclear Language, Culture, and Propaganda," in Chilton, ed., *Nukespeak: The Media and the Bomb* (London: Comedia, 1982), p. 97. Churchill is quoted in Spencer R. Weart, *Nuclear Fear: A History of Images* (Cambridge, Mass.: Harvard University Press, 1988), p. 102.

2. See Chilton for a discussion of how this view has been expressed in public statements regarding nuclear weapons. Chilton argues that when military officials today use terms like *Poseidon,* it is a more or less deliberate effort on their part to obscure the human origins of the weapons, thus removing them from the realm of political controversy. I am not distinguishing here between such a deliberate and guileful use of religious language and its apparently more innocent use by earlier scientists, like Oppenheimer.

3. I will follow common practice here in using the term *the bomb* to refer to the global system of nuclear deployments, the integration of these into national strategies, and their overall readiness for use in warfare. Similarly, *antinuclear* refers to opposition to current policies pertaining to nuclear weapons, not nuclear power.

4. Herman Kahn's *Thinking about the Unthinkable in the 1980s* (New York: Simon and Schuster, 1984) is a revealing exposition of some of the premises of these views. There are some who question the directness of Kahn's influence on policy, but he clearly looms large within the school of thinking that leads highly respected strategic theorists like Colin S. Gray and Keith Payne to promote "rational" preparations for the waging of nuclear war. Although this book is not principally about these schools of thinking, the specifics of current U.S. nuclear policy are discussed further in chapter 5.

5. Jonathan Schell, *The Fate of the Earth* (New York: Avon, 1982), p. 115.

6. Kahn, p. 38; the Harvard Nuclear Study Group, *Living with Nuclear Weapons* (New York: Bantam, 1983), pp. 253–54. The precise Einstein quote is: "The unleashed power of the atom has changed everything save our modes of thinking."

7. The quoted phrases are from Thomas Powers, "What Is It About?" *Atlantic*, January 1984, p. 55, but they are also to be found in any number of other accounts.

8. There are minority or dissenting strategy professionals who are not complacent. They comprise a school of which Bernard Brodie is sometimes named founder and spokesman, and it is no coincidence that Brodie's views, for instance in *War and Politics* (New York: Macmillan, 1973), in important ways overlap with my own. But I am here speaking of the currently dominant voices in the discourse.

9. Leo Marx, *The Machine in the Garden: Technology and the Pastoral Ideal in America* (Oxford: Oxford University Press, 1964), p. 4.

10. Brodie, p. 277.

11. Peter Wyden, *Day One: Before Hiroshima and After* (New York: Simon and Schuster, 1984), p. 43.

12. Mary Midgley's phrase, from "To What End?" (review of several books), *Guardian* (London), 10 July 1987.

13. Powers, p. 55.

14. John E. Mack, "The Perception of U.S.-Soviet Intentions and Other Psychological Dimensions of the Nuclear Arms Race," *American Journal of Orthopsychiatry* 52:4, October 1982, p. 594.

15. The Eisenhower, McNamara, and Carter stories are told in Peter Pringle and William Arkin, *SIOP: Nuclear War from the Inside* (London: Sphere Books, 1983). Quotes are from pp. 77, 132–33. Herbert Scoville, formerly of the CIA, tells the MIRVing story in Robert Scheer, *With Enough Shovels: Reagan, Bush and Nuclear War* (New York: Random House, 1982), p. 98.

16. Melissa Healey, "Even with Targets Gone, U.S. Missile Has a Future," *Los Angeles Times,* 29 November 1987; David Evans, "Arms Pact's Hidden Gains," *Chicago Tribune,* 20 September 1987.

17. Lord Zuckerman, "Nuclear Fantasies" (book review), *New York Review of Books,* 14 June 1984; Assistant Secretary of Defense Richard Perle as quoted by Christopher Hitchens, *The Nation,* 22 October 1983, p. 358; Theodore Draper (discussing Secretary of State Alexander Haig), "How Not to Think about Nuclear War," reprinted in *Present History: On Nuclear War, Detente, and Other Controversies* (New York: Vintage Books, 1984), p. 18.

18. Christopher Lasch, *The Minimal Self: Psychic Survival in Troubled Times* (New York: W. W. Norton, 1984), p. 241.

19. Also see Jonathan B. Stein, *From H-Bomb to Star Wars: The Politics of Strategic Decision-Making* (Lexington: Lexington Books, 1984), esp. pp. 48–49, for another example of a focus on conscious intentions.

20. David Dellinger, "The Bread Is Rising," in Michael Albert and Dellinger, eds., *Beyond Survival: New Directions for the Disarmament Movement* (Boston: South End Press, 1983), p. 13.

21. Namely in his denunciations of MAD, to be discussed in chapter 5.

22. Robert McNamara, "Surviving the Nuclear Age's First Century," *Guardian* (London), 29 June 1987. The civil-disobedience case in question was heard in the Lake County, Illinois, criminal courts in the spring of 1985.

23. Brodie, chapter 7, pp. 276ff.

24. For a full exposition see Robert Jay Lifton and Richard Falk, *Indefensible Weapons: The Political and Psychological Case Against Nuclearism* (New York: Basic Books, 1982). I will not deal here with the problem of how psychic numbing theory is derived, though it seems questionable to analogize, as Lifton does, from the experience of victims of actual blast, heat, and radiation to the behavior of people whose victimization consists solely of living with the threat of such things.

25. Also in a neologistic vein, R. J. Lifton uses the term *nuclearism,* a word I will also borrow, but for quite different purposes, in chapter 6.

26. Robert Paul Wolff, *The Ideal of the University* (Boston: Beacon Press, 1969), p. 71, emphasis in original.

27. Reported by Conor Cruise O'Brien in the *Times* (London), 10 June 1987, p. 16.

28. Kahn, p. 63.

29. Robert Wuthnow, *Meaning and Moral Order: Explorations in Cultural Analysis* (Berkeley: University of California Press, 1987), p. 339.

30. A point Sherry Turkle repeated, as it happens, with respect to Freud's own ideas: "Psychoanalysis has taught us that resistance to a theory is part of its cultural impact." Turkle, *The Second Self: Computers and the Human Spirit* (London: Granada, 1984), p. 323.

31. From Foucault's *The Archeology of Knowledge,* trans. A. M. Sheridan Smith (New York: Pantheon, 1972) and other writings.

32. Richard Rorty, "The Contingency of Language," *London Review of Books,* 17 April 1986, pp. 3–6, emphasis in original.

33. Ian Hacking, "The Archeology of Foucault," in David Couzens Hoy, ed., *Foucault: A Critical Reader* (New York: Basil Blackwell, 1986), p. 28.

34. Richard Rorty, "Foucault and Epistemology," in Hoy, ed., *Foucault: A Critical*

Reader. Rorty calls this a "deflationary interpretation" of Foucault's "insistence on texts" and links it to a tradition that includes Wittgenstein and others as well.

35. Dana Gioia, "Strong Counsel" (book review), *The Nation*, 16 January 1988, p. 59.

36. Terry Eagleton, *Literary Theory: An Introduction* (London: Basil Blackwell, 1983), p. 203.

37. Eagleton, p. 213.

38. For instance, E. D. Hirsch, Jr. in "Back to History," in Gerald Graff and Reginald Gibbons, eds., *Criticism in the University* (Evanston: Northwestern University Press, 1985), pp. 189–97. Several other contributions to this volume, including the editors' own introduction, deal interestingly with these same issues.

39. Wayne C. Booth, "Reversing the Downward Spiral: Or, What Is the Graduate Program *For*?" *Profession 87* (a publication of the Modern Language Association of America), pp. 37–38, emphasis in original.

40. Robert Scholes, "Some Problems in Current Graduate Programs in English," ibid., p. 42.

41. Edward W. Said, *The World, the Text, and the Critic* (London: Faber and Faber, 1984), pp. 170 and 177; Eagleton, pp. 210 and 194–217; Gerald Graff, *Professing Literature: An Institutional History* (Chicago: University of Chicago Press, 1987), p. 257.

42. Graff, p. 256.

43. For Eagleton "it is surely becoming apparent that without a more profound understanding of such symbolic processes, through which political power is deployed, reinforced, resisted, at times subverted, we shall be incapable of unlocking the most lethal power-struggles now confronting us." *The Function of Criticism: From the Spectator to Post-Structuralism* (London: Verso, 1984), p. 124. And for the very influential Jacques Derrida, "specialists in discourse and in texts" are "doubly" entitled "to concern ourselves seriously with the nuclear issue" in this time when "the frontier is more undecidable than ever" between different fields and between rhetoric and the exercise of power. Derrida, "No Apocalypse, Not Now: (full speed ahead, seven missiles, seven missives)," *Diacritics* 14:2, summer 1984, p. 24.

44. See the essays by Hayden White, *Tropics of Discourse: Essays in Cultural Criticism* (Baltimore: Johns Hopkins University Press, 1978), and in Dominick LaCapra, *History and Criticism* (Ithaca: Cornell University Press, 1985).

45. For one classic example, see H. Stuart Hughes's "Is Contemporary History Real History?" *American Scholar* 32:4, autumn 1963, pp. 516–25.

46. "Eccentric" as it may seem to believe nuclear weapons and literature are related, says Eagleton, they inevitably are in the sense that "any body of theory concerned with human meaning, value, language, feeling and experience will inevitably engage with broader, deeper beliefs about the nature of human individuals and societies, problems of power and sexuality, interpretations of past history, versions of the present and hopes for the future." *Literary Theory*, p. 195.

47. Brodie, p. 380. As a major assumption of Jonathan Schell's, this idea that the technologically possible is also the inevitable is analyzed more closely in chapter 3.

2. Antinuclear Psychology and Antinuclear Theology

1. See Jim Garrison, *The Darkness of God: Theology After Hiroshima* (London: SCM, 1982).

2. Morris Schwartz, "The Social-Psychological Dimension of the Arms Race," in Paul Joseph and Simon Rosenblum, eds., *Search for Sanity: The Politics of Nuclear Weapons and Disarmament* (Boston: South End Press, 1984), p. 272.

3. John E. Mack, "The Perception of U.S.-Soviet Intentions and Other Psychological Dimensions of the Arms Race," *American Journal of Orthopsychiatry*, vol. 52, no. 4 (October 1982), p. 594.

4. Garry Wills, *Reagan's America: Innocents at Home* (Garden City: Doubleday, 1987).

5. Jack Beatty, "A Country of the Mind" (review of Wills's *Reagan's America*), *Atlantic Monthly*, March 1987, p. 90.

6. Ted Koppel, *The Jennings-Koppel Report: Memo to the Future*, ABC News, 23 April 1987.

7. William Greider, "The Lonesome Drifter," *Rolling Stone*, 12 March 1987, p. 26. Greider adds, "Americans are smarter than that, surely," but doesn't seem to know what to do with this insight, except to suppose that "we" simply have let our guard down in this particular case.

8. Chellis Glendinning, *Waking Up in the Nuclear Age: The Book of Nuclear Therapy* (New York: Beech Tree Books/William Morrow, 1987), p. 15.

9. Gail Sheehy, "Reality? Just Say No," *New Republic*, 30 March 1987, p. 18, emphasis added.

10. Joel Kovel, whose writing will be discussed below, believes it is no mistake that "we" thinking tends to endorse the present system of power: the creation of a "we" is basic to what Kovel calls technocratic politics. Kovel, *Against the State of Nuclear Terror* (London: Pan Books, 1983), pp. 120, 161, 166.

11. Dorothy Rowe, *Living with the Bomb* (London: Routledge and Kegan Paul, 1985), p. 221.

12. Alasdair C. MacIntyre, *After Virtue: A Study in Moral Theory* (Notre Dame, Ind.: University of Notre Dame Press, 1981, rev. ed. 1984), p. 71, emphases in original.

13. Edward P. Thompson, "Europe, the Weak Link in the Cold War," in *Exterminism and Cold War*, a New Left Review book (London: Verso, 1982), p. 330.

14. See Robert Jay Lifton and Richard Falk, *Indefensible Weapons: The Political and Psychological Case Against Nuclearism* (New York: Basic Books, 1982).

15. George Kennan, "On Nuclear War," *The New York Review of Books*, 21 January 1982, reprinted in *Nato, Nuclear War and the Soviet Threat*, ed. by Phil Braithwaite (Evesham, England: West Midlands CND, 1985), p. 39. Kennan also speaks in psychologically loaded language (using terms like *schizophrenia*) in his foreword to Norman Cousins's *Pathology of Power* (New York: W. W. Norton, 1987), pp. 9–15.

16. William Stringfellow, "The Nuclear Principalities: A Biblical View of the Arms Race," in Jim Wallis, ed., *Waging Peace: A Handbook for the Struggle to Abolish Nuclear Weapons* (San Francisco and Sydney: Harper and Row, 1982), p. 109.

17. Helen Caldicott, *Missile Envy: The Arms Race and Nuclear War* (New York: William Morrow, 1984), pp. 174–75.

18. David P. Barash and Judith Eve Lipton, *The Caveman and the Bomb: Human Nature, Evolution, and Nuclear War* (New York: McGraw-Hill, 1985), p. 22, emphasis in original.

19. Marcus Raskin, "Nuclear Extermination and the National Security State," in *Exterminism and Cold War*, p. 207.

20. An interesting recent review of this position, including excerpts from the 1986 "Seville Statement" in which several scientists took issue with it, is contained in Alfie Kohn, "Make Love, Not War," *Psychology Today*, vol. 22, no. 6 (June 1988), pp. 34–38. The sociobiological debate is taken up in Ian Fenton, ed., *The Psychology of Nuclear Conflict* (London: Coventure, 1986), particularly in the implicitly opposed essays "Archetypes of War" by Anthony Stevens and "Prenuclear Age Leaders and the Arms Race" by Jerome Frank.

21. Barash and Lipton, p. 267.

22. Brian Easlea, *Fathering the Unthinkable: Masculinity, Scientists and the Nuclear Arms Race* (London: Pluto Press, 1983), pp. 10–11.

23. Easlea, p. 135.

24. Kovel, p. 52.

25. Kovel, pp. 57–58.

26. Kovel, p. 131.

27. Kovel, p. 59, emphasis in original.

28. Paul Rogat Loeb, *Hope in Hard Times* (Lexington, MA: Lexington Books, 1987), pp. 241, 245.

29. Dale Aukerman, *Darkening Valley: A Biblical Perspective on Nuclear War* (New York: Seabury Press, 1986), p. 161. Also see chapter 23 in particular.

30. Elaine Pagels, "The Politics of Paradise," *New York Review of Books*, 12 May 1988, p. 28. See also her book *Adam, Eve, and the Serpent* (New York: Random House, 1988). As the "first philosopher of the will," in Hannah Arendt's words, Augustine is logically the figure whose discourse one would expect to figure centrally in the nuclear problem, which (as discussed in chapter 1) is partly a problem of the gap—so worried over by Augustine—between willing something and being able to act on it. See Arendt, *The Life of the Mind*, vol. 2 (New York: Harcourt, Brace, Jovanovich, 1978), pp. 84–110.

31. Geoffrey Aggeler, *Anthony Burgess: The Artist as Novelist* (University: University of Alabama Press, 1979), p. 161. A discussion of Augustinian and Pelagian ideas with specific reference to the arms race occurs in Edward LeRoy Long, Jr.'s little-regarded book, *The Christian Response to the Atomic Crisis* (Philadelphia: Westminster Press, 1950).

32. Bernice Martin, "Invisible Religion, Popular Culture and Anti-nuclear Sentiment," in David Martin and Peter Mullen, eds., *Unholy Warfare: The Church and the Bomb* (London: Basil Blackwell, 1983), p. 110.

33. Ira Chernus, "The Symbolism of the Bomb," *Christian Century*, 12 October 1983, pp. 907–10. Chernus has put a somewhat more elaborately developed version of this argument in book form, qualifying his proposals but still basically keeping them (and speaking throughout in "we"s). See Chernus, *Dr. Strangegod: On the Symbolic Meaning of Nuclear Weapons* (Columbia: University of South Carolina Press, 1986).

34. Perry Miller, *Errand into the Wilderness* (New York: Harper Torchbooks, 1956), pp. 217ff.

3. Perpetrators and Prophets

1. The films to be discussed at length here are *Dr. Strangelove: Or, How I Learned to Stop Worrying and Love the Bomb*, produced by Stanley Kubrick for Hawk Films, directed by Stanley Kubrick (Columbia Pictures, 1964) and *WarGames*, produced by Harold Schneider for Leonard Goldberg Productions, directed by John Badham (MGM/UA, 1983).

2. Geoffrey Aggeler has made this point about the most naive versions of each view: "Pelagianism and detheologized Augustinianism actually share a great deal." Aggeler, *Anthony Burgess: The Artist as Novelist* (University: University of Alabama Press, 1979), p. 183. Aggeler notes that both philosophies are dehumanizing, since both are "machines that seek to destroy the 'self' to save 'man.'"

3. Jonathan Schell, *The Fate of the Earth* (New York: Avon, 1982); Schell, *The Abolition* (New York: Alfred A. Knopf, 1984); Freeman Dyson, *Weapons and Hope* (New York: Harper and Row, 1984). Page citations throughout the text are to these editions. All three of these books, incidentally, originally appeared as *New Yorker* magazine serials.

4. Aggeler, *Anthony Burgess*, p. 159.

5. Rudolph Peierls, summarizing Richard Rhodes's *The Making of the Atomic Bomb*, in "Making It," *New York Review of Books*, 5 November 1987, pp. 47–48.

6. Schell accepts the mistaken notion that, to borrow William Stringfellow's words, "science is morally neutral or, to put it in some traditionally theological terms, that science as a principality somehow enjoys exemption from the Fall." Stringfellow points out that this notion has been "inculcated profusely in the culture since the start of this century." William Stringfellow, "The Nuclear Principalities: A Biblical View of the Arms Race," in Jim Wallis, ed., *Waging Peace: A Handbook for the Struggle to Abolish Nuclear Weapons* (San Francisco and Sydney: Harper and Row, 1982), p. 110.

7. See Lewis Mumford, *Technics and Civilization* (New York: Harcourt, Brace and Co., 1934).

8. Lynn White, Jr., *Dynamo and Virgin Reconsidered: Essays in the Dynamism of Western Culture* (Cambridge, Mass.: M.I.T. Press, 1968), pp. 83–84, emphasis added.

9. See chapter 4.

10. He also critiques Schell, mainly because he doesn't believe that Schell's thesis of utter destruction has been proven. See pp. 22ff.

11. Freeman Dyson, *Disturbing the Universe* (New York: Harper and Row, 1979), p. 91 and *Weapons and Hope*, p. 248.

12. Northrop Frye, *The Great Code: The Bible and Literature* (London: ARK, 1983), pp. 221 and xvi. Subsequent parenthetical page citations are to this edition of the text.

4. "A Largess Universal"

1. Jonathan Schell, *The Fate of the Earth* (New York: Avon Books, 1982), pp. 226 and 186–87, emphasis added.

2. New Historicist literary critics, however, have accomplished some of this work, and (unrelated to their efforts) some serious analysis of the state does appear in the nuclear debate thanks to a few of the books discussed in chapter 2, particularly Joel Kovel's *Against the State of Nuclear Terror*.

3. My use of the term *anxieties* in what follows partly comes from Jonathan Dollimore and Alan Sinfield's "History and Ideology: The Instance of *Henry V*," in John Drakakis, ed., *Alternative Shakespeares* (London: Methuen, 1985), though the historical concerns driving my analysis are a bit different from Dollimore and Sinfield's. Without the concept of anxieties, critics have either looked at *Henry V* as muddled or dichotomous, or they have had to adopt a notion like Norman Rabkin's "complementarity," which is based on the idea that the celebratory and anxious dimensions of the play simply reflect Shakespeare's sense of the "duality of things" and the "inscrutability of history"—as if Shakespeare were reporting on universals, not particular historical conditions of his time. The discussion in this chapter should make it obvious how that analysis fails. (See Rabkin, "Rabbits, Ducks, and *Henry V*," *Shakespeare Quarterly* 28:3, summer 1977, reprinted in Mark W. Scott, ed., *Shakespearean Criticism*, vol. 5 [Detroit: Gale Research, 1987].)

4. *Henry V* is the Shakespeare play which "more than any other," as one editor puts it, echoing others, "takes war as its theme." A. R. Humphreys, ed., *Henry V* (Harmondsworth: Penguin, 1968, repr. 1980), p. 32. All references to the play throughout this discussion are from this edition and reflect its scene and line numberings.

5. See F. H. Hinsley, *Sovereignty*, 2nd ed. (Cambridge: Cambridge University Press, 1986).

6. Alasdair C. MacIntyre, *A Short History of Ethics* (New York: Macmillan, 1966), pp. 131–32.

7. It was perceived in Shakespeare's time that war was changing. *Henry V* was written in the same decade in which Sir Roger Williams wrote that it was impossible any longer to learn from the example of great war heroes of the past, so different

had warfare become. See Gordon A. Craig, "The Art of War" (review of several books), *New York Review of Books*, 28 April 1988, p. 16.

8. See, for instance, James Turner Johnson, *Can Modern War Be Just?* (New Haven: Yale, 1984), pp. 76ff.

9. Humphreys, for instance, puts forward such a justification, in his introduction to the Penguin *Henry V*, pp. 34–37.

10. Hinsley, a historian of sovereignty, sees sovereignty as having arisen in early modern times to replace older segmentary states through a process whereby government and community come to interpenetrate. Medieval European communities had stood in important ways in opposition to their own kings, even to the point of retaining rights of rebellion against him if he violated custom or God's will. The king was an exceptionally powerful lord among other lords, and was expected to accord those others the customary honors they were due.

Under sovereignty, government comes to be viewed as the expression of the whole community, rather than as merely one privileged sector within it. It becomes the source of "positive law," which supersedes the more static ideas of natural law, divine law, and ancient custom.

And for this to happen, the central authority must come to be seen as absolute within its own realm, not bound by any larger, "universal" authority like a pope or emperor, nor by traditional social hierarchies and realms of privilege within the society itself. And along with all this, sovereignty redefines warfare, which eventually comes to be seen as less a private affair of the ruling nobility and more a contest of fundamental values, one involving the strength and survival of whole nations.

11. For example Falstaff's famous "honor" speech in *I Henry IV*, and act IV, scene i of the current play—see discussion later in this chapter.

12. This point is further buttressed by two variations on it. First, Henry also acknowledges that the opposite is possible, that the "gentle" can prove vile. He confronts his three would-be assassins with this idea, noting that their "fall hath left a kind of blot / To mark the full-fraught man and best endued / With some suspicion" (II.ii.138–40). And second, the leveling effect of war is to have an ironic counterpart even among the less enlightened French:

MONTJOY:
For many of our princes—woe the while!—
Lie drowned and soaked in mercenary blood;
So do our vulgar drench their peasant limbs
In blood of princes. . . .

[IV.vii.73–76]

Henry's war, which levels and unites the different British peoples, ironically does the same to the French, if only post mortem.

Also, the famous passage "Once more unto the breach" (III.i) has Henry addressing his armies familiarly, as "dear friends," as if to assert that their relationship to him is independent of social rank. And these "friends" include both the "noblest English" and the "good yeomen." The transitional view of "social landmarks" is very clear here—they are acknowledged, and in the proper order (nobility first), but both classes are claimed as equally fit to the military task at hand (an important point to be discussed further in this chapter).

13. See Robert Weimann, *Shakespeare and the Popular Tradition in the Theater: Studies in the Social Dimension of Dramatic Form and Function* (Baltimore: Johns Hopkins University Press, 1978), p. 169 and part V, sections 1 and 2.

14. Jean Bodin, *Six Books of the Republic*, in Michael Curtis, ed., *The Great Political Theories*, vol. 1 (New York: Avon Books, 1961), p. 279; Thomas Hobbes, *Leviathan* (1651), The Library of Liberal Arts (Indianapolis: Bobbs-Merrill, 1958, reprinted 1976), p. 151. Of course, the ruler as sun has a much more ancient image, but

Shakespeare's use of it in connection with the idea of social leveling would not have had the same long history.

15. Philippe de Mézières, *Letter to Richard II* (1395), introduced and translated by G.W. Coopland (Liverpool: Liverpool University Press, 1975), pp. 46, 51, 53.

16. *Henry V* was written at a time when England "had made little advance as yet from this fundamental conviction of the Middle Ages [that king and people were separate] towards the conception of the visible Ruler as the personification of the body politic or towards the conception of the People as being something more than a mere collection of individuals." Hinsley, p. 130.

17. This same point applies to the play's care in excusing Henry's invasion of France, as if troubled to find an excuse that will stick. There is the notion that Henry is carrying out God's will, that he is personally charitable toward the French, that he "loves" France, and that the French unfairly mock his claims, which are in accordance with the medieval Salic Law. But the Salic Law speech (I.ii) is dry, unheroic; Henry's charitableness is to be radically questioned at Harfleur; "God's will," as Mézières warned, is a sword hung *over* the king; and Henry's "love" for a country he has just overrun is almost transparently ironic: "I love France so well," he says, "that I will not part with a village of it—I will have it all mine" (V.ii.172–73). By act IV, when Henry conducts his nighttime disputation with the soldiers, the issue has not been settled (although the dramatic situation provides one quick retort to Williams: the hapless soldier becomes comic by telling the king himself—in disguise—that the king never hears the "poor and private displeasure" of people like him).

18. It is interesting to trace the presentation of Harfleur, and of Henry's whole war, in prose histories from Shakespeare's time and afterwards. Holinshed, the chronicler from whom Shakespeare himself got most of his information, reports that Harfleur actually was sacked; Shakespeare apparently deliberately altered this. Also, Holinshed is concerned with the reasons that justify Henry's actions; he takes the Salic law speech very seriously, and argues that Henry hopes to succeed because "victory for the most part followeth where right leadeth" (the forerunner to the notions that victory proves one *was* right and, finally, that victory *makes* one right). By the eighteenth century a historian like Goldsmith can put the whole war down to Henry's domestic troubles and his resolution "to take advantage of the troubles" in France—not reasons any longer, which don't seem to be needed, but merely motives, as we expect today.

19. Francis Bacon, *History of Henry VII*, 1622, in Arthur Johnston, ed., *Francis Bacon* (London: Batsford, 1965), p. 186.

20. Ibid.

21. Hinsley, p. 130.

22. Dwight Macdonald, essays reprinted in *Politics Past* (New York: Viking, 1957), pp. 56–57ff. What Macdonald calls animism is similar to what others have called reification, the pathetic fallacy, or the fallacy of misplaced concreteness.

23. Macdonald, p. 174.

24. Macdonald, p. 160.

25. Macdonald, p. 53.

26. Brian Martin, *Uprooting War* (London: Freedom Press, 1984), p. 127.

27. Quoted in John Dillin, "Reagan Courts 'Disaster,' Says Mr. Conservative," *Christian Science Monitor*, 31 August-6 September 1987.

28. Don Cook and Stanley Meisler, "Fears of Denuclearized Europe Pose Dilemma," *Los Angeles Times*, 28 February 1988.

29. *Newsweek International*, 15 June 1987, p. 7.

30. These examples are from Bill Barol, "The Eighties Are Over," *Newsweek*, 4 January 1988, p. 46; Ian Aitken, "Radical Designs on a Selfish Society," *Guardian* (London), 7 September 1987; and Jack Smith, "Getting Out of Line," *Los Angeles Times Magazine*, 24 April 1988, p. 6.

31. Neither, historically, did Katherine consent to marry Henry, though Shakespeare—again, perhaps, reflecting the anxiety produced by this knowledge—has his Henry actively woo her, as if there were some doubt about his power to politically compel the marriage.

32. Tom Brokaw on the *NBC Nightly News*, 12 January 1988.

33. Julian Amery MP, quoted in Karl Miller, "State-Sponsored Counter-Terror," *London Review of Books*, 8 May 1986, p. 23.

34. Augustine, *City of God*. In Mary T. Clark, trans., *Augustine of Hippo: Selected Writings* (London: SPCK, 1984), p. 460, emphasis added.

35. Edward R. Norman, "Christian Morality and Nuclear Arms," in Raymond English, ed., *Ethics and Nuclear Issues: European and American Perspectives* (Washington: Ethics and Public Policy Center, 1985), p. 116. Norman's reading of Christian morality is what Alan Kreider calls post-Constantinian in his interesting essay, "Rediscovering our Heritage: The Pacifism of the Early Church," in Jim Wallis, ed., *Waging Peace: A Handbook for the Struggle to Abolish Nuclear Weapons* (San Francisco: Harper and Row, 1982), pp. 122–125.

36. Neuhaus's actual phrase is "the chief idolatry of our time." In "A Crisis of Faith," in English, ed., *Ethics and Nuclear Arms*, p. 62. See also Robert W. Tucker's discussion of the irony that the bombing of Hiroshima was justified under the "principle of humanity": "Thus a doctrine that begins by insisting upon the continued validity in war of the imperative requirements of humanity ends by justifying in the name of the principle of humanity measure having no discernible limits save those imposed by force itself." Tucker, *The Just War: A Study in Contemporary American Doctrine* (Baltimore: Johns Hopkins University Press, 1960), pp. 90–91.

37. For instance, see Bernard Brodie's *War and Politics* (New York: Macmillan, 1973).

38. For Bodin (as for Shakespeare's own patron, King James I), kingly power is quasi-divine; the king "is the image of God" and has no peer in his realm for the same reason that "Almighty God cannot create another God equal to Himself." (*Great Political Theories*, p. 278). Since Bodin's was a Christian theory, it superficially would seem to hold the sovereign to a higher authority, God's. But "Jean Bodin had indeed submitted the Sovereign to the law of God, but the inner logic of the concept was to make Sovereignty free from every—even heavenly—limitation. From the fact alone that he existed, was not the Sovereign always, as Rousseau put it, all that he ought to be? In actual fact Sovereignty required that no decision made by the Mortal God, or law established by the General Will, could possibly be resisted by the individual conscience in the name of justice. Law did not need to be *just* to have force of law. Sovereignty had a right to be obeyed, whatever it might command. Sovereignty was above moral law." Jacques Maritain, *Man and the State* (Chicago: Phoenix Books, 1956/1966), p. 48, emphasis in original.

The Bodinian and Hobbesian derivations of sovereignty roughly correspond to the view of the state as natural and the state as representative, both of which, as I said early in this chapter, can wind up producing the same results.

39. Bodin, in *Great Political Theories*, pp. 274, 280.

40. Hobbes, *Leviathan*, pp. 146, 272.

41. Hobbes, p. 142.

42. Hobbes, pp. 135, emphasis in original.

43. Hobbes, p. 172.

44. Hobbes, p. 272.

45. Shakespeare, *Henry VI Part I*, act I, scene i.

46. Hobbes, pp. 135, 144, emphasis in original.

47. Theodore Roszak, *Where the Wasteland Ends* (Garden City, N.Y.: Anchor, 1973), p. 165.

48. Interestingly, the "rights of society" idea doesn't translate to other societies; Russian society doesn't have rights. People seem to have a firm sense of their own personal rights, which leads them to anthropomorphize their own society as rights bearing; but having, by the same token, anthropomorphized the other society, they lose sight of the individuality of *its* citizens and hence of their rights, and thus they forget to assign rights to those citizens' government.

49. Herman Kahn, *Thinking About the Unthinkable in the 1980s* (New York: Simon and Schuster, 1984), pp. 216, 224, emphases added.

50. For a careful account of the claim that this way of thinking is characteristically modern, see Alasdair C. MacIntyre, *After Virtue: A Study in Moral Theory* (Notre Dame, Ind.: University of Notre Dame Press, 1981, rev. ed. 1984).

51. Nor, as implied above, would they accept the fundamental philosophical presupposition of deterrence: that any kind of threat is acceptable so long as it works.

52. Thus is excused Henry's execution of the French prisoners, a pragmatic move which has been criticized by commentators from Fluellen ("'Tis expressly against the law of arms") (IV.vi.36-vii.10) to the present.

53. From Friedrich Klemm, ed., *A History of Western Technology* (Cambridge, Mass.: M.I.T Press, 1964), pp. 102–7.

54. Shakespeare may be satirizing such skirmishes in *Troilus and Cressida*; He has Fluellen express admiration for Greek heroes in act III, scene vi; he also seems to have drawn Fluellen from *An Arithmeticall Militare Treatise, Named Stratioticos* by Leonard Digges, whose title speaks to the new interest in methods. See Humphreys.

55. Gwynne Dyer, *War* (London: Bodley Head, 1986), pp. 54ff.; also John Keegan, "Grand Illusions" (book review), *New York Review of Books*, 17 July 1986, p. 38.

56. See Dyer, *War* and Johnson, *Can Modern War Be Just?*

57. Macdonald, p. 159.

58. From the German Fireworkbook in Klemm, ed., *History of Western Technology*.

59. Bacon, *History of Henry VII* in Johnston, and "Of the True Greatness of Kingdoms and Estates," *Bacon's Essays* (Edinburgh: W. and R. Chambers, 1884), p. 70.

60. Bacon is discussed this way, for instance, by Roszak in *Wasteland*, and by Joel Kovel, *Against the State of Nuclear Terror* (London: Pan Books, 1983).

61. Bacon, *The Advancement of Learning*, in Johnston, p. 53.

62. See, for instance, Marina Warner, *Joan of Arc: The Image of Female Heroism* (Harmondsworth: Penguin, 1983).

63. Paracelsus is quoted in Hugh Kearney, *Science and Change 1500–1700*, World University Library (New York: McGraw-Hill, 1971), p. 124; also Johannes Kepler, *Epitome of Copernican Astronomy IV*, trans. Charles Glenn Wallis, in *Great Books of the Western World*, vol. 16 (Chicago: Encyclopedia Brittanica, 1952), p. 897.

As to the persistence of this confusion of the spiritual and physical up to the present, Spencer R. Weart has written, "Well into the twentieth century most people spoke of 'energy' without distinguishing the physicists' term, which was now precisely defined, from spiritual energy, sexual energy, and so forth." Weart, *Nuclear Fear: A History of Images* (Cambridge, Mass.: Harvard University Press, 1988), p. 42.

64. See chapter 2.

65. Donne's poem merges several social and intellectual themes of the period, or rather shows their intrinsic interconnectedness. There is the chaos of new ideas, the sinful "corruption" of both man and the cosmos, and the upsets in the traditional social hierarchies caused by the upward strivings which a new mobility and a new individualism encouraged:

As mankind, so is the world's whole frame
Quite out of joint, almost created lame:
For, before God had made up all the rest,
Corruption entered, and depraved the best:
It seized the angels, and then first of all
The world did in her cradle take a fall,
And turned her brains, and took a general maim
Wronging each joint of th'universal frame.
The noblest part, man, felt it first; and then
Both beasts and plants, cursed in the curse of man.
So did the world from the first hour decay,
That evening was beginning of the day,
And now the springs and summers which we see,
Like sons of women after fifty be.
And new philosophy calls in all doubt,
The element of fire is quite put out;
The sun is lost, and th'earth, and no man's wit
Can well direct him where to look for it.
. . . .
For every man alone thinks he hath got
To be a phoenix, and that then can be
None of that kind, of which he is, but he.
This is the world's condition now.

66. Bacon, *In Praise of Knowledge*, in Johnston, p. 15.

67. In *The Tempest* (II.ii.), for instance, the courtier Gonzalo muses over how he would run things on the island where his party has been shipwrecked. There would be "no sovereignty," he says, and no need of any, since

All things in common nature should produce
Without sweat or endeavour. Treason, felony,
Sword, pike, knife, gun, or need of any engine,
Would I not have; but nature should bring forth,
Of its own kind, all foison, all abundance,
To feed my innocent people. . . .
I would with such perfection govern, sir,
T'excel the golden age.

Gonzalo unselfconsciously mixes together visions of an anarchist utopia with visions of nature producing in abundance. In his view, scarcity in nature is what compels work, which gives rise to idleness, luxury, and crime (and weapons), which require government (more weapons), which gives rise to treason (and perhaps still more weapons—Gonzalo mentions several by name). Shakespeare himself, modern and pragmatic, gently undercuts Gonzalo's dreams, but only by way of recognizing that they are a commonplace of his age.

Of course, the belief that methods *could* be found for all these problems reflects a residual *Pelagian* idea of human capability.

68. Bacon, *Doctrine of Idols*, Book 1, L, in Johnston, p. 88. Even Bodin's divine-right theories were protoscientific in their use of concepts from medieval sorcery, another effort to "command" nature. (Machiavelli is also relevant here, but I have left him out of this discussion because, unlike Hobbes and Bodin, he did not propound a complete theory of sovereignty in terms of its origin and nature.) In the same vein, Ernst Cassirer speaks of the "close connection between the new *cosmology* and the new *politics* of the Renaissance." Cassirer, *The Myth of the State* (New Haven: Yale University Press, 1946, repr. 1975), p. 136, emphases in original.

69. Marina Warner has argued that the medieval sense of war was precisely this. See Warner, *Joan of Arc*.

70. David P. Barash and Judith Eve Lipton, *The Caveman and the Bomb: Human Nature, Evolution, and Nuclear War* (New York: McGraw-Hill, 1985), p. 260.

71. Jonathan Schell, *The Abolition* (New York: Alfred A. Knopf, 1984), p. 77. See discussion in chapter 3.

72. Thomas Powers, *Thinking About the Next War* (New York: New American Library, 1982), p. 115.

5. Nostalgia for Industry

1. References here are to a report quoted by John Tirman in *Empty Promise: The Growing Case against Star Wars* (Boston: Beacon, 1986), p. 2; David Watt, "Why CND Could Mushroom Again," *Times* (London), 12 April 1985; Julia A. Moore, "Scuttling SALT—The Real Debacle," *Chicago Tribune*, 12 December 1986; Stephen S. Rosenfeld, "SDI: On The Other Hand, Not So Fast," *Cleveland Plain Dealer*, 21 October 1986, and syndicated; E. P. Thompson, "The Ideological Delirium Which Strikes Chords in the Worst Traditions of American Populism," *Guardian* (London), 18 February 1985; and Stephen M. Walt, "Politicians and Professors: A Double Standard," *Bulletin of the Atomic Scientists*, July/August 1987, p. 3.

2. Reagan interview with four correspondents, 3 December 1987. "Paradoxical" is from a *Chicago Tribune* editorial, "Going the Last, Decisive Inch," 14 October 1986; the same piece said there were several possible answers to the question of what Reagan "might truly believe." Reporting on the Reykjavik summit on 12 October 1986, Sam Donaldson and Peter Jennings of ABC News wondered if Reagan really meant what he "apparently" believed. And Broder's claim is from his syndicated column, "SDI and Reagan: What a Dream; What a Dreamer," *Chicago Tribune*, 15 October 1986. For sources of Reagan's speeches, see Bibliography.

3. Martin Gardner, "Giving God a Hand," *New York Review of Books*, 13 August 1987, p. 17.

4. See Robert Scheer, "Teller's Obsession Became Reality in 'Star Wars' Plan," *Los Angeles Times*, 10 July 1983; also George W. Ball, "The War for Star Wars," *New York Review of Books*, 11 April 1985, p. 39 ("it was a top-down speech"). Hedrick Smith of the *New York Times* reported that Reagan's enthusiasm for the project came across in his "body language" during an interview shortly after Reagan's second inauguration in 1985. Arms-control expert Paul Warnke told Cable News Network that "it has proved almost impossible for anyone to talk President Reagan out of his Star Wars scheme" (CNN-2, 14 January 1987). And the fact that SDI was Reagan's own personal initiative would explain the widely reported fact that the proposal was never run through normal channels with the European allies nor even Reagan's own Joint Chiefs of Staff. See, for instance, Mark Schapiro, "The Selling of Star Wars to Europe," *The Nation*, 16 January 1988, p. 54. (As will be shown later in this chapter, Reagan was promoting the general idea of strategic defense long before his famous meetings with Edward Teller in 1982 and 1983.)

It is scarcely the case that all this is only clear in retrospect. Even before the evidence of the various summits had accumulated, I pointed out Reagan's sincerity and predicted some of its consequences in "Reagan's Missionary Dream: The Meaning behind Star Wars," *The Cresset* 48:6, April 1985. At that time, though, it was a difficult thesis to sell to the mainstream press, which was still too busy debating SDI's technical merits and puzzling over what Reagan "really" meant.

5. Lance Morrow, "Yankee Doodle Magic," *Time*, 7 July 1986, p. 14.

6. In the summer of 1984 Reagan called "Man does not live by bread alone" an "old saying," suggesting that he was not aware of its origin—as a phrase of Jesus'

from the Gospel of Luke. (By contrast, when Jimmy Carter displayed a knowledge of Scripture by speaking of lust in his heart in 1976, this was held up as a gaffe, largely because the press no more recognized this phrase as a Biblical allusion than it would later recognize Reagan's.)

On the general question of whether leaders and elites represent popular views, see my discussion of the post-Reykjavik fallout in chapter 1 and of the leaders-versus-people argument in chapter 2.

7. The phrase is from Lord Zuckerman, "Reagan's Highest Folly," *New York Review of Books*, 9 April 1987, p. 36. Additional details about plans to keep SDI going and to accelerate deployment of a partial system are given in R. Jeffrey Smith, "SDI Comes Down to Earth," *Washington Post* (National Weekly Edition), 4–10 April 1988, pp. 9–10, and in Charles E. Bennet, "The Rush to Deploy SDI," *Atlantic Monthly*, April 1988, pp. 53–61.

8. Tirman, *Empty Promise*, p. 1.

9. Examples: Phyllis Schlafly brought a campaign called "Americans for SDI" to the Geneva summit; Congressman Delbert Latta (Ohio), in a March 1987 questionnaire to constituents, posed the intriguing question, "Since we have not perfected a missile defense system, do you agree it is in our national interest to aid the freedom fighters presently fighting communism in Nicaragua?"; and "moderate" Robert Dole, campaigning for the New Hampshire primary, said he challenged his fellow Republican candidates "to join me in this clear and unequivocal pledge: I will develop SDI. I will test SDI. I will deploy SDI" (reported by William Schneider in the *Los Angeles Times*, 14 February 1988).

10. Both terms were used, for instance, in a *Chicago Tribune* post-Reykjavik editorial, "Getting beyond the Iceland Impasse," 19 October 1986.

11. See Ball, "Star Wars," *New York Review of Books*, 11 April 1985.

12. From Weinberger's letter to the *Chicago Tribune*, 26 February 1987, sec. 1, p. 10. I will call the ability to make statements like this "intellectual dishonesty" and will analyze it further in chapter 6. (In the same letter, incidentally, Weinberger also reaffirms that the president's original vision of a comprehensive global defense was still intact, and he continued to make the same point in published articles right up until he left the administration—further suggesting how well entrenched SDI had become in the U.S. defense establishment.)

13. "Reagan Views Star Wars' as Peaceful Technology, Like Radar Development" (New York Times News Service), *The Blade* (Toledo, Ohio), 18 October 1986.

14. Reagan speech to the nation, 13 October 1986. Compare with Reagan news conference, 17 September 1985; Reagan interview with the BBC, 30 October 1985; Reagan interview with Soviet journalists, 4 November 1985; Reagan interview with European TV journalists, 12 November 1985.

15. Reagan interview with Robert Scheer during the 1980 primaries, in Scheer, *With Enough Shovels: Reagan, Bush and Nuclear War* (Random House, 1982), pp. 232ff.

16. Reagan interview with Robert Scheer. Also see Scheer, "Teller's Obsession," and Strobe Talbott and Michael Mandelbaum, *Reagan and Gorbachev*, A Council on Foreign Relations Book (New York: Vintage Books, 1987), p. 126. One of Reagan's claims on the 1980 campaign trail was that the United States was in more danger of surprise attack then than it had been at the time of Pearl Harbor.

17. Reagan speech to the nation, 27 October 1983. Reagan also called the U.S. presence in Central America a "defensive shield." Weekly radio address, 13 August 1983.

18. The controversy over "winning" nuclear wars flared up in 1982 in part over the leaked "Fiscal Year 1984–1988 Defense Guidance," a document which—though this was widely overlooked—also spoke of the U.S. developing ballistic missile defense systems.

19. Quoted in Peter Pringle and William Arkin, *SIOP: Nuclear War from the Inside* (London: Sphere Books, 1983), p. 196. The authors point out that this was not so much "bombast" to be contrasted with President Carter's reassuring "homilies" as it was a return full circle to the strategic thinking of the 1950s.

20. Michael Krepon, "The Surprise Defense Initiative," *Bulletin of the Atomic Scientists*, July/August 1987; "What the West Should Say to Mr Gorbachov," *Observer* (London), 6 October 1985. David Watt reported in the *Times* (London) on 29 March 1985 that "the real view of [British officials] in unbuttoned moments is that the Administration behaved with astounding arrogance in foisting an entirely new doctrine onto the alliance without the slightest consultation." The arrogance follows from the alleged newness of the doctrine, which I am claiming is the opposite of Reagan's own perception of the matter.

21. Foreign policy debate with Walter Mondale, October 1984. Also compare Reagan's remarks in his interview with the BBC, 30 October 1985, and in his interview with Soviet journalists, 4 November 1985.

Interestingly, Reagan was flatly contradicted by the director of the U.S. Space Command, Brig. Gen. Wayne Knudson, an SDI supporter, who nonetheless said in 1988: "I don't think you'll ever have a time without offenses." See R. Jeffrey Smith, "The 30 Percent Solution: It Was a Military Goal," *Washington Post* (National Weekly Edition), 4–10 April 1988, p. 10.

22. *Observer* (London), "What the West Should Say to Mr Gorbachov," 6 October 1985.

23. Caroline L. Herzenberg, letter to the *Chicago Tribune*, 26 January 1987.

24. Quoted in an Ellen Goodman syndicated column, 19 November 1983.

25. For instance, see his address to the nation on Nicaragua, 16 March 1986. Cynics have recalled that Reagan spent World War II in Hollywood, and have suggested that his image of war was borrowed from movies, hence superficial. But such arguments tend to confuse two very different things: superficiality with respect to the real truth about war, and superficiality of commitment or conviction. Reagan believed profoundly in the images conveyed by the movies. Lots of people did—that's why the movies were made that way.

26. Reagan speech to the European Parliament, 8 May 1985.

27. Edward T. Linenthal, "Moral Rhetoric, Moral Confusion in the Star Wars Debate," *Christian Century*, 25 November 1987, p. 1059. In his interview with Soviet journalists in November 1985, Reagan spoke of "the kind of armed warfare that has occurred between nations" as if this history contained norms of morality that the war in Afghanistan had violated.

28. William H. Kincade pointed out that, indeed, Reagan's *own* offensive nuclear weapons programs were undercutting the chances for success with SDI. "History is against Star Wars," *Chicago Tribune*, 20 January 1985, sec. 5, p. 3.

29. For instance, in his second inaugural address and in the post-Reykjavik speech of 13 October 1986, with similar allusions in many other statements.

30. Pringle and Arkin, *SIOP*, p. 192. Mainstream journalists, of course, treat the president's statements on U.S. defense policy as authoritative, even if the president doesn't know what he's talking about. This is a fact that also bore upon Reagan's "weapons/missiles" muddle, discussed below, and one that I will analyze further in chapter 6.

31. For summaries of the debate, see Pringle and Arkin, *SIOP*; Jeffrey Porro, "The Policy War: Brodie vs. Kahn," reprinted in Donna Gregory, *The Nuclear Predicament: A Sourcebook* (New York: Bedford/St. Martin's, 1986), pp. 108–14; and William J. Broad, "Star Wars' Defense Idea Launched by Eisenhower" (New York Times News Service), *Chicago Tribune*, 2 November 1986. Actually Reagan was factually correct in viewing Robert McNamara as the official who had come closest to committing the U.S. to MAD.

32. "What possible bearing can the urge to idealize a simple, rural environment

have upon the lives men lead in an intricately organized, urban, industrial, nuclear-armed society?" asks Leo Marx in his classic study *The Machine in the Garden*. The answer is that by clarifying "the root conflict of our culture," the American writers discussed by Marx outline one task of modern American politics: creating "new symbols of possibility," a job which is "in some measure the responsibility of artists, [but] in greater measure the responsibility of society. The machine's sudden entrance into the garden presents a problem that ultimately belongs not to art but to politics." Leo Marx, *The Machine in the Garden: Technology and the Pastoral Ideal in America* (Oxford: Oxford University Press, 1964), pp. 5, 365.

33. Reagan and Richard G. Hubler, *Where's the Rest of Me?* (New York: Duell, Sloan and Pearce, 1965), pp. 3f; quotes are from pp. 13 and 17.

34. Reagan speech to the nation, 14 November 1985, and address to the UN General Assembly, 24 October 1985. For older examples other than those given by Marx, see Henry Nash Smith, *Virgin Land* (Cambridge: Harvard University Press, 1950, repr. 1970).

35. Fitzgerald, pp. 131 and 139.

36. Loren Baritz, *Backfire: A History of How American Culture Led Us into Vietnam and Made Us Fight the Way We Did* (New York: Ballantine, 1985), p. 11.

37. Fitzgerald, p. 56.

38. James Nuechterlein, "The Intervention in Grenada," *The Cresset* 47:2 (December 1983), p. 4. Nuechterlein offers a related statement of this view relative to Vietnam in "The Legacy of Vietnam" in the preceding issue, November 1983, pp. 3–4.

39. Soviet military ideologies differ from American in many ways. See Stephen Shenfield, *The Nuclear Predicament: Explorations in Soviet Ideology* (London: Routledge and Kegan Paul, 1987).

40. Abraham Lincoln address on "The Perpetuation of Our Political Institutions" before the Young Men's Lyceum of Springfield, Illinois, 27 January 1837; from Arthur Brooks Lapsley, ed., *The Writings of Abraham Lincoln* (New York: P. F. Collier & Son, 1905), pp. 148–60. It will be of passing interest to readers of Garry Wills's *Reagan's America* that these otherwise obscure lines from Lincoln's early career are quoted by the mechanical Lincoln at Disneyland—a contraption Wills interestingly ascribes to the same cultural tendencies that produced the Reagan presidency.

41. Of course there *were* fears at the time of threats from outside the country, especially of the "popish" designs of European Catholics; Richard Hofstadter famously documented some of these fears in "The Paranoid Style in American Politics" (1963), reprinted in *The Paranoid Style in American Politics and Other Essays* (New York: Vintage Books, 1967). Lincoln may have been speaking to such fears with his mention of Bonaparte. But precisely by emphasizing the insidiousness and invisibility of foreign plots, and by focusing on immigrants rather than invaders, "paranoid" fears indirectly confirmed the general belief that America was basically immune to direct conquest.

42. Leo Marx, p. 32.

43. See Michael Kammen, *People of Paradox: An Inquiry Concerning the Origins of American Civilization* (New York: Vintage, 1973), p. 34.

44. John F. Kasson, *Civilizing the Machine: Technology and Republican Values in America, 1776–1900* (Harmondsworth: Penguin Books, 1977), pp. 35, 40–41, 166, 174.

45. R. Keith Schoppa, "Vietnam Memoirs: 1980," *The Cresset* 44:7 (May 1981), p. 35.

46. Simon Hoggart, in a column titled "Reagan Assumes the Royal Motley" from the *Observer* (London) shortly after the bombing.

47. Roger Simon, "Now the Shoe's on the Other Table" (syndicated column), *Chicago Tribune,* 19 October 1986. The "biblical quality" is what *New York Times*

editor A. M. Rosenthal deliberately sought to give his paper's shuttle headline. See "Covering the Awful Unexpected," *Time*, 10 February 1986, pp. 42, 45.

48. Reagan news conference, 17 September 1985.

49. See Garry Wills's discussion of Reagan by analogy to Henry Ford in *Reagan's America: Innocents at Home* (Garden City, N.Y.: Doubleday, 1987), pp. 373–74.

50. First inaugural address, 20 January 1981. Later Reagan said that in America's brief slice of world history, "not only would a new concept of society come into being, a golden hope for all mankind, but more than half the activity, economic activity in world history, would take place on this continent. Free to express their genius, individual Americans . . . would perform such miracles of invention, construction, and production as the world had never seen." Reagan address at commencement exercises at the University of Notre Dame, 17 May 1981.

51. Since my language here stresses Reagan's somewhat solitary role in promoting SDI, it bears repeating that there were certainly military and economic interests allied with him and with the program. But I believe my analysis makes clear that Reagan was driven to push the program quite apart from such alliances of convenience.

52. Alan Brinkley, "The Bomb and Balm" (review of Paul Boyer, *By the Bomb's Early Light*), *New Republic*, 23 December 1985, pp. 36. I agree with Brinkley that Americans' new-found enthusiasms toward atomic technology "are too characteristic of other American stances on other issues to be dismissed as defensive rationalizations." Brinkley, p. 37.

53. Thomas Powers, "Rabi: Bomb Had No Part in Greater Glory of Physics," *Los Angeles Times*, 17 January 1988. See also Lawrence Freedman, *The Evolution of Nuclear Strategy* (New York: St. Martin's, 1981, 1983), esp. chapter 4. Bernard Brodie suggests that the real change that occurred in Reagan's lifetime was the shift to "total war" thinking after World War I. Brodie, *War and Politics* (New York: Macmillan, 1973), p. 49.

54. Reagan interview with four correspondents, 3 December 1987. In the same interview we see Reagan's persistence in unorthodoxies, like calling strategic weapons destabilizing (when professional strategists would say the opposite—that they are stabilizing if correctly deployed). This is further evidence that he is not *politically* calculating what he says, but speaking what he feels.

55. Reagan spoke of there having been major historical developments "during my lifetime" in his 1982 "New Year's Remarks to Foreign Peoples," quoted in Paul D. Erickson, *Reagan Speaks: The Making of an American Myth* (New York: New York University Press, 1985), p. 68. "Turning back" is from the "Star Wars" speech (Reagan speech to the nation on national security), 23 March 1983.

56. Thompson, "Ideological Delirium." After reading an earlier version of my argument, Thompson backed away slightly from this thesis; his *Star Wars* (Penguin, 1985) even incorporates the "machine in the garden" language brought to his attention by my manuscript.

57. See Richard Hofstadter, *Anti-Intellectualism in American Life* (New York: Vintage, 1962, 1963).

58. Reagan news conference, 17 September 1985.

59. All this follows from what I have been saying. Reagan passionately rejected the central tenet of the nuclear age; MAD was just his name for it. As to the technical and the strategic debate, they were also variations of this tenet. The technical argument against SDI said that offense would always dominate defense, hence vulnerability would always remain. To answer this in technical terms would be to suggest that it might be true, that the success of defense depended on accidents of technology instead of some inherent historic principle. Worse was the situation posed by the strategic objection, which said it would be "destabilizing" to deploy an effective defense. This objection amounted to: You *must* let your people

be held hostage by the other side. The strategy traditionalist's answer would be to argue that the premise was wrong—the basic current structure of vulnerability wasn't really threatened. It is no wonder Reagan refused to enter this debate on either side. When Gorbachev raised the fear of destabilization at Reykjavik, Reagan is reported to have told an aide in frustration, "I don't know why this guy believes this, because it is just not true." It is hardly likely Reagan would grasp fears rooted in "ordinary" geopolitics, even when he himself was responsible for raising them. (See Bernard Weinraub, "In Iceland: How Grim Ending Followed Hard-Won Gains," *New York Times,* 14 October 1986, p. A11.)

60. Reagan remarks at Quebec luncheon, 18 March 1985. Scheer reports that Edward Teller, the father of the H-bomb, who played a major role in alerting Reagan to SDI as a concrete programmatic possibility, is thought by colleagues to be pursuing a similar agenda of showing that his own nuclear technology can save the world as well as threaten it. Scheer, "Teller's Obsession," p. 6.

61. Reagan speech at Fallston High School, 4 December 1985.

62. Reagan interview with the BBC, 30 October 1985.

63. Reagan speech to the nation on national security ("Star Wars" speech), 23 March 1983, and "The President's Strategic Defense Initiative," official publication of the Office of the President, January 1985.

64. Terry Atlas, "How Many Nuclear Weapons Almost Got Banned in Iceland?", *Chicago Tribune,* 19 October 1986. Aleksandr Bessmertnykh, Soviet deputy foreign minister, complained about U.S. efforts to change its account of Reykjavik by saying the discussion involved elimination only of missiles, when in fact it involved "all nuclear explosive devices." Bessmertnykh, "Reykjavik Revisited: Window on a Nuclear-Free World," *Disarmament* 10:1 (Winter 1986/87) (United Nations Department of Disarmament Affairs).

65. For instance, on 30 October and 12 November 1985.

66. Reagan State of the Union address, 25 January 1988.

67. "And if the Soviet Union and the United States both say we will eliminate our offensive weapons, we will put in this defensive thing in case some place in the world a madman some day tries to create these weapons again—nuclear weapons—because, remember, we all know how to make them now. So, you can't do away with that information. But we would all be safe knowing that if such a madman project is ever attempted, there isn't any of us that couldn't defend ourselves against it." Reagan interview with Soviet journalists, 4 November 1985.

68. See Garry Wills's discussion of this in *Reagan's America,* especially chapter 2, and Reagan's own account in Reagan and Hubler.

69. Garry Wills points out that Reagan's temperament very much inclined toward conserving and restoring rather than innovating. Wills also paints GE as peculiarly committed to fostering a kind of secular religion around technology and progress. *Reagan's America,* pp. 281–83.

70. See Friedrich Klemm, *A History of Western Technology* (Cambridge, Mass.: M.I.T Press, 1964), p. 105; the specific reference is to the German Fireworkbook (also cited above in chapter 4).

71. Reagan speech to the National Association of Evangelicals, 8 March 1983.

72. Reagan interview with Robert Scheer, in Scheer, *With Enough Shovels,* p. 233; Reagan news conference, 17 September 1985.

73. See Reagan interview with Scheer, *With Enough Shovels,* and the quotations in George W. Ball, "White House Roulette," *New York Review of Books,* 8 November 1984, p. 5.

Possessing an impossible Pelagian strength, the adversary, says Richard Hofstadter, "wills, indeed he manufactures, the mechanism of history himself, or deflects the normal course of history in an evil way." He is effectual where we good people somehow aren't. This is the paranoid style, and it accords with Reagan's anxiety about America as history's trustee. Precisely what made Communists "monsters" for him was their subversive approach to history. Pressed to discuss them (even, early on, the Chinese) in traditional geopolitical terms, Reagan had an urge not to; instead he would stress their refusal to give up "the basic principles of Marxism" that called for world revolution—as if these ultimate purposes are at every moment present to a Marxist's mind.

Also as to "changed history": Reagan is reported to have associated nuclear weapons with Armageddon, explicitly so in 1971. See Daniel Schorr, "Reagan Recants: His Path from Armageddon to Detente," *Los Angeles Times*, 3 January 1988.

74. Erickson, *Reagan Speaks*, pp. 68–69.

75. Reagan speech to the nation, 14 November 1985, emphasis added.

76. *Platoon*, produced by Arnold Kopelson for Hemdale Film, directed by Oliver Stone (Orion, 1986). It is interesting that the counterpoint to *Platoon*, as to *War-Games*, was provided by Stanley Kubrick, with his contemporaneous Vietnam film *Full Metal Jacket*—a movie devoted precisely to exposing the presumptions of American virtue that drove the Vietnam adventure: "Inside every gook is an American straining to get out," as one character in the film puts it.

77. The example is from Loren Baritz, *Backfire: A History of How American Culture Led Us into Vietnam and Made Us Fight the Way We Did* (New York: Ballantine Books, 1985), p. 9. Henry Kissinger had also contributed to the demonizing of Vietnam with puzzled declarations of how the mystery of "that distant monochromatic land" confounded the kind of geopolitical calculation that he had helped make famous. Baritz, pp. 5–6.

78. For actual examples see Reagan's news conference of 18 September 1985, or his post-Reykjavik speech to the nation, 13 October 1986. Also see note 59.

79. Alexander Cockburn, "Ashes and Diamonds," *Metro Times* (Detroit), 21–27 January 1987.

80. George W. Ball, "Sovietizing U.S. Policy" (book review), *New York Review of Books*, 2 February 1984. Ball points out that this analysis, with which he obviously agrees, is shared by Leon Wieselter, whose book is under review in the article.

81. Quoted in Robert Chesshyre, "A Red-Necked Novice Can Win Missile Votes Too," *Observer* (London), 31 March 1985.

82. As, for instance, Mark Green and Gail MacColl, with Robert Nelson and Christopher Power, try to do in *There He Goes Again: Ronald Reagan's Reign of Error* (New York: Pantheon, 1983).

83. Reagan sounded a similar theme in remarks he made shortly before leaving for the June 1988 Moscow summit.

84. See my discussion of this in chapter 1.

85. Enoch Powell, "Why Europe Dances to Reagan's Tune," *Guardian* (London), 21 October 1985.

6. Breaking the Wall of Virtue

1. This journalistic tendency is discussed in Michael Schudson, "The Politics of Narrative Form: The Emergence of News Conventions in Print and Television," *Daedalus* 111:4 (fall 1982), p. 110.

2. George Orwell, *1984* (New York: Signet, 1949, repr. 1961). On the surface, *1984* posits that some sort of "atomic wars" have already occurred. But, as I will argue here, it is really about the conditions which underlie the possibility of such wars occurring in the first place. (Page references hereafter are to this edition.)

3. See chapter 4.

4. Christopher Hitchens, "The Moral High Ground," *Spectator* (London), 15 December 1984, p. 9.

5. I don't mean here that they refuse to grade students' work, a potentially conscientious and admirable (if rare) move, but that they claim, at least, to be unable

to hold up *any* standard of value before students—though of course they must do so anyway, despite themselves; for it is impossible for a teacher not to represent for students some system of value or other.

Also, though my notion of relativism no doubt has some similarities to Allan Bloom's in *The Closing of the American Mind* (New York: Simon and Schuster, 1987), my analysis of the problem is meant to contrast with his; Bloom practices the false alternative to relativism that below I call fundamentalism.

6. For instance, see Frances Fitzgerald, *America Revised: History Schoolbooks in the Twentieth Century* (Boston: Little, Brown, 1979); E. D. Hirsch, Jr., *Cultural Literacy: What Every American Needs to Know* (Boston: Houghton Mifflin, 1987).

7. Of course some left academic theories, particularly in feminist and women's studies, question the naturalness even of these relationships, right down to the gender distinctions on which the nuclear family is most fundamentally built.

8. Terry Eagleton, *Literary Theory: An Introduction* (London: Basil Blackwell, 1983), p. 210.

9. David Rieff, "The Colonel and the Professor," *Times Literary Supplement*, 4 September 1987, p. 950.

10. John F. Maclean, "Rapping the Knuckles of Academia," *Chicago Tribune Sunday*, 6 September 1987.

11. James Turner Johnson, *Can Modern War Be Just?* (New Haven: Yale University Press, 1984), p. 205 (footnote).

12. Schudson, p. 110.

13. Noam Chomsky, *Turning the Tide: U.S. Intervention in Central America and the Struggle for Peace* (Boston: South End Press, 1985), p. 215.

14. See chapter 5.

15. Noam Chomsky argues that something like the dynamic I am describing also presented itself as a "threat" after Vietnam, and that efforts by policy intellectuals and the media since then have been aimed at heading off this threat by restoring America's lost aura of virtue. See Chomsky, *Towards a New Cold War: Essays on the Current Crisis and How We Got There* (New York: Pantheon, 1982). Reagan, who as noted in the previous chapter saw SDI as such a project in restoring virtue, also (it should be remembered) campaigned in 1980 on the argument that Vietnam had been "a noble cause," and entered office pardoning government officials accused of abuses of power—that is, of acting on allegedly ignoble purposes of the state.

16. I am here borrowing the concept of earth- or world-abstraction from Hannah Arendt and the notion of the heath and its importance from Michael Ignatieff, who makes extensive use of it in *The Needs of Strangers* (London: Chatto and Windus, 1984).

17. See chapter 3.

18. Essentially these same questions were posed (in 1984 as it happens) in Christopher Lasch's book *The Minimal Self: Psychic Survival in Troubled Times* (New York: W. W. Norton), and the answer there is similar to Orwell's in its pessimism. It also seems they are what Sherry Turkle was speaking of when she said (on *Voices*, BBC Television, 3 June 1987) that free will (basically the Pelagian/Augustinian issue) is an "urgent and hot" problem for our culture today, as sexuality was for the Victorians.

19. I am indebted for this idea to Dr. David Morris.

20. It is difficult to tell whether Orwell himself agrees with the novel's apparent conclusion. He presents Winston Smith as defeated, yet the style throughout is realism, meaning that the text everywhere ratifies Winston Smith's view that truth exists and is knowable. The authorial voice, in effect, undercuts its own statement.

21. Foucault in *The Archeology of Knowledge* and Richard Rorty in his essays "The Contingency of Language/The Contingency of Selfhood" (*London Review of Books*, 17 April/8 May 1986) present something like these views, although Rorty, at least, is

addressing slightly different issues and might not actually raise this objection to the view I have been stating.

22. Joel Kovel presents such arguments for "community" in *Against the State of Nuclear Terror* (London: Pan Books, 1983), and Theodore Roszak synthesized many of these arguments at length in *Where the Wasteland Ends* (Garden City, N.Y.: Anchor Books, 1973).

23. See Ellen Goodman, "Apartheid: A 'Safe' Cause for Protest?", *Chicago Tribune*, 17 January 1986; and Joan Beck, "Shanties: New Campus Symbol," *Chicago Tribune*, 17 April 1986.

24. Jon Margolis, "For Most People, the Big Picture Is What Really Matters," *Chicago Tribune*, 30 December 1986.

25. Of course, the relationship is reciprocal: nuclear weapons also support American ideology, both by validating beliefs in national technical prowess and by forming part of the worldwide military presence of the United States. A state's ideology is compelling to the extent that the state seems successful; "white man's burden" was more compelling to more people in the days when there was still a worldwide British empire. So if nuclear weapons help preserve American power in the world, they may ensure greater longevity for the assumptions about American virtue that currently underwrite that power.

26. Rousseau, quoted in Alfie Kohn, "Make Love, Not War," *Psychology Today*, vol. 22, no. 6 (June 1988), p. 36.

27. Caldicott, *Missile Envy*, p. 338. I say "risk" here because in many ways Caldicott is on the right track; my differences with her argument are perhaps matters of emphasis and phrasing, though, I believe, important ones.

28. John Lewis Gaddis, "How the Cold War Might End," *Atlantic Monthly*, November 1987, p. 99.

29. Caldicott, p. 339.

30. See chapter 4.

31. A Turin Films production, 1983.

32. From transcript in "The Nuclear Debate," *Chicago Sun-Times*, 27 November 1983, "Views" section, p. 1.

Bibliography

Aggeler, Geoffrey. *Anthony Burgess: The Artist as Novelist*. University: University of Alabama Press, 1979.

Albert, Michael, and Dellinger, David, eds. *Beyond Survival: New Directions for the Disarmament Movement*. Boston: South End Press, 1983.

Auerbach, Erich. "The Weary Prince." In *Mimesis: The Representation of Reality in Western Literature*. Garden City, N.Y.: Doubleday Anchor Books, 1957.

Aukerman, Dale. *Darkening Valley: A Biblical Perspective on Nuclear War*. New York: Seabury Press, 1981.

Bacon, Francis. *Advancement of Learning* (1605); *History of Henry VII* (1622); *In Praise of Knowledge* (1592); *Novum Organum* (1620). In Johnston, Arthur, ed., *Francis Bacon*. London: Batsford, 1965.

———. *Bacon's Essays*. Edinburgh: W. and R. Chambers, 1884.

Barash, David P., and Lipton, Judith Eve. *The Caveman and the Bomb: Human Nature, Evolution, and Nuclear War*. New York: McGraw-Hill, 1985.

Baritz, Loren. *Backfire: A History of How American Culture Led Us into Vietnam and Made Us Fight the Way We Did*. New York: Ballantine Books, 1985.

Bodin, Jean. *Six Books of the Republic*. In Curtis, Michael, ed. *The Great Political Theories*, vol. 1. New York: Avon Books, 1961.

Boyer, Paul. *By the Bomb's Early Light: American Thought and Culture at the Dawn of the Atomic Age* New York: Pantheon Books, 1985.

Brians, Paul. *Nuclear Holocausts: Atomic War in Fiction 1895–1984*. Kent, Ohio: Kent State University Press, 1987.

Broad, William J. *Star Warriors: A Penetrating Look into the Lives of the Young Scientists behind Our Space Age Weaponry*. New York: Simon and Schuster, 1985.

Brodie, Bernard. *War and Politics*. New York: Macmillan, 1973.

Caldicott, Helen. *Missile Envy: The Arms Race and Nuclear War*. New York: William Morrow, 1984.

Cassirer, Ernst. *The Myth of the State*. New Haven: Yale University Press, 1946, 13th printing 1975.

Charlton, Michael. *From Deterrence to Defense: The Inside Story of Strategic Policy*. Cambridge, Mass.: Harvard University Press, 1987.

Chernus, Ira. *Dr. Strangegod: On the Symbolic Meaning of Nuclear Weapons*. Studies in Comparative Religion, edited by Frederick M. Denny. Columbia: University of South Carolina Press, 1986.

———. "The Symbolism of the Bomb," *Christian Century*, 12 October 1983, pp. 907–10.

Chilton, Paul. "Nukespeak: Nuclear Language, Culture, and Propoganda." In Aubrey, Crispin, ed. *Nukespeak: The Media and the Bomb*. London: Comedia Publishing Group, 1982.

Chomsky, Noam. *Towards a New Cold War: Essays on the Current Crisis and How We Got There*. New York: Pantheon Books, 1982.

Diacritics, vol. 14, no. 2 (Summer 1984—nuclear criticism).

Dollimore, Jonathan, and Sinfield, Alan. "History and Ideology: The Instance of *Henry V*." In Drakakis, John, ed. *Alternative Shakespeares*. London: Methuen, 1985.

———. *Political Shakespeare: New Essays in Cultural Materialism*. Ithaca: Cornell University Press, 1985.

Draper, Theodore. *Present History: On Nuclear War, Detente, and Other Controversies.* New York: Vintage Books, 1984.

Dyson, Freeman. *Weapons and Hope.* New York: Harper and Row, 1984.

Eagleton, Terry. *The Function of Criticism: From the Spectator to Post-Structuralism.* New York: Schocken Books, 1984.

———. *Literary Theory: An Introduction.* Minneapolis: University of Minnesota Press, 1983.

Easlea, Brian. *Fathering the Unthinkable: Masculinity, Scientists and the Nuclear Arms Race.* London: Pluto Press, 1983.

English, Raymond, ed. *Ethics and Nuclear Issues: European and American Perspectives.* Washington: Ethics and Public Policy Center, 1985.

Erickson, Paul D. *Reagan Speaks: The Making of an American Myth.* New York: New York University Press, 1985.

Fallows, James. *National Defense.* New York: Vintage Books, 1981.

Fenton, Ian, ed. *The Psychology of Nuclear Conflict.* London: Coventure, 1986.

Fitzgerald, Frances. *America Revised: History Schoolbooks in the Twentieth Century.* Boston: Little, Brown and Co., 1979.

Foucault, Michel. *The Archeology of Knowledge.* Translated by A. M. Sheridan Smith. New York: Pantheon Books, 1972.

Freedman, Lawrence. *Atlas of Global Strategy.* New York: Facts on File, 1985.

———. *The Evolution of Nuclear Strategy.* New York: St. Martin's Press, 1981, 1983.

Frye, Northrop. *The Great Code: The Bible and Literature.* New York: Harcourt Brace Jovanovich, 1981.

Garrison, James. *The Darkness of God: Theology After Hiroshima.* London: SCM Press, 1982.

Graff, Gerald. *Professing Literature: An Institutional History.* Chicago: University of Chicago Press, 1987.

——— and Gibbons, Reginald. *Criticism in the University. Triquarterly.* Series on Criticism and Culture, no. 1. Evanston: Northwestern University Press, 1985.

Gregory, Donna. *The Nuclear Predicament: A Sourcebook.* New York: Bedford/St. Martin's, 1986.

Hinsley, F. H. *Sovereignty,* 2nd ed. Cambridge: Cambridge University Press, 1986.

Hobbes, Thomas. *Leviathan* (1651). The Library of Liberal Arts. Indianapolis: Bobbs-Merrill, 1958.

Hofstadter, Richard. *Anti-Intellectualism in American Life.* New York: Vintage Books, 1962, 1963.

———. *The Paranoid Style in American Politics and Other Essays.* New York: Vintage Books, 1967.

Hoy, David Couzens, ed. *Foucault: A Critical Reader.* New York: Basil Blackwell, 1986.

Ignatieff, Michael. *The Needs of Strangers.* New York: Viking, 1985.

Jacoby, Russell. *The Last Intellectuals: American Culture in the Age of Academe.* New York: Basic Books, 1987.

Johnson, James Turner. *Can Modern War Be Just?* New Haven: Yale University Press, 1984.

———. *Ideology, Reason, and the Limitation of War: Religious and Secular Concepts, 1200–1740.* Princeton: Princeton University Press, 1975.

———. *Just War Tradition and the Restraint of War: A Moral and Historical Inquiry.* Princeton: Princeton University Press, 1981.

———. *The Quest for Peace: Three Moral Traditions in Western Cultural History.* Princeton: Princeton University Press, 1987.

Joseph, Paul, and Rosenblum, Simon, eds. *Search for Sanity: The Politics of Nuclear Weapons and Disarmament.* Boston: South End Press, 1984.

Kahn, Herman. *Thinking about the Unthinkable in the 1980s.* New York: Simon and Schuster, 1984.

Kammen, Michael. *People of Paradox: An Inquiry Concerning the Origins of American Civilization.* New York: Vintage Books, 1973.

Kearney, Hugh. *Science and Change 1500–1700.* World University Library. New York: McGraw-Hill, 1971.

Kennan, George. *George Kennan on Nato, Nuclear War and the Soviet Threat.* Edited by Phil Braithwaite. Evesham, England: West Midlands Campaign for Nuclear Disarmament, 1985.

Klemm, Friedrich, ed. *A History of Western Technology.* Cambridge, Mass.: M.I.T. Press, 1964.

Kovel, Joel. *Against the State of Nuclear Terror.* Boston: South End Press, 1984.

LaCapra, Dominick. *History and Criticism.* Ithaca: Cornell University Press, 1985.

Lasch, Christopher. *The Minimal Self: Psychic Survival in Troubled Times.* New York: W. W. Norton, 1984.

Lifton, Robert Jay, and Falk, Richard. *Indefensible Weapons: The Political and Psychological Case Against Nuclearism.* New York: Basic Books, 1982.

Loeb, Paul Rogat. *Hope in Hard Times.* Lexington, Mass.: Lexington Books, 1987.

Long, Edward Leroy, Jr. *The Christian Response to the Atomic Crisis.* Philadelphia: Westminster Press, 1950.

Macdonald, Dwight. *Politics Past.* New York: Viking, 1957.

MacIntyre, Alasdair C. *After Virtue: A Study in Moral Theory,* 2nd ed. South Bend, Ind.: University of Notre Dame Press, 1984.

Mandelbaum, Michael, and Talbott, Strobe. *Reagan and Gorbachev.* A Council on Foreign Relations Book. New York: Vintage Books, 1987.

Maritain, Jacques. *Man and the State.* Chicago: Phoenix Books, 1956, 1966.

Martin, Bernice. "Invisible Religion, Popular Culture and Anti-nuclear Sentiment." In Martin, David and Mullen, Peter, eds. *Unholy Warfare: The Church and the Bomb.* London: Basil Blackwell, 1983.

Marx, Leo. *The Machine in the Garden: Technology and the Pastoral Ideal in America.* Oxford: Oxford University Press, 1964.

Miller, Perry. *Errand into the Wilderness.* New York: Harper Torchbooks, 1956.

National Conference of Catholic Bishops. *The Challenge of Peace: God's Promise and Our Response.* A Pastoral Letter on War and Peace, 3 May 1983.

Office of the President. *The President's Strategic Defense Initiative.* Washington: U.S. Government Printing Office, January 1985.

Orwell, George. *1984.* New York: Signet, 1949, reprinted 1961.

Pagels, Elaine. *Adam, Eve, and the Serpent.* New York: Random House, 1988.

Powers, Thomas. *Thinking About the Next War.* New York: New American Library, 1982.

Pringle, Peter, and Arkin, William. *SIOP: The Secret U.S. Plan for Nuclear War.* New York: W. W. Norton, 1983.

Rabkin, Norman. "Rabbits, Ducks, and *Henry V.*" *Shakespeare Quarterly* 28:3, summer 1977, pp. 279–96. Reprinted in Scott, Mark W., ed. *Shakespearean Criticism,* vol. 5. Detroit: Gale Research, 1987.

Reagan, Ronald. Selected speeches, statements, and interviews. United States Information Service, *Official Texts* and *European Wireless Files; Weekly Compilation of Presidential Documents; New York Times* (and index); Scheer, *With Enough Shovels* (appendices); Erickson, *Reagan Speaks;* Fred L. Israel, Compiler, *Ronald Reagan's Weekly Radio Addresses: The President Speaks to America.* Wilmington, Del.: Scholarly Press, 1987.

———. *Where's the Rest of Me?* With Richard G. Hubler. New York: Duell, Sloan and Pearce, 1965.

Rollins, Peter C., ed. *Hollywood as Historian: American Film in a Cultural Context.* Lexington: University of Kentucky Press, 1983.

Rorty, Richard. "The Contingency of Language." *London Review of Books,* 17 April 1986, p. 3.

———. "The Contingency of Selfhood." *London Review of Books,* 8 May 1986, p. 11.

Roszak, Theodore. *Where the Wasteland Ends.* Garden City, N.Y.: Anchor Books, 1973.

Rowe, Dorothy. *Living with the Bomb.* New York: Methuen, 1985.

Said, Edward W. *The World, the Text, and the Critic.* Cambridge, Mass.: Harvard University Press, 1983.

Scheer, Robert. *With Enough Shovels: Reagan, Bush and Nuclear War.* New York: Random House, 1982.

Schell, Jonathan. *The Abolition.* New York: Alfred A. Knopf, 1984.

———. *The Fate of the Earth.* New York: Avon Books, 1982.

Schudson, Michael. "The Politics of Narrative Form: The Emergence of News Conventions in Print and Television." *Daedalus* 111:4 (fall 1982—print culture and video culture), pp. 97–112.

Shakespeare, William. *Henry V.* Edited with an introduction by A. R. Humphreys. Harmondsworth, England: Penguin, 1968, reprinted 1980.

Shenfield, Stephen. *The Nuclear Predicament: Explorations in Soviet Ideology.* London: Routledge and Kegan Paul, 1987.

Smith, Henry Nash. *Virgin Land: The American West as Symbol and Myth.* Cambridge, Mass.: Harvard, 1950, reprinted 1970.

Stein, Jonathan B. *From H-Bomb to Star Wars: The Politics of Strategic Decision-Making.* Lexington, Mass.: Lexington Books, 1984.

Talbott, Strobe. *Deadly Gambits: The Reagan Administration and the Stalemate in Nuclear Arms Control.* New York: Vintage Books, 1985.

Thompson, E. P. et al. *Exterminism and Cold War.* A New Left Review Book. New York: Schocken Books, 1982.

———. "The Ideological Delirium Which Strikes Chords in the Worst Traditions of American Populism." *Guardian* (London), 18 February 1985, p. 18.

———, ed. *Star Wars: Science Fiction, Fantasy or Serious Probability?* New York: Pantheon Books, 1986.

Tirman, John. *Empty Promise: The Growing Case against Star Wars.* Boston: Beacon Press, 1986.

Wallis, Jim, ed. *Waging Peace: A Handbook for the Struggle to Abolish Nuclear Weapons.* San Francisco: Harper and Row, 1982.

Warner, Marina. *Joan of Arc: The Image of Female Heroism.* New York: Alfred A. Knopf, 1981.

Weart, Spencer R. *Nuclear Fear: A History of Images.* Cambridge, Mass.: Harvard University Press, 1988.

Weimann, Robert. *Shakespeare and the Popular Tradition in the Theater: Studies in the Social Dimension of Dramatic Form and Function.* Baltimore: Johns Hopkins University Press, 1978.

Wells, Robin Headlam. *Shakespeare, Politics and the State.* Context and Commentary Series, edited by Arthur Pollard. Houndmills and London: Macmillan Education, 1986.

White, Hayden. *Tropics of Discourse: Essays in Cultural Criticism.* Baltimore: Johns Hopkins University Press, 1978.

White, Lynn, Jr. *Dynamo and Virgin Reconsidered: Essays in the Dynamism of Western Culture.* Cambridge, Mass.: M.I.T Press, 1968.

Wills, Garry. *Reagan's America: Innocents at Home.* Garden City, N.Y.: Doubleday, 1987.

Films:

Doctor Strangelove: Or, How I Leaned to Stop Worrying and Love the Bomb. Produced by Stanley Kubrick for Hawk Films. Directed by Stanley Kubrick. Columbia Pictures, 1964.

In the King of Prussia. Produced and directed by Emile de Antonio for Turin Films, 1983.

Platoon. Produced by Arnold Kopelson for Hemdale Film. Directed by Oliver Stone. Orion, 1986.

WarGames. Produced by Harold Schneider for Leonard Goldberg Productions. Directed by John Badham. MGM/UA, 1983.

Index